Early Years
Management

actice

edition

Early Years
Management
in Practice

2nd edition

Maureen Daly
Elisabeth Byers
Wendy Taylor

www.heinemann.co.uk
✓ Free online support
✓ Useful weblinks
✓ 24 hour online ordering

01865 888118

Heinemann

Part of Pearson

Heinemann is an imprint of Pearson Education Limited, a company incorporated in England and Wales, having its registered office at Edinburgh Gate, Harlow, Essex, CM20 2JE. Registered company number: 872828

www.heinemann.co.uk

Heinemann is a registered trademark of Pearson Education Limited

Text © Elisabeth Byers, Maureen Daly, Wendy Taylor 2009

First published 2004

12 11 10
10 9 8 7 6 5 4 3 2

British Library Cataloguing in Publication Data
A catalogue record for this book is available from the British Library

ISBN 978 0 435402 47 1

Edited by Maria Anson
Designed by Hicks Design
Typeset by Tek-Art, Crawley Down, West Sussex
Original illustrations © Pearson 2009
Illustrated by Paule Trudel
Cover design by Pearson Education
Picture research by Virginia Stroud-Lewis
Cover photo © TongRo Image Stock/Alamy
Printed in China (GCC/02)

Acknowledgements

The author and publisher would like to thank the following individuals and organisations for permission to reproduce photographs:

Alamy/Horizon International Images Limited p213; Alamy/Stock Connection Blue/Jim Pickerell p69; Art Directors and Trip/Michael Melia p221; Art Directors and Trip/Tony Freeman p143; Corbis/moodboard p23; Getty Images/Stone/Rosanne Olson p38; moodboard/Alamy Images p276; Pearson Education Ltd/ Arnos Design p247; Pearson Education Ltd/Bea Ray p191; Pearson Education Ltd/Gareth Boden pp82, 83, 113; Pearson Education Ltd/Gerald Sunderland p45; Pearson Education Ltd/Haddon Davies pp4, 88, 125; Pearson Education Ltd/Jules Selmes pp48, 92, 97, 146, 209, 284; Pearson Education Ltd/Mark Bassett p140; Photolibrary.com p271; photos.com/Jupiter Images p28; PhotoStock-Israel/Ilan Rosen/Alamy p177; Sally and Richard Greenhill p264; Zac Macaulay/Getty Images p163

Every effort has been made to contact copyright holders of material reproduced in this book. Any omissions will be rectified in subsequent printings if notice is given to the publishers.

pp4, 12, 25, 200, 201, 211 Extracts from 'Leadership in Early Childhood 3rd Edition' by Jillian Rodd ©1998: Reproduced with the kind permission of Open University Press. All rights reserved.

pp10, 216 Extracts from 'Effective Leadership and Management in the Early Years' by Janet Moyles © 2007: Reproduced with the kind permission of Open University Press. All rights reserved.

pp12, 21, 25, 165 Extracts from 'Leadership in Early Childhood 2nd Edition' by Jillian Rodd © 1998: Reproduced with the kind permission of Open University Press. All rights reserved.

pp28, 29, 95, 210, 228 Extracts from 'Effective Leadership in the Early Years Sector' by Siraj-Blatchford, I. and Manni: © The ELEYS Study. (London: Institute of Education) / Siraj-Blatchford, I. and Manni

pp96, 102 Extracts from 'Developing Learning in Early Childhood / Paul Chapman publishing by Tina Bruce: Reproduced by permission of SAGE Publications, London, Los Angeles, New Delhi and Singapore, from Tina Bruce, Developing Learning in Early Childhood © Paul Chapman, SAGE Publications 2004.

p136 Extract from 'Start Right, the Importance of Early Learning' by Sir Christopher Ball and Professor Kathy Sylva, published by the RSA.

p162 'Team Role Descriptions' by Dr R. Meredith: Reproduced from www.belbin.com with kind permission of © Belbin Associates, 2008.

p164 'Five-stage theory', Group and Organizational Studies Volume 2, 1977 by BW Tuckman and MAC Jenson © 1977, Sage Publications. Reproduced by permission of SAGE Publications.

pp213, 214 Extracts from 'The Learning Styles Helper's Guide' by Peter Honey and Alan Mumford: © Peter Honey Publications / Peter Honey and Alan Mumford

pp287, 288 Extracts from 'Understanding Early Years Policy' by Baldock, Fitzgerald and Kay: Reproduced by permission of SAGE Publications, London, Los Angeles, New Delhi and Singapore, from Baldock, Fitzgerald and Kay, Understanding Early Years Policy, © Paul Chapman, SAGE Publications 2005.

p238 Extract from 'Practice Guidance for the Early Years Foundation Stage' © Crown copyright 2008. Published by the Department for Children, Schools and Families. Reproduced under the terms of the Click-Use Licence.

p267 Extract from 'Early Years, the First National Picture' © Crown copyright 2003. Reproduced under the terms of the Click-Use Licence.

The websites used in this book were correct and up to date at the time of publication. It is essential for tutors to preview each website before using it in class so as to ensure that the URL is still accurate, relevant and appropriate. We suggest that tutors bookmark useful websites and consider enabling students to access them through the school/college intranet.

The authors

Elisabeth Byers qualified as a nursery nurse and then started her career in the United States, where she worked in a kindergarten and in a hospital for sick children as a volunteer. She returned to the UK to work in a school, when she worked with nursery, reception and Year 1 children. She has been a lecturer in early years at Oaklands College in Hertfordshire since 1998, teaching on a range of courses, including those leading to the CCE, DCE and NVQ. She is currently the programme director for the Foundation Degree in Early Years.

Maureen Daly spent over 20 years working in a variety of childcare settings and has also managed an early years establishment. She has been a lecturer in early years in colleges of further education, teaching on a variety of courses at all levels. In the last two years she has been External Examiner for Thames Valley University (TVU). Since 2006, she has been Head of School for Care and Early Years at West Herts College.

Wendy Taylor has been involved in childcare and education since 1976 when she started training as an early years teacher at the University of East Anglia. Since then she has worked with children and adults aged 0 to 85 through teaching, childminding, managing a pre-school, lecturing in a further education college, and is currently working at CACHE as the Chief Examiner for Children's Services. She has trained classroom assistants, nursery nurses, nannies, childminders, babysitters, pre-school workers and lecturers, written qualifications and assessments and still has a lot to learn about children.

Contents

Authors' acknowledgements

The authors would all like to thank the team at Pearson, who have once again provided so much support and advice during the writing of this new edition. Particular thanks must go to Virginia Carter and Beth Baker, who are both very patient and understanding when life gets in the way of deadlines.

Elisabeth Byers would like personally to thank her son Joseph, who was beginning to think that play was no longer important at home, and her new baby daughter Alice for napping frequently, allowing the writing of this book.

Maureen Daly would like to thank her children – Emma, James, David, Katy and Sophie – and her family for all their patience and support. She would also like to say a special thank you to her dad, J, for being understanding and encouraging.

Wendy Taylor would like to thank her family again for understanding her strange obsession with the computer, and writing at peculiar times. They are remarkably indulgent. She would also like to mention two new additions to the family – great nephew Jack and great niece Amelia Grace – both of whom will probably wish their great aunt knew nothing about childcare.

Introduction

> Childcare can make a positive difference to children, parents and communities –
> helping to tackle child poverty, improve children's achievements at school, enable
> parents to choose work as a route out of poverty, improve health and reduce crime.
> (Department for Education and Skills and Department for Work and Pensions, 2002)

Since this statement was written many changes have occurred in the childcare sector and continue to take place. At the time of writing, the prime minister, Gordon Brown, has announced the government's intention to provide free childcare places for all children aged from 2 years with the aim of increasing social mobility through childcare opportunity. The first to be targeted for this provision will be 20,000 children of parents within a low income bracket. Changes that have taken place since 2002 include:

- the provision of more Sure Start children's centres
- the expectation for continuous professional development for all staff
- the creation of the Early Years Professional Status
- changes to the curriculum, such as the Early Years Foundation Stage
- legislation that reflects the status of children through the *Every Child Matters* programme.

These initiatives reflect the widely held view that the long-term future prosperity for children can be improved by high-quality childcare and education provision. It also shows that influential people are raising awareness of the importance of the early years in the development of the individual and also in the growth of the country as a whole. There are implications here for the early years manager. Firstly, managers must be able to cope with the concept of continual growth and change. This may generate excitement, but can also bring added pressure for managers as they struggle to keep up with different legislation and regulatory expectations. They will also need to develop ways of coping with possible increases in stress, and methods of motivating their staff to accommodate and respond positively to change.

Children and their families are at the heart of these changes to legislation and practice and it is essential, therefore, that all childcare workers and managers have as much knowledge as possible to carry forward the latest strategies and plans for the care and education of children. An early years manager in particular needs to have the vision, knowledge and experience to lead a team and to stay informed about current thinking and expectations.

This book aims to clarify some of the issues that concern new and prospective managers, and provides in-depth knowledge of the current framework for early years services. It considers some of the expectations and responsibilities associated with the manager's role, but will also consider other facets of management roles – for instance practitioners who have just taken on some management responsibilities.

Frequently asked questions that are investigated within the book include:

- What do I need to do to ensure there is good practice in my setting?
- How do I prepare for an Ofsted inspection?
- How do I recruit, select, support and train staff?
- What knowledge do I need to meet current government targets for delivering curriculum requirements and good-quality provision?
- How do I manage relationships with the parents/carers and families?
- How do I ensure the children are treated fairly and kindly within the setting?

- How should I manage the staff team effectively and ensure that we are a cohesive team with a clear vision?
- What personal strengths and attributes do I need to be a good manager?

From time to time you will probably ask yourself these and many more questions. The confidence you have when you manage a situation or group of people will depend upon the reasons why you became a manager (or are seeking to become one) in the first place. These could include any of the following:

- You were an experienced childcare and education worker who was qualified to Level 3, you had the opportunity to cover for a manager while they were absent and then the post became vacant.
- You were a deputy manager with post-qualifying experience (Level 3 qualifications and at least two years' experience, as required by Ofsted).
- You wanted to move away from working solely with the children and become involved in the running of the setting.
- You were inspired by another manager (a role model).
- You felt that you had been poorly managed and that, given the opportunity, you could do a better job!
- You have a particular skill or interest and would like to pursue the management of a certain area.
- You were interested in the status and better salary.
- You set up your own early years setting and thus became a manager.
- You had been on an advanced course and felt you had the knowledge to take on a new role.

Whatever your reasons for becoming a manager, you will no doubt be eager to build on your skills and further your knowledge in order to do an effective job and enhance the experience being offered to the children in your care.

Many experienced managers have never actually attended any formal management training, and more recently appointed managers may not have had the opportunity to do so. The Early Years Development and Childcare Partnerships in all areas are a good source of training opportunities for staff in early years settings and occasionally run courses for managers that are specific and designed to support managers with certain aspects of the work. The local further education college or training agency will also provide training opportunities for people working at this level, but management may be just one element of a course that also explores other areas of early childhood studies. There is also the option of doing a generic management course, designed for people managing in all walks of life. This, however, has limitations, as such courses will not be designed to meet the specific needs of an early years manager.

If you are a learner or practitioner on an advanced course in childcare, Foundation Degree, BA or working towards Early Years Practitioner Status, you will also be able to use this book as a study guide for many of the subjects you will be exploring in your course, not only those directly looking at management.

As authors we have used our own experience to produce a book for current or potential managers in early years settings. We have summarised the core issues for childcare practice and linked these issues to generic management practice. We wanted to recognise the reader's existing experiences while drawing attention to new and developing theories as well as long-standing and tested theories. The aim is to give you practical ideas on how to manage while ensuring you have opportunities to reflect on your current practice and review it in light of theorists who have based their findings on research.

We have also highlighted the statutory requirements for early years settings. To varying degrees the four nations comprising the UK have their own legislation. That relating to England is generally presented by way of explication, and readers are advised to check what applies in their own area.

To make the book 'researcher friendly' the following features have been included:

- case studies – scenarios and examples from practice, with questions to encourage you to reflect on your current practice
- figures and tables – to highlight examples, summarise theories and demonstrate models of working
- 'think it over' boxes – opportunities to look back at what you have read and collect your thoughts (these would also be useful as subjects for a seminar or discussion within a taught class or to provide a focus for team meetings or in-house training)
- points for reflective practice – questions or suggestions designed to encourage you to reflect on how your current practice matches up to the best standards, and to consider ways in which it could be improved or developed
- key terms – definitions of frequently used terminology, or 'jargon', explained in early years context
- good practice checklists
- top tips
- 'find it out' ideas for further research
- 'check your understanding' – questions at the end of every chapter to check your learning, consolidate your ideas and reflect on practice
- lists of references and further reading
- a selection of useful websites, including those of the principal organisations, within each chapter.

The early years curriculum has changed significantly over the last few years and workers must have up-to-date knowledge of the legislation governing the education of the children they are working with. The Early Years Foundation Stage curriculum provides staff with a clear framework from which to plan activities and leads into the National Curriculum. Managers must ensure that the children in their care benefit from a carefully planned, inclusive environment that reflects national expectations and meets their developmental needs. This means having experience and working knowledge of child development and the ability to encourage staff to reflect upon their practice and provide a stimulating, exciting and challenging environment in which children want to learn. There is also a need for managers to understand the ways in which children learn, and this will require knowledge of the work of theorists such as Jean Piaget, Lev Vygotsky and more current theorists in order to make comparisons.

The quality of the provision will depend greatly on the ability of the team to plan successfully and to use observational techniques to evaluate its success. Many early years professionals find the cycle of planning, implementing and evaluating daunting. Indeed, it can be a confusing aspect of the job. Many people also find it difficult to document the processes. Difficulties can arise when the team is not clear about the terminology used, and time needs to be given to working together to decide on the following points:

- What do we mean by 'the curriculum'?
- How do we plan to cover all aspects of the Early Years Foundation Stage?
- What are the differences between long-term, medium-term and short-term planning?
- What forms can be used to record the plans for each session?

- How can play be incorporated?
- How can individual educational plans be incorporated?
- How will the child's progress be monitored and assessed?
- What records will be kept?

All these issues are discussed within the book, as it is necessary for managers to have a clear understanding of these points in order to lead and guide their team.

As part of the present guidelines for high-quality learning and care, the manager is required to ensure that there is an effective and productive partnership with parents. Parents are the most important people in children's lives. They are children's first educators and generally know their children best of all. It is, therefore, not surprising that research has shown that high-quality relationships between the setting and parents, carers and families have a positive effect on children and their long-term learning. Through high-quality relationships, settings are able to help parents to increase their understanding and knowledge of their children's development and education, as well as enable early years practitioners to build a profile of each child. This valuable knowledge of each child informs the selection and planning of appropriate activities and experiences. High-quality partnerships with parents and families are too important to be left to chance and should be carefully planned and managed.

Managers are also accountable for ensuring that they maintain high-quality provision. Quality encompasses all areas of the setting, not just those linked directly with children. The environment, staffing, resources, finances and relationships with parents, carers and families all affect the standard of provision. The level of quality and availability in each of these areas can differ greatly between settings; therefore, it could be argued that there cannot be a universal measure of quality. However, there are guidelines and quality indicators drawn from good practice that enable you to develop the best possible practice for young children and their families.

The management of an early years setting is not an easy task. It is fraught with everyday hurdles and potential difficulties that even the most experienced manager will find a challenge. For most, this challenge is a worthwhile one and managers gain a great deal of job satisfaction in running a setting, even on the difficult days. To be an effective manager you need to have a cohesive team. Managers cannot do it alone and they need to ensure that they are working with their team to create the right kind of atmosphere for cohesiveness. In any early years setting the quality of management and team working will have a profound effect on the service offered to children, parents and carers. It is essential in a climate of accountability that the manager is aware of the importance of creating a vision within the setting, and that the staff team are committed to it and share the same ethos and set of goals and standards.

To do this, managers have both to learn leadership skills and to create their own style of management. This book explores the notion of leadership and clarifies the skills a manager needs to lead a team effectively. How you set about learning such skills will depend upon your previous experiences and on the expectations of the post. There is a plethora of research and theory on how the manager's role is best implemented. The role of a manager is to manage the day-to-day workings of the setting; but it is also to inspire and motivate the staff team to provide high-quality care for young children. An effective manager will work with the team and ensure that they are all involved in the development of good practice. In this way the individual team members will take ownership of what is going on in their setting and feel valued as a result. It is also necessary for the manager to be able to encourage evaluation as part of the process of building a team, as this can be a very useful tool in implementing further changes. Evaluation and review are good practice and will need to be evidenced for the purpose of inspection by Ofsted.

Today's managers also need to be able to review their own performance within a constantly changing environment, and to be evaluative and reflective thinkers. They must constantly research practice and make the necessary changes in order to develop and broaden their skills. For this reason, we have devoted a whole new chapter to the management and development of self, which aims to explore the importance of self-development for the individual practitioner and considers ways in which the manager can support members of the team to reflect on and develop their own practice.

Managers of early years settings must be open to new ideas and prepared to initiate change within their setting. The *Every Child Matters* programme highlights the need for inter-agency collaboration and early intervention. This call for professionals to work together will mean that today's early years manager will need a broad and in-depth knowledge of their setting and the services available to the children and their families. Early years managers have a very important role to play in the national picture and in supporting this drive to make each child 'matter'.

Since the Children Act 2004 local authorities are required to produce a Children and Young People's Plan that demonstrates how they will integrate local children's services. Early years, health, social services and play and leisure services are part of this plan. As an early years manager it is vital that you build strong links with your local authority. It will be a very useful source of information on further training and funding and may help to publicise your provision for children.

The general public are well informed about what they should expect in terms of good-quality childcare. Parents and carers are more aware of their right to be involved in the care and education of their children and will want to know that the setting will provide a flexible and accessible service which involves them if they wish and which respects them as the child's first educator. The setting will need a strong ethos to convince parents, carers and children that it is a place worth coming to and that children are treated with respect and kindness. The diverse needs of individual children and their families will need to be paramount, within an inclusive ethos.

Historically, children were not valued as part of society. In the UK this is changing and there is now legislation that protects children as vulnerable members of society.

Early years managers are constantly striving to make current provision better by evaluating and reviewing:

- the ethos of the setting – a mission statement and supportive atmosphere are required
- kindness to children – all of the setting's policies should reflect the need for kindness towards and respect for individual children and their families
- values and attitudes – these underpin working practices and staff should be given the opportunity to reflect upon them
- skills of managers – all managers need good communication and leadership skills
- qualities of teams – good working practices can be used not only internally but in working with wider teams and the community when necessary
- parental input – a basic requirement of the Children Act 1989 and a prerequisite for a child to settle into a setting
- children's self-esteem – research has shown that giving children this good start will ensure that they have a better chance to become well-rounded and confident adults
- the development and personal growth of staff – so that they can feel valued and confident in their role as professionals.

This book explores all these issues in detail. You will be asked to reflect on your own ideas and ways of working, and relate them to theories relating to early years management, care and education. The purpose of this is to help you broaden your theoretical knowledge and reflect on your present and future practice. Happy reading and researching!

A note on terminology

First, the 'manager' is the person in day-to-day charge of the setting. The manager is generally, but need not be, the 'registered person' (the one whose name appears on the certificate of registration for the setting). For example, in the case of privately owned nurseries a manager is often recruited by an owner (the registered person) who does not wish to perform the management role in the day-to-day running of the setting. A 'nominated person' is required to act as the point of contact for the Office for Standards in Education – referred to as Ofsted throughout the text.

The term 'setting' is generally used in the text to refer to any sort of organisation that provides early years care and education, such as nurseries, pre-schools and children's centres.

The terms 'parent', 'carer' and 'family' collectively refer to anyone who is responsible for the child, whether on a long- or short-term basis. Sometimes these responsible adults are the child's biological parents but they could be other adults who are involved in caring for and bringing up the children. Children's primary carers may be:

- grandparents
- childminders
- older siblings
- foster carers
- guardians
- step-parents
- members of the extended family.

In this book the term 'parents and carers' is used to refer in shorthand to the child's primary carers.

Elisabeth Byers
Maureen Daly
Wendy Taylor
March 2009

References

Department for Education and Skills and Department for Work and Pensions (2002)
Birth to Three Matters: A Framework to Support Children in their Earliest Years. London: DfES.

Useful websites

Department for Children, Schools and Families: www.dcsf.gov.uk

Every Child Matters: www. everychildmatters.gov.uk

Ofsted: www.ofsted.gov.uk

Sure Start: www.surestart.gov.uk

1 Management and Leadership

There has been an immense amount of material written about management and leadership over the last 50 years. There is clear evidence of the relationship between how staff are managed and how they perform. The deeper the commitment of the staff to their organisations, the better their performance will be. In the early years sector today's leaders and managers are required to manage the related areas of health, care and family support and integrate these with education. Good-quality leadership and management are vital in raising the standards of learning and achievement.

The work of managers and leaders in the early years and care sector has been researched and looked at in terms of the unique approach taken and required expertise. Many of the managers in the past have become so by moving through the ranks within their establishment and will not necessarily have been trained for the job. These managers will have the unique expertise in working with children and young people but may feel overwhelmed by the necessary leadership and management skills. Latest research has identified a set of skills and attributes that managers will need to meet the future challenges of the sector. Standards have been written to enable them to lead high-quality provision and meet the requirements of the Care Standards and the latest government initiatives and legislation.

This chapter will consider the role of the manager as a leader who has the necessary skills to lead and support a team and provide a good-quality service with sound monitoring systems.

The chapter covers the following areas:

1.1 What is a manager? What is a leader?

1.2 Management theory

1.3 What makes an effective early years manager and leader in practice?

1.4 Self-assessment of management skills

1.1 What is a manager? What is a leader?

There has been a great deal of research and debate into the possible differences between leadership and management in the early years sector. Although the terms tend to be used interchangeably, there are many schools of thought on how they differ, which we will be considering in this chapter. Gillian Pugh (2001) has told us that changes which have taken place in providing an expansion of flexible services for children and their families have in turn changed the role that early childhood practitioners undertake. 'Such changes require strong leaders of high calibre who are capable of leading and meeting the interpersonal professional challenges of multi-professional teams' (cited in Rodd, 2007, p. 3).

Put very simply this means:

- *management* is operational – it deals with the organisation of people and resources
- *leadership* is to inspire and influence the vision to meet future challenges.

These very different skills may be affected by the context of the setting, that is:

- the *private sector* – leadership may come from the owner of the business
- the *voluntary sector* – the manager may be responsible to a committee of volunteers that oversees the vision
- the *public sector* – the manager may be responsible for leading quality practice and moving the setting on.

It is evident that managers and leaders in the early years sector work in a variety of contexts and perform many different roles.

Most managers of early years settings are keen to show them off to visitors.

What is a manager?

All of us manage at some time in our everyday lives, perhaps by organising an evening out, a journey or a holiday with others. You will no doubt have had conversations with your tutor about your 'time management skills' and ways of improving them, for example. We all manage situations and resources every day before we leave home in the morning.

In your working life you will also have had widely different experiences of being managed by others and will be aware of the difference a manager can make to how effectively you are able to do your job. It may seem difficult to define precisely what a manager is or does, but the manager should be the linchpin to the smooth running of any organisation.

A manager is often perceived as:

■ the person who makes the decisions

■ the person who is ultimately responsible

■ the person everyone goes to with their problems

■ someone who passes on information given by a higher authority

■ a person who controls and organises the people in the team

■ someone who has to come up with ideas and set examples for the team.

In order to understand what a manager does, it may be helpful first to consider your own experiences to ascertain why you might react in the way you do to instructions or requests from a manager. It could be that you have had a poor experience in the past that has left you feeling that you cannot trust managers, or you may have had good experiences of being managed and feel open to a manager's ideas and plans. You may have had a managerial or coordination role within an early years setting and therefore have some empathy for the manager's role and responsibilities.

A day in the life of Marla, manager of a children's centre

I am the manager of a children's centre. I begin my day today at 8.00 a.m. When I arrive at my desk I have a call on my mobile phone to tell me that a member of staff will be off sick today, so I first need to sort out some cover for her today and possibly for tomorrow. I have an appointment with a parent at 8.30 to discuss some issues with her child's behaviour at home. The meeting with this parent goes on a little longer and I am aware that I have failed to catch up with another parent I wanted to see this morning. When the first parent leaves I begin to sort out today's post, prioritising items as urgent for attention today, not so urgent and things that can be passed to the staff room. Because I don't have any teaching or cover sessions this morning, I visit a couple of the rooms to chat to the children and have a quick chat to staff to offer encouragement and support. I want the staff to know I have noticed their efforts day to day. While I am in the rooms it also gives me the opportunity to observe practice. At about 11.30 I go back to my desk and check my emails – good, only 40 today! I do have to do some work on the budget this week, but as it is now lunchtime and parents are starting to arrive I want to be accessible to them, so I go into reception and chat to some parents as they arrive.

At lunchtime, a member of staff made an appointment to see me. I am aware that this member of staff has been a little unhappy for a while and needs encouragement. We talk and she tells me that she would like to take up the opportunity I had offered her in a previous meeting to do some further training. This is really good news and we talk through the advantages for her – but I must remember to sort out the funding and cover for her to do this as it has to be booked quite quickly. I eat a sandwich at my desk and check a few more emails.

After lunch I have a planned meeting with some of my team. I have been concerned that we need to make some improvements in speech and language development with some of the younger children. I have sent one of the team on a BLAST (Boosting Language Auditory Skills and Talking) training programme, and she has been working with a focus group on ideas for good practice. The group has lots of really good ideas and I need to harness those while keeping the issues of resources and future management in mind. It is a fruitful meeting but goes on a little longer than expected. I was hoping to work on my budget for half an hour, but instead have to leave as I have a meeting with some other children's centre managers across town and only have 45 minutes to get there. I check with one of the coordinators that all is under control for tomorrow and go to the meeting. This finishes at 6.30 as there are many strategic issues to discuss. I arrive home at 7.00 p.m. with the budget draft in my bag. I need to look at that tonight as I have a meeting first thing tomorrow with the county council's budget adviser.

Think it over

When you have read this case study think about the following.

- Identify where Marla was using management skills.
- Identify when Marla was using leadership skills.
- What are the advantages of being able to use both these skills sets as a manager of a children's centre?
- Where does Marla meet the requirements of the Care Management Standards in this case study?

The management of early years settings requires particular skills and knowledge. An early years manager will need a wide range of both in order to:

- ensure a good-quality service is provided and evidenced through sound quality assurance (QA) and monitoring systems
- know the legislative requirements covering childcare, employment and premises
- lead and support the staff team
- provide adequate resources to ensure the smooth running of the setting
- work in partnership with parents and carers
- actively liaise with external agencies to support children and their families
- provide a strong framework of supervision and appraisal to ensure that staff are kept up to date with relevant training and development and are set appropriate targets
- provide a safe, secure and stimulating environment for the children, including responsibility for safeguarding children as the designated person in most cases
- ensure that the manager's own practice is reflective and updated regularly through continuing professional development
- manage change.

Later chapters look at many of these aspects of the manager's role in more detail, but by way of introduction each of these aspects is discussed briefly below.

Ensure a good-quality service is provided and evidenced

Managers need to be in tune with the needs of people using the setting. They need to ensure that the wishes of the parents, carers and children can be met, and that the setting is a place where parents and carers will want to leave their children and where, indeed, the children will be happy to stay. Without knowing the expectations of the 'customers' (prospective as well as current) the setting will find it very difficult to provide a quality service. The quality of the provision can be measured only against the views of the customers, which requires an evaluation of their needs.

Every aspect of the early years setting contributes to the quality of the provision. This will include:

- the premises
- the people
- the standards of care and welfare

- children's learning and development

- relationships with parents, families, carers and the local community.

The key to providing good quality is to ensure that there are robust policies and procedures within the setting – this will help achieve the quality standard the setting aims to achieve. The working practices of the setting will be designed to meet these standards. These should comply with the requirements of the statutory guidance set out in the following documents:

- Day Care and Childminding (National Standards) (England) Regulations 2003

- Statutory Framework for the Foundation Stage 2007

- *Birth to Three Matters* Framework 2003 and the Early Years Foundation Stage (EYFS).

Raising quality is an ongoing process and the manager of the setting will need to ensure that there is:

- a system of clear lines of management for the setting: business planning; development planning; legal responsibilities

- effective staff development: training and development; clear performance management

- a safe and secure environment: meeting the legal requirements of health and safety; use of indoor and outdoor spaces

- the meeting of individual needs: inclusion; welfare needs; learning and development

- a good working relationship between staff; effective relationships with parents and carers; multi-agency working.

In addition to the requirements of the Ofsted inspection process, managers can also use self-evaluation tools to ensure they are providing quality service, such as:

- Common Core of Skills and Knowledge for the Children's Workforce: Every Child Matters – Change for Children

- National Occupational Standards: Leadership and Management for Care Services

- Sure Start Children's Centres Practice Guidance.

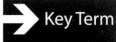 **Key Term**

Multi-agency – different services, agencies and teams of professionals working together to provide support that meets the needs of children and their families.

The Investors in People (IIP) standard is also well recognised, and IIP offers advice and guidance to its members. The guidance it produces on leadership and management can be a useful tool for managers. Investors in People (2003, p. 5) states that the quality of management and leadership has a direct impact on the delivery of the key indicators of success, such as staff productivity and performance and, as these indicators improve, the need for better leaders and managers will increase accordingly. This increasing need led IIP to produce a leadership and management model as part of its family of support models to help managers and leaders work effectively to manage change, and increasing pressure and responsibility.

Investors in Children has been replaced by the National Quality Improvement Network (NQIN) and is managed by the National Children's Bureau (NCB). All of the key organisations are interested in maintaining and promoting high standards in early years provision. The NQIN has determined a set of 12 principles that determine quality and have practical guidance for managers of early years settings.

Know the legislative requirements covering childcare, employment and premises

An effective manager will have a good working knowledge of all the legislative requirements covering childcare, employment and premises and ensure that they have regular updates of their knowledge for their own professional development. (This will be explored further in Chapters 6 and 7.)

Lead and support the staff team

It will be the responsibility of the manager to lead, motivate and support the members of the team. The staff will need support for further professional development, as well as support in performing their own roles within the setting. Some of this support can be implemented during appraisal, whereby the manager highlights areas of strength and areas for improvement. This particular area is considered further in Chapter 7.

Provide adequate resources to ensure the smooth running of the setting

The principal resource of an early years setting is its staff, be they childcare workers, teachers, unqualified care assistants, students on placement, kitchen staff, caretakers, gardeners, contracted workers or agency staff. Proper use of this resource will involve the manager in:

- timetabling work rotas for part-time and full-time staff
- the recruitment and selection of staff
- professional development and statutory training in, for example, first aid and food hygiene
- the appraisal and mentoring of staff (see Chapter 7)
- leading staff meetings (see Chapter 6).

The manager will need to look at priorities for resources. These will depend on the type of setting. Ofsted requires health and safety to be a priority and this is always checked during inspections. The manager may not be the budget holder, but will have responsibility for ensuring that new equipment is purchased as and when necessary. The staff will need to understand how to use the equipment for the benefit of the children and this could require special training.

Not all resources are financial. For example, the manager should work with the staff to make use of all the space available to them. It is also important to maximise the use of staff time as a resource, and to match the staff to the needs of the children. It is the manager's job to ensure that there are the correct staff ratios, as set out in current legislation. Thus, as part of the process of drawing up budgets for resources, the manager will take responsibility for ensuring:

- that there are sufficient qualified staff to meet the Ofsted requirements
- that resources are replenished and replaced
- health and safety requirements
- training and staff development
- plans for improvements to the service.

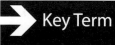

Key Term

Mentor – trusted and experienced professional person who can provide training, advice and support in an organisation or institution.

Work in partnership with parents and carers

Partnership with parents and carers is of paramount importance in providing a quality service for children. The manager will probably be one of the first points of contact with prospective parents and carers (that is, customers). Above all, the manager must make parents and carers feel welcome, and appear professional yet friendly. Every opportunity must be taken to work inclusively and encourage an ethos of inclusivity in the setting. Managers need to have the skill to inform prospective customers about the ethos of the setting while making them feel that their children's needs are going to be met. This very important aspect of management in early years settings is dealt with in detail in Chapter 5.

Actively liaise with external agencies to support children and their families

The manager of any early years setting will need to liaise with a variety of external agencies and professionals: social services, the local Early Years Development and Childcare Partnership, schools, training establishments, health visitors, general practitioners, speech and language therapists, physiotherapists, psychologists, family therapists and numerous others. This liaison could be for a number of reasons – emergencies, training needs, supporting a family in crisis, child protection issues, special needs advice or supporting children settling into school. In meeting with other professionals, the manager must remain professionally focused on the needs of individual children, families and staff, while maintaining confidentiality and meeting legal and statutory requirements (see below and Chapter 8).

Ensure that relevant policies, procedures and records are maintained

The National Standards (Standard 14, Documentation) specifically relates to the records early years settings must keep, and for each of the other 13 standards there are policies and procedures that need to be in place in the setting. There are 30 such policies and procedures required by the National Standards, and another 11 are recommended by Ofsted to provide evidence of compliance with the standards. There are also requirements within the Leadership and Management for Care (LMC) Services requirements (particularly units LMC B1; LMC B3; LMC E2; LMC E9).

Provide a strong framework of supervision and appraisal

The manager will be required to ensure that there is an auditable framework of supervision and appraisal so that staff are kept up to date with relevant information and given the opportunity for evaluation and reflection. Solly (2003) states that: 'management is related more to maintenance tasks, concerned with carrying on, keeping up, perpetuating and sustaining' (cited in Moyles, 2007, p. 21).

Provide a safe, secure, and stimulating environment for the children

The manager's role is to ensure that the children in the setting feel safe and secure and that their developmental needs are being met. This will include overseeing the planning of activities and short-, medium- and long-term plans for the curriculum (more details of this are given in Chapter 3). Each child's progress must be monitored by members of staff, and the manager should support the staff team to do this.

The manager will almost certainly be the designated person for safeguarding children and will, therefore, need an in-depth knowledge of the safeguarding children procedures (see Chapter 9 for more details).

Ensure that the manager's own practice is reflective and updated regularly

In reality, performing all of these tasks does present quite a challenge for a manager, who may have received very little training for the job or have little experience. Many of the skills needed to perform in this way will develop over time and with experience.

In the Effective Provision of Pre-School Provision project (Sylva et al., 2004), it was found that the higher the qualifications of managers, the higher the quality of children's curriculum experiences, the more effective the programme structure and the better the relations with, and between, staff and parents (Taggart et al., 2000).

Think it over

Consider the various pieces of legislation relating to providing a safe, secure and stimulating environment for children. Make a list of all those the manager may need to consider, and identify what training may be required to keep updated.

Manage change

Changes are taking place constantly within the sector. The leader can be the orchestrator of change, having the ability to adapt to changing circumstances themselves and supporting staff to do so. (You can read more about managing change in Chapter 6.)

We have discussed, then, aspects of the roles, responsibilities and tasks managers are asked to perform. Each of these aspects can be summarised as in Table 1.1.

Table 1.1. Facets of the manager's job

Fixer	Administrator
Ensures everything works	Understands all the paperwork
Negotiates for the staff and among the staff	Makes sure all the staff timetables are done
Finds the resources	Disseminates information
Ensures the setting has a good reputation	Deals with all outside agencies and demands
Understands people's personal problems	Organises and plans effectively
Asks for opinions	Writes good, workable policies

What is a leader?

Whitaker (1998) states that a leader's role is to create an environment that values commitment and challenge in which all members of the team can give their best.

We have seen that there are many practical aspects, then, to being a manager – certain tasks must be completed and responsibilities met. Managers in early years settings have traditionally been reluctant to identify with the concept of leadership as part of their professional role (Rodd, 1998). Leadership is, by contrast, about vision and influence. Leaders influence and inspire people to develop openness and become part of their shared vision. Rodd (1998) says that 'Leaders are able to balance the concern for work, task, quality and productivity with concern for people, relationships, satisfaction and morale.' She also goes on to describe a list of key elements in effective leadership (Figure 1.1).

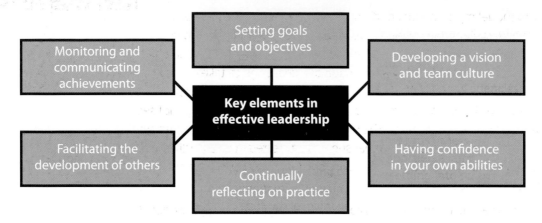

Figure 1.1. Key elements in effective leadership

It could be argued that leadership skills are especially important in early years settings because teams require more than being managed, as their motivation is in the main different from that of workers in more commercial organisations. Early years workers are motivated in general by a commitment to working with children and their families. Early years services require innovative leaders who are able to carry forward a set of values and principles because staff will need guidance in finding the way forward, especially in the ever-changing early years climate.

There have been many inspirational leaders throughout history: Napoleon Bonaparte, Nelson Mandela, Martin Luther King, Margaret Thatcher, to name but a few. You may not have agreed with some of these leaders' views or politics but you cannot refute their *very* strong leadership qualities. It could also be argued that leaders, however visionary, are not always necessarily good and efficient managers! They are very often successful in leading people towards a common goal, but perhaps not so successful in the day-to-day running of an organisation.

Good leaders of organisations tend to lead by example, by being a role model for their staff. They inspire trust and work in consultation with their teams, even when challenging the status quo. They have a long-term view and are open to new ideas and projects. Leaders can also be very persuasive, as they are often passionate about their work; this passion can be infectious and motivate others around them. Jillian Rodd (2007) has noted that leadership is about interacting with others and says that 'Leadership can be displayed in a range of early childhood contexts by people who have vision, drive, energy, commitment and positive relationships with others' (Rodd, 2007, p. 13). Rodd also tells us that managers are leaders when they:

- offer inspirational and credible values, vision and mission
- encourage open communication
- develop a team culture

- set realistic and achievable goals and objectives

- monitor and celebrate achievements

- foster and facilitate the development of others (ibid., p.12).

The model manager

I always try to model my own management on a manager I had some years ago. She was an excellent role model for all the people in her team, her own performance in her job was exemplary, she was an excellent teacher and she had integrity. When there was a decision to be made or a challenge to take on, she would gather us all together and ask, 'How shall we go about this?' She appeared to manage the day-to-day, mundane things adequately, but these things did not seem a problem as we all worked together. She utilised individual strengths to meet any targets set. We felt she knew us all and that she was interested in us as individuals. We felt valued. I worked really hard for the team because she ensured that we realised our full potential.

- Do you think that the manager in this case was a leader or a manager or both?

- What would you say were her strengths and weaknesses?

It may appear at this stage that 'managing', on its own, implies a lack of skills and that leaders are better to work for. This, of course, may not always be the case. Some efficient managers may make staff feel secure in their roles, for example.

To be a 'leader' suggests that one must have followers. Leadership has been studied by looking at effective leaders, such as the ones mentioned above, to attempt to define what makes a leader, but this approach has produced disappointing results. Most people in their first management role draw on their personal experience of being managed. So, if you have been managed poorly you will have probably decided to manage your staff in a very different way. Managers who are willing to continue learning and are aware of their strengths and weaknesses are more likely to adapt their approach to meet the needs of their team and the organisation.

The distinction between managers and leaders could be, then, that one manages (copes) while the other leads (points the way).

- The manager looks after the day-to-day running of the organisation or establishment, which involves planning, organising, coordinating and being ultimately responsible.

- The leader leads the team to an ultimate goal or set of targets, will have a vision for the future and a picture of how they would like the organisation to move forward. The leader can be an inspirational, even charismatic, character.

The kind manager

The manager of our centre was extremely kind. She was a very likeable person. The systems she put in place were well organised and efficient, but I did not feel I was consulted about them. She always seemed to have a million reasons as to why we had to follow these ways of practising, telling us that it was 'because of the inspection' or 'social services state that… ' It appeared that decisions had been made and then directives were passed on to us. Sometimes I felt that it would be pointless bringing things to her, as new ideas appeared to make her feel uneasy.

- In your view does it appear there was anything lacking in this person's management skills?

- How would you compare this manager to the one in the case study 'The model manager', above?

- Which person would you prefer to have as a manager?

Table 1.2. Managers v leaders (Jillian Rodd: 2006)

Managers	Leaders
Plan – set objectives, forecast, analyse problems, make decisions, formulate policy	Give direction – find a way forward, communicate a clear direction, identify new goals, service and structures
Organise – determine what activities are required to meet objectives, classify work, divide it up and assign it (i.e. decide who does what)	Offer inspiration – have ideas and articulate thoughts that motivate others
Coordinate – inspire staff to contribute both individually and as a group to the organisation's objectives	Build teamwork – use teams as the most effective form of management, spending their time building and encouraging collaboration
Control – check performance against plans, develop people and maximise their potential to achieve agreed outcomes (i.e. they get the work done through and by other people)	Set an example – model what leaders do and how they do it
	Gain experience – act in ways that arouse acknowledgement of their leadership status in followers

It could be assumed that all managers are leaders and that those chosen to manage are people who were 'born to lead' – that is, who have a natural aptitude for the job. To a degree, this is true, as managers today cannot simply expect total, unquestioning compliance from their teams. People in the team are the organisation's most valuable asset and can make the difference between success and failure. Nonetheless, good management is important to the people in the team, as they can be reassured by a manager who can plan, coordinate and control what is going on in the setting.

The way in which managers perform their role will of course vary according to personality. For this reason it is useful to analyse the experiences you have had of managing and being managed. This in turn might suggest to you some of the strategies and skills that are necessary for the management of early years settings. To this end, consider the statements below. These are drawn from *Good Practice in Childcare. 14: Teamworking* (Department for Education and Employment, 2000). Read each statement and see whether it applies to you. If you already have experience as a manager, this exercise may help you to see how you lead your staff and whether or not you allow them to help with decision-making. If you are not presently in a management role you could base your responses on a past or present line manager. It should give you some ideas of contrasting approaches to management and leadership.

- I trust my staff.
- The carrot is more effective than the stick.
- I see myself as part of a team.
- The success of my team will reflect well on me.
- My key role is to give the team a direction and support them in heading towards it.
- I expect my staff to put forward ideas without prompting and to contribute to decision-making.
- I need to monitor my staff closely.
- Following the appropriate rules is essential for discipline.
- I need to distance myself from staff to keep rules clear.
- My successes will reflect well on my staff.
- My role is to give my team clear, specific objectives and to monitor achievement of them.
- Leaders have to take key decisions on their own.

Think it over

Consider the series of statements relating to management style.

- Which points match the management strategies used within your organisation?
- Does this indicate that the manager has 'power'? If so, is the manager aware of the power they have?
- If you are a team member, how do these strategies make you feel?

You probably have seen a variety of these strategies in use and you may even have employed some of them. The role of the manager is to lead the team and guide and support them without abusing power. A manager who feels they are above the staff and uses discipline as a method of control can create problems, as this encourages a 'them and us' culture, which is likely to be negative. The manager who does not feel threatened and is confident in their own ability can lead the team effectively while also being very much a member of the team.

Many people become managers in early years settings because they want to progress in their career, but when they begin in a management role they realise that it actually requires a very different set of skills and that they are no longer able to do the 'hands-on' work with the children that they previously found so rewarding. Much of their time will be filled with paperwork and administrative duties. Also, the manager is required to take ultimate responsibility and so may often feel that they have to be a 'Jack of all trades'. The case study 'The childminder who became the boss' relates to a manager who has found herself in just this position.

The childminder who became the boss

Case study

Ellie owns a private day nursery. The nursery offers sessional care and the building has been purpose-built. Ellie was a qualified nursery nurse, but when she had her own children she decided to do some childminding in order to keep her practical expertise up to date. As a childminder she became more and more popular with parents. She then decided to take on some staff so that she could take on more children; this she continued to do in her own home. Very soon her home was being 'taken over' by the children, so she decided to move and start a purpose-built nursery in the same locality. Ellie maintains that it was never her intention to become a manager or a 'boss' and that she still feels more comfortable working with the children, even though she rarely has the time to do so. She has a strong vision for her nursery and a set of values and principles she is able to justify to potential parents. Ellie has a management structure within the nursery that promotes and values the staff who use their initiative. She tries hard when introducing new ideas to discuss them fully with the staff and get them on board. Although some of the practice is not exactly as she would like it to be, she is working slowly to train and educate her staff and give them opportunities to learn more.

- Would you say Ellie was fairly typical of today's early years manager?

- Would you say that Ellie is more a manager or a leader? Give some reasons for your choice.

Figure 1.2. The facets of a manager's role

1.2 Management theory

Many researchers have looked at what constitutes a good manager and leader. They have tried to identify characteristics which could enable employers to select and train effective leaders, but no clear characteristics have been found. It is apparent, however, that to be a leader a person requires a certain kind of interpersonal behaviour and that strong leaders are often people who inspire confidence in others and support team members or colleagues to achieve their full potential. Leadership involves getting the very best from people. Leadership in early years settings is promoted by the common goal or ethos of meeting the needs of children.

Before the chapter moves on to consider what it is that makes an effective early years manager and leader it is important to look at the various ways in which management and leadership have been interpreted. There have been many theories concerning managers and leaders. Most of the research we will consider will be generic management theory that has influenced the world of business for some time. Although not aimed directly at early years management, many of the outcomes and developments are pertinent. We will all have been managed in a variety of job roles and worked in other contexts, experiencing a variety of management styles and organisational cultures. A selection is presented in Table 1.3. You can use this table as a point of reference for research. It gives only a small sample of the plethora of information on management theory.

Table 1.3. Some notable management theories and theorists

Name	Work	Comments
Fayol (1841–1925)	Henri Fayol was a French mining engineer. He spent his life with one company and became its managing director. It is said that he invented management, by distinguishing it as a separate activity. He identified 14 principles of management and initiated a theoretical analysis appropriate to a wide range of organisations. He suggested that all activities to which industrial undertakings give rise are divided into six groups. He said that 'without principles there is darkness and chaos.'	Fayol is the earliest known proponent of a theoretical analysis of managerial activities – an analysis which has withstood years of critical discussion. His ideas, along with others, are collectively called classical management theory. They are somewhat limited to industrial management and therefore do not represent a coherent body of thought.
Herzberg (1959)	Frederick Herzberg was research director of a psychological consulting firm. He worked on industrial mental health and focused on areas such as the individual, attitudes and motivation to work, which led to his theories of 'hygiene' and motivation. The hygiene factors were essentially environmental and he labelled those 'dissatisfiers'. He argued that removing the dissatisfiers did not motivate people to work harder or make them happier. The five principal motivation factors (satisfiers) were: achievement; recognition; whether work is meaningful; responsibility and advancement. After a number of studies within a cross-section of industry he came to the conclusion that pay was not a motivator – just the most important hygiene factor.	Herzberg's ideas were well received at the time and led to considerable work on 'job enrichment' so that jobs contained more motivators.
McGregor (1960)	According to Douglas McGregor, 'theory X' bosses believe their employees dislike work and try to avoid it; they assume people have to be bullied into work. 'Theory Y' bosses feel that people do like work and value it as part of their lives. McGregor said that the employees behaved in the way their bosses expected them to, so if they had a theory Y boss they would enjoy and value their work.	Some of the problems with this theory could be that it makes assumptions about the employees. For example, would all people be influenced by their boss in this way? The two types of boss could be seen as extremes, whereas in real life a blend of the two types is more likely.
Likert (1961)	Rensis Likert's 'Michigan studies' theorised about high-producing and low-producing managers. The research indicated that high-producing managers tended to build their success around interlocking and tightly knit groups of employees who had been motivated by a range of forces, such as money, security, ego and creativity ('self-actualisation'). Likert looked at four systems of management.	Some of this work is still valid today, as it looks at the essential elements of teams and the motivation of teams.

Name	Work	Comments
Peters (1989)	Tom Peters wrote an international bestseller, *Thriving on Chaos*. He looked at innovative ways of dealing with change in the world of management, and targeted five key areas – responsiveness, innovation, people power, leadership and systems.	Peters challenged many of the traditional theories on management, and could even be said to be revolutionary, but is nonetheless highly respected.
Jeffers (1991)	Susan Jeffers wrote about the challenges of life. She held that the motivators were no longer the same as they were – quality of life and a better sense of balance between job, family, friends and contribution to society were taking precedence.	Society may well be moving towards this, but the bottom line of money and status still applies to much of the workforce.
Senge (1994)	Peter Senge suggested that managers should works towards: 'organisations where people continually expand their capacity to create results they truly desire, where new and expansive patterns of thinking are nurtured, where collective aspirations are set free, and where people are continually learning to see the whole together'.	These theories are currently very popular with early years researchers in leadership and management, and are being utilised to train and develop managers and leaders in early years centres of excellence.
Salovey and Mayer (1950) Goleman (1995)	Discussed theory of emotional intelligence and identified five main domains: 1 Knowing own emotions – self-awareness 2 Managing emotions 3 Recognising emotions – empathy 4 Handling relationships – becoming a change catalyst 5 Interacting with people effectively.	This is a theory which has become well respected and known – most of us are aware of the emotional intelligence of others. This is a useful theory to work with as a manager in early years settings.
Tannebaum and Schmidt (1973)	The leadership continuum – discussion of the leadership continuum, ranging from autocratic to democratic. This theory works on a model whereby the manager is involved in directing teams to achieve something.	Does not directly relate to early years settings – more useful for large organisations with large teams within the workforce.
Irving Janis (1972)	Groupthink – the cohesive thinking of a group of people, isolated from other company or options. The directive leader makes their wishes known.	Does not relate to early years settings – does not allow for reflective thinking or adverse opinion.
Paul Hersey (1960)	A behavioural approach – situational leadership. Teams are directed to improve skills application and are supported throughout with feedback and recognition of willingness on part of team.	This theory relates well to task-led activity.

Management theorists over the years have looked at the key concepts of organisations – such as culture, motivation, leadership, power, group working – and discussed ways of helping managers to find solutions to familiar problems experienced in all organisations. It is useful to look in some detail at a range of theories because, at this level of study, you will need to understand how organisations work and how this links directly to leadership and management styles.

Handy's 'have a go'

Handy (1992) stated that there had formerly been three general categories of theory on leadership – trait, style and contingency theories.

- *Trait theories*. By 1950 there had been over 100 studies of the personality traits of managers and leaders. These had found that they had in common the following: intelligence; initiative; self-assurance and, in more recent studies, 'the helicopter factor' (the person had the ability to 'rise above' a situation and see it in its relation to the overall environment). However, possession of all of these traits became an impossible ideal. These theories were also criticised on the grounds that they seemed to imply that there were elite groups of people who could become managers and leaders because they had inherited these characteristics.

- *Style theories*. These theories predicted that employees would work harder for a person who adopted a certain style of leadership, but it was found that style alone was not an answer to effective leadership. Nonetheless, it was shown that a supportive style of leadership led to more contentment and greater involvement on the part of employees. This would not necessarily generate higher productivity, but it would be a good basis on which to build. It became evident that the effectiveness of a workforce came from more than leadership style alone, and this led to the development of 'contingency theories'.

- *Contingency theories*. These concentrated on the relationship between the manager and the employee, but also took into account the task, the work group and the position of the leader within that group. Thus, for example, employees would be most effective in situations where the leader was well liked and the task to be done was clearly defined.

Handy looked at all these theories but concluded that the only way to train people to become effective leaders and managers was by simply 'letting them have a go', provided they were given good support. Handy advocated the use of mentors to support new managers.

Think it over

Which of the above theories fits best with the early years sector?

Peters' tools for effective leadership

Tom Peters has written a number of successful books about the world of management and the ways in which managers can be most successful. He maintains that leaders require three 'tools' for effective leadership:

- establishing direction

- channelling interest by living the vision – that is, motivating staff to love change and be inspired by the positive development which takes place as a consequence of change

- practising 'visible management' for the purpose of preaching the message and enhancing the leader's understanding of the context; this is done by the manager being visible and being aware of all that happens 'on the shop floor'.

Peters sees the principal challenges as empowering other people and cherishing those who are at the front line. He says that it is important for leaders to be vocal about their main vision in order to inspire team members to become involved and develop it. Although some may argue that Tom Peters is extreme in his expectations, a manager in an early years setting may find some of his strategies useful (see Peters, 1989).

Key Term

Reflective practice – thinking about your role and practice with the aim of evaluating it and making any changes to improve its quality.

Points for reflective practice

- How can the information and advice of management specialists be used in your present role?

- If you were researching management theory for an assignment or work-based project, what would you look at in more detail because it directly related to your work practices?

- Has this look at management theory made you feel any differently about the skills and abilities needed to be an effective manager or leader?

1.3 What makes an effective early years manager and leader in practice?

Bogue (1997), cited in Rodd (1998, p. 15), said that 'leaders are organisers of time, talent and task'. This explains in one short statement all the functions of a leader or manager – the manager will have to complete the tasks on hand, in timely fashion, by making the best use of the talent, skills and attributes of the people in the team.

It is possible to draw some conclusions as to what skills make an effective early years manager. These ideas concern not only effective management but also ensuring that the *team* is successful. It is important that the manager is aware that we can ensure good practice through leadership:

Jillian Rodd undertook comprehensive research into early childhood practitioners. She concluded that there appeared to be three different aspects identified from her research which emerged as part of leadership as a 'collaborative and shared endeavour' (1998, p. 52). She grouped together characteristics, skills and responsibilities that emerged in leaders at certain stages of their development. These stages she named as:

- Direct care – novice. These practitioners were 'kind, warm and friendly. Technically competent as a practitioner responsible for delivery of a quality service.'

- Direct care – advanced. These confident practitioners were more self-aware and knowledgeable. They had also gained the skills of financial and general administration and were able to engage in collaborative and partnership approaches.

- Indirect care. These assertive, proactive practitioners had become visionary and were sensitive and responsive to the need for change. They were able to lead the change effectively and advocate for staff, children and parents as well as the community.

This typology effectively describes the perhaps unique way in which managers in early years settings develop through their careers into visionary leaders.

Think it over

Think about Jillian Rodd's typology of an early childhood leader and compare it to your own practice. Can you identify ways in which you apply these skills as a manager or leader on a daily basis? Think of ways in which you can develop these skills.

You might want to compare these skills and attributes with the tool for managers and leaders identified in the Effective Leadership and Management Scheme (ELMS) (see Moyles, 2007).

There are various ways in which you can identify the skills needed to be a manager or leader in a variety of settings. This is the point at which we start to turn some of the theories of leadership and management into models for good practice in a variety of settings. Listed below are some of the assets and skills that can lay the foundations for effective management (depending upon the context of your setting and the role you perform).

- *Defining a mission*. This is an ability to see a vision for the future, a bigger picture view which encapsulates the values and principles of the setting. This vision will need to be communicated to the team regularly and to service users.

- *Having good communication skills*. Managers must be able to communicate and have the ability to pass on information and share ideas in a clear and understandable way to everyone they deal with.

- *Creating an atmosphere*. The manager should create a setting with a 'family atmosphere', in which trust and confidence can be nurtured.

- *Respecting confidentiality*. All managers need to prioritise confidentiality, as this will inspire trust in children, parents/carers and staff.

- *Being prepared to delegate*. Manager who are interested in the development of the team will delegate duties and responsibilities to other team members, and put their expertise to good use. This need not make the manager feel threatened; on the contrary, it will support them in the role, knowing that experienced staff are able to share some of the burden of responsibility. It will also build the self-esteem of team members and confirm that they are trusted and valued.

- *Representing the views of the team*. A good leader will ensure that the setting reflects the views of all members of the team, and will be ready to listen to new ideas and to discuss old ones.

- *Finding out what motivates the team*. Managers need to know what makes the team tick, what interests them, what their personal goals and ideals are.

- *Providing support to team members.* Support can be offered in many different ways, for example in the form of a 'listening ear', taking on new ideas, offering staff opportunities for training and networking with other professionals.

- *Being a good role model.* A leader needs to be someone people are prepared to follow, and they will follow only someone in whom they have confidence.

- *Being prepared to take risks.* Sometimes being a manager and leader means taking calculated risks for the good of the setting and the team.

- *Thinking strategically.* The manager should have a plan which the team can work to. Implementation of the plan should be monitored and the results evaluated. All the team need to show commitment to and understanding of the plan. This is strategic thinking.

- *Encouraging a 'can do' culture.* This will involve inspiring confidence in the team and making them feel valued and useful – then all team members will feel more confident to take on new challenges.

- *Sharing success.* A good manager does not take personal credit for success; it is important to involve the team so that they have the opportunity to celebrate their contribution, no matter how small.

- *Ensuring optimum use of resources.* The manager will need to make sure that all resources (including human resources) are made the best use of.

- *Financial awareness.* This means a good understanding of how to make best use of the budget available.

- *A positive attitude to change.* This is the ability to reflect on previous experiences, evaluate progress and make decisions so that you can plan for the future.

The manager's job involves a variety of tasks.

An effective leader needs to put all of the above into place, but this takes time and cannot be rushed. People expect their leaders to have integrity and to be credible; this can be achieved only by ensuring that you keep promises and by doing what you say you will do. To be trusted, the manager will need to be prepared to tell the truth and to show humility, which involves admitting when they have got things wrong. This will require self-evaluation and looking at your own strengths and weaknesses before you take on such a responsibility. The people you manage need to know where they stand, and this means it is not always possible for the manager to be 'one of the team'. Moreover, if the manager forms too close a relationship with particular members of the group, this can cause jealousies and sometimes conflict.

The qualities of an effective manager

It has been suggested that effective managers do require certain qualities, but what are they? Can they be learned or are some of us 'born to lead'? Handy (1992) and Jameson and Watson (1998) looked at some specific qualities a person might need in order to be an effective manager. Figure 1.5 presents this collection of qualities; it represents, of course, a wish-list – we are only human, after all! Many practitioners will have experienced working with managers with some (if not all) of these qualities. Why are these qualities so important, then?

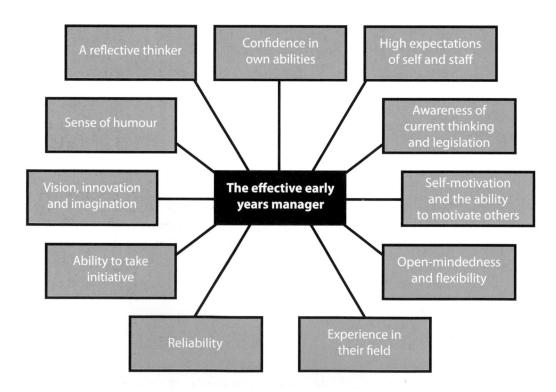

Figure 1.3. Ideal attributes and qualities of an effective manager in early years settings

Think it over

Consider the attributes and qualities shown in Figure 1.3. Can you think of any others? Perhaps you feel some of these qualities would conflict with being efficient. If so, which ones?

Today's early years manager therefore will need to be sensitive to the ever-changing needs of the children, their parents and families and the staff team. Confidentiality and trust are paramount. A good manager will also be aware of the staff and their personal and professional development. There will always be a need to balance a sensitive approach with sound, trustworthy management, which is a challenge for the most experienced and effective manager and requires practice.

Managers who know their limitations can draw on other team members for support in those areas where they are not so strong. A manager does not need to be the leader in all aspects of running the setting. The recognition and realisation of the qualities and skills of other members of staff will be seen as a sign of strength on the part of the manager.

A good manager with a strong team will need a real vision and a sense of conviction to carry it forward. But this will need to be joined with the ability to see the 'other point of view' by fostering open dialogue with staff, parents, carers and children.

A reflective practitioner is one who reviews and evaluates their work. This is especially important for those who work with children. If the staff in the team are to be expected to carry out evaluation and reflection, then the manager should also demonstrate the ability to do this, as a role model. The work of managing a setting in any case benefits from a reflective approach. The theme of reflective practice is taken up in Chapter 2.

It is evident that effective leaders and managers require certain skills and qualities to support them to be reflective leaders. Ongoing professional development will assist this process, as will a capacity to demonstrate:

- emotional intelligence
- the ability to listen and respond appropriately.

We can now look at these particular attributes in more detail.

Emotional intelligence

Maxwell (1999), cited in Rodd, 2007, tells us that 'leaders are effective because of who they are on the inside – in the qualities that make them up as people' (p. 51). In research completed by Jillian Rodd, she noted that individuals working in management of early years settings need to develop 'emotional intelligence'. Goleman (1996, ibid.) clarifies emotional intelligence as:

- knowing your own feelings
- being able to manage your emotions
- having a sense of empathy
- being able to repair emotional damage in yourself and others
- being emotionally interactive – that is tuning into people so that you can interact with them effectively (Rodd, 2007, p. 69).

It is believed that leaders and managers who are emotionally intelligent are able to raise standards and foster organizational stability.

Listening and responding appropriately

The National Occupational Standards for Leadership and Management in Care Services 2007, unit LMC B2.1 is entitled 'Lead and manage provision that promotes the well being of people'. The way in which a manager or leader listens and responds to staff, children and their families is crucial for effective communication.

Listening

To overcome barriers to communication effectively Jillian Rodd suggests using the strategies shown in Figure 1.4.

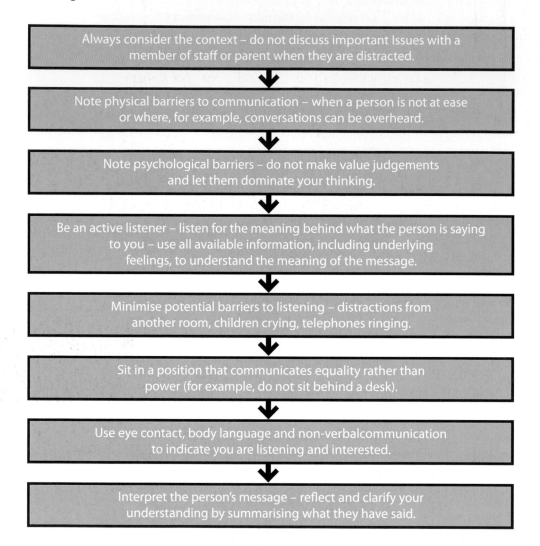

Figure 1.4. Overcoming barriers to communication

Rodd maintains that this process will communicate interest and encourage further interaction.

Responding

Carl Rogers (1961) tells us that there are approximately five response styles that account for 80 per cent of our verbal communication. These are shown in Table 1.4.

Table 1.4. Appropriate response styles in verbal communication

Response style	Sample
1 Advising and evaluating	'What you should do now…'
2 Interpreting and analysing	'The problem you have here is…' or 'You have missed the point, the real reason is…'
3 Supporting and placating	'Don't worry, they all go through that stage…' or 'Forget it – he'll get over it…'
4 Questioning and probing	An interrogation such as: 'Did she have a disturbed night?'; 'Did anything unusual happen at home this morning?'; 'Is everything all right at home?'
5 Understanding or reflecting	The listener focuses on the underlying feelings as well as the content and indicates their understanding in a short paragraph: 'You're concerned about Sam's adjustment to childcare…'

Rogers maintains that professionals use the first four responses most frequently, with the fifth response one of the most rarely used. The first four do not consider the person's feelings and can lead to their feeling as if they have not been listened to.

Case study

Gemma's new job

Gemma had come to work in the nursery a month ago. She told team members that she was extremely experienced. On numerous occasions team members had tried to give Gemma advice but Gemma very often talked over them and did not appear to listen. The manager of the setting, Mita, could see that Gemma was not helping herself. She called Gemma into her office for a talk.

- What would be the best approach for Mita to take when talking to Gemma?
- What are the possible pitfalls of Gemma's behaviour for the setting?
- Should the manager advise the team? If so, how?

The provision of early years services has traditionally been a female domain, with women in society often taking the role of placator. This can sometimes lead to feelings being suppressed until the person gets to the point where they explode. It is therefore important that early years managers develop emotionally intelligent ways of coping with and managing feelings. One of the ways in which this can be achieved is by using the correct listening strategies to empower the person at the offset. We will be looking at further strategies for managing teams and resolving conflict later in Chapter 6.

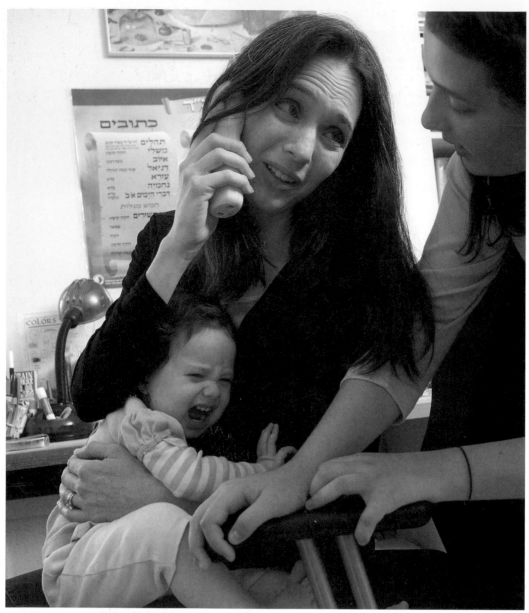

A manager might be distracted so they might not listen properly to staff.

Think it over

'The Daycare Trust reports that 97.5 per cent of the sector's workforce is female.' Siraj-Blatchford and Manni (2007) suggest that '… women's leadership style tends to be more democratic and participatory, encouraging inclusiveness and a broader view of the curriculum' (Scrivens, 2002).

Look at other research which has focused on specific studies of women such as Acker (1999), Hall (1996) and Shakeshaft (1987/89).

- What did these studies have in common?

- Do you think our expectations are influenced by gender?

1.4   Self-assessment of management skills

In recent years there has been an immense amount of work, research and development in early years services. Legislation in the Children Act 2004 was introduced to support a framework that sets out to improve the life chances of every child. With this at the heart of all the work a leader or manager is involved in, there is an identified need for evaluation and reflection of one's own performance. Until recently there was little opportunity for reflective training at manager level in early years settings. Very busy managers and leaders were unable to spare time for further training and funding was hard to find. Now the government's proposed Children's Workforce Strategy (CWS) aims to have one member of staff in every setting trained to graduate level by 2015. There is no doubt, therefore, that appropriate training for this role is an increasingly important element in providing 'high-quality provision for the early years, especially as we move to larger and sometimes more complex, multi-professional teams of staff [see Siraj-Blatchford et al, forthcoming 2007] across the early years sector' (Siraj-Blatchford and Manni, 2007, p. 29).

It was noted that there was a need for an assessment tool which would support managers and leaders to be more reflective. The Effective Leadership and Management Scheme (ELMS) is a tool for those who lead and manage early years settings to help them become more critically reflective in their practice. The ELMS also supports them to evaluate their effectiveness in their role as manager. The ELMS 'tree' (Figure 1.5) has four main sections called branches representing:

Figure 1.5. The ELMS model of management skills

1   leadership skills

2   management skills

3   professional skills and attributes

4   personal characteristics and attitudes.

This system also has four levels of grading:

Level 1 Acceptable – intuitive and pragmatic

Level 2 Good – reasoned and articulate

Level 3 Very good – involved and collaborative

Level 4 Exemplary – reflective and philosophical.

The levels of grading help support the manager to look at areas that need improvement or development.

Think it over

Investigate the ELMS typology and the four levels of grading. Consider the system's uses and benefits and whether you could apply it to your current job role (see Moyles, 2007).

Conclusion

This chapter has looked at what is meant by management and leadership, and examined various aspects of the roles in the light of the need for leadership skills within early years settings. This chapter has also reviewed some of the many theories linked to leadership and management and shown how they can be used to inform good practice. You will have had the opportunity to reflect on your own management skills and what it takes to be an effective manager. This will be explored in more detail in Chapter 6.

Check your understanding

1 Name eight of the skills required to be a leader and a manager.

2 Give a brief outline of three pieces of legislation managers of settings will need to know well, i.e. Statutory Framework for the Foundation Stage 2007.

3 Which external agencies might a manager need to work with to support children and their families?

4 What are the key elements of effective leadership?

5 Briefly describe McGregor's (1960) theory of management.

6 What are Tom Peters' (1989) tools for effective management?

7 Name six of the key assets and skills of today's manager.

8 Describe strategies a manager can adopt in listening to the team.

9 What is meant by the term 'emotional intelligence'?

10 What is the 'ELMS' model of management skills?

References and further reading

Acker, S. (1999) *The Realities of Teachers' Work*, London: Cassell

Bogue, R.J. (ed.) (1997) *Health Network Innovations: How 20 Communities Are Improving Their Systems Through Collaboration.*

Chicago: American Hospital Publisher. *Department for Education and Employment* (2000)

Good Practice in Childcare. *14: Teamworking*, London: DfEE.

Department for Education and Skills (2003) *Every Child Matters*. London: DfES

Goleman, D.P. (1995). *Emotional Intelligence: Why It Can Matter More Than IQ for Character, Health and Lifelong Achievement*, Bantam Books, New York.

Hall, V. (1996) *Dancing on the Ceiling*, London: Paul Chapman

Handy, C. (1992) *Understanding Organizations*. Harmondsworth: Penguin.

Handy, C. and Aitken, R. (1986) *Understanding Schools as Organizations*. London: Penguin.

Herzberg, F., Mausner, B. and Snyderman, B. (1959) *The Motivation to Work*. New York: Wiley.

Investors in People (2003) *Leadership and Management. The Investors in People Guide to Supporting the Development of Your Leaders and Managers*. London: IIP.

Jameson, H. and Watson, M. (1998) *Starting and Running a Nursery*. Cheltenham: Nelson Thornes.

Jeffers, S. (1991) *Feel the Fear and Do It Anyway*. London: Random House.

Likert, R. (1961) *New Patterns of Management*. New York: McGraw-Hill.

McGregor, D. (1960) *The Human Side of Enterprise*. New York: McGraw-Hill.

Moyles, J. (2007) *Effective Leadership and Management in the Early Years*. Maidenhead: Open University Press.

Peters, T. (1989) *Thriving on Chaos*. London: Macmillan.

Rodd, J. (1998) *Leadership in Early Childhood* (2nd edn). Buckingham: Open University Press.

Rodd, J. (2007) *Leadership in Early Childhood* (3rd edn) Maidenhead: Open University Press.

Rogers, C. (1961) *On Becoming a Person: A Therapist's View of Psychotherapy*, London: Constable.

Senge, P. et al. (1994) *The Fifth Discipline Fieldbook: Strategies for Building a Learning Organization*. London: Nicholas Brealey.

Shakeshaft, C. (1989) *Women in Educational Administration*, Newbury Park, CA: Corwin.

Siraj-Blatchford and Manni (2007) *Effective Leadership in the Early Years Sector: The ELEYS Study*. London: Institute of Education.

Smith, A. and Langston, A. (1999) *Managing Staff in Early Years Settings*. London: Routledge.

Sylva et al. (2004) *The Effective Provision of Pre-School Education (EPPE) Project: Final Report*, Nottingham: DfEE Publications

Taggart et al. (2000) *The Effective Provision of Pre-School Education (EPPE) Project: Technical Paper 5 – Characteristics of the Centres in the EPPE Sample: Interviews*, London: DfEE/Institute of Education, University of London.

Whitaker, P. (1998) *Managing Schools*. Oxford: Butterworth Heinemann.

Useful websites

BLAST (Boosting Language Auditory Skills and Talking): www.blastprogramme.co.uk

Investors in People (IIP): www.investorsinpeople.co.uk

National Children's Bureau (NCB): www.ncb.org.uk

National Occupational Standards: www.standards.dfes.gov.uk

Ofsted: www.ofsted.gov.uk

2 Providing a High-Quality Service

Early childhood care and education have become increasingly recognised as playing a vital role in laying the foundation for successful later learning. Research has shown that high-quality early childhood care and education can affect subsequent academic achievement and social behaviour. In the last few years we have seen significant developments in the early years curriculum and standards, most significantly the introduction of the Early Years Foundation Stage (EYFS). The Statutory Framework for the Early Years Foundation Stage aims to set the standards for learning, development and care for children from birth to five, and replaces previous frameworks. However, practitioners will recognise many of the key principles, pedagogy and good practice from *Curriculum Guidance for the Foundation Stage* (Qualifications and Curriculum Authority, 2000), the *Birth to Three Matters* framework and the *National Standards for Under 8s Day Care and Childminding* (DfES, 2003). The EYFS is a central part of the government's ten-year child care strategy and aims to improve outcomes for children and reduce inequalities. It is mandatory for all schools and early years providers in Ofsted-registered settings attended by young children to meet the EYFS requirements.

The EYFS provides us with a framework of quality; however, if quality is viewed through an imposed framework this will give only a partial view of practice. Inspection, rating scales and quality checklists can measure only those areas of practice that can be easily observed, and tend to impose changes to practice externally, rather than change being initiated by practitioners. Therefore this chapter focuses on assessing, evaluating and building quality from the inside. There is no doubt that encouraging practitioners to evaluate their own work closely results in a heightened awareness of high-quality practice.

Quality encompasses all areas of the setting, not just those directly linked to the children. These include:

- the physical environment
- materials and equipment
- the characteristics of staff–child relationships
- the qualifications of the staff and staff turnover
- health and hygiene procedures and standards
- relationships with parents and carers
- systems of observation, assessment and record-keeping
- systems of planning.

This chapter explores strategies that the early years manager may use in order to enable the team to meet the requirements of the Early Years Foundation Stage Framework, as well as to improve quality, in a way that maintains the setting's own ethos. It also identifies key quality indicators that managers and teams must meet in order to provide the best possible service for children and families.

The chapter covers the following areas:

2.1 Definition of quality
2.2 Identifying quality indicators
2.3 Identifying current good practice
2.4 Maintaining quality
2.5 Welfare requirements of the Early Years Foundation Stage
2.6 Meeting the requirements of *Every Child Matters* within the setting
2.7 Leading and managing continuous improvement in the provision

2.1 Definition of quality

Moss and Penn (1996) define quality as being both subjective and relative. Quality is fluid, as it is determined by (in the early years setting):

- the professional and personal values and beliefs of those who work directly with the children
- the environment in which the children learn
- the resources available to the setting.

Therefore it can be argued that there is no universal measure of quality – only guidelines and indicators (discussed in the next section) for each setting to follow and implement.

In relation to the first point, early years practitioners' values and beliefs will affect how they interact with children and how children learn. Most early years practitioners recognise that in order for children to develop to their full potential the adults need to interact actively and sensitively with the children, supporting and extending their learning. However, in order for children to develop to their full potential, all adults in the setting need to share the same professional values and beliefs, as well as having a shared concept of good practice. By encouraging regular reflection and evaluation of practice and training it is possible to ensure a common and consistent approach between the adults in the setting.

Quality provision can exist only when early years practitioners work towards incorporating the principles of early years education into all aspects of the setting. Managers also need to carry out regular reviews and assessments of practice, the environment, resources and procedures, and make any necessary changes. This section considers those areas of practice that will principally determine the quality of provision:

- a child-centred approach
- meeting the needs of children
- treating children as individuals
- equal opportunities
- inclusion
- enhancing self-esteem
- play as a vehicle for learning.

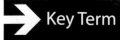

Key Term

Child-centred approach – an approach that has the child at its centre, with all aspects of the setting being informed and influenced by children's interests and needs.

A child-centred approach

A child-centred approach aims to incorporate children's interests as the focus of all aspects of learning and care within the setting. A child-centred approach relies on the adults in the setting interacting with and responding to the children in the following ways.

- They support and extend children's learning sensitively and appropriately.
- They appreciate what children can do for themselves and that this differs among children.

- They enable children to enjoy their childhood.

- They have consideration for the children as individuals.

- They are respectful and caring, and they ensure the welfare and safety of each child without being overprotective.

- They provide an environment that allows children to progress and develop at their own pace to fulfil their potential.

- They plan and implement a range of learning experiences that encourage and support all areas of development.

Think it over

Use the list of ways in which adults should interact with and respond to children to evaluate whether your setting has a child-centred approach. In order to gain an accurate picture, gather evidence for each point. This can be through either observation or discussion with your team.

- Are there any points you are unable to find supporting evidence for?

- How can you address this in your setting?

- Compare your answers with someone from another setting and share any points of good practice.

Meeting the needs of children

Early years settings should offer a range of learning opportunities that meet the diverse needs of children, to enable them to achieve their full potential. All activities and learning experiences should be responsive to and respectful of individual differences and promote acceptance of each person, positive self-esteem and a strong personal identity. The planning of activities and the curriculum (which is dealt with fully in Chapter 3) must therefore take account of the needs of:

- both boys and girls

- children with special educational needs

- more able children

- children with particular needs

- children from all social, cultural and religious backgrounds.

In order to meet the diverse needs of the children, the *Practice Guidance for the Early Years Foundation Stage* (Department for Education and Skills, 2007) highlights the importance of practitioners doing the following.

- Practitioners should deliver personalised learning, development and care to help children get the best possible start in life.

- Practitioners must promote positive attitudes to diversity and difference within all children. This includes making sure that all children and families feel included, safe and valued; that children and adults are treated as individuals and are not discriminated against; and that all children are listened to and respected.

■ Practitioners must plan for the needs of children from black and other minority ethnic backgrounds, including those learning English as an additional language, and for the needs of children with learning difficulties or disabilities.

■ Practitioners must plan for each child's individual care and learning requirements. The focus should be on removing or helping to counter underachievement and overcoming barriers for children where these already exist. There must be appropriate challenges for gifted and talented children.

It is the responsibility of the early years manager to ensure that the team is fully aware of these key principles and that they are put into practice. One effective way of achieving this is to allocate responsibility for monitoring individual areas to different team members. Regular feedback during team meetings will ensure that everyone is familiar with each key principle, responsibility for which can be regularly rotated. Copies of statements of these key principles can be included in information packs for new staff and students, with examples of good practice taken from the corresponding Principles into Practice cards (1.2 and 2.1) from the EYFS resource pack.

> ## Key Term
>
> **Personalised learning** – embraces every aspect of the child's experience in the setting, including teaching and learning strategies and assessment techniques.

Treating children as individuals

Early years practitioners have an essential role to play in helping each child develop to her or his full potential. A profile of each child is built from the first meeting between manager and parents and child, and is added to through observation of the child and discussion with parents throughout the child's time in the setting. These profiles inform the planning of appropriate activities and experiences, which should also take into account the individual interests of each child. It is important to remember that all children develop along a determined continuum but at different rates. A high-quality early years setting would ensure that the social, emotional, physical and intellectual aspects of the continuum are incorporated into the planning of appropriate activities. It is vital for early years practitioners to have an in-depth knowledge and understanding not only of child development in general, but also of the likes and dislikes, interests and preferences of each child in their care.

> ## Key Term
>
> **Key person** – a practitioner who is mainly responsible for providing lead support, contact and communication for a child and their family within the setting, with the aim of enabling and supporting close attachments between individual children and staff.

Many early years settings use the key person approach to enable children to develop a strong relationship with an individual adult. Research has demonstrated that this system supports children when they are separated from their primary carers. Experience has shown that early years practitioners can really get to know individual children and families through this system and use any information gained to inform planning. The key person approach is discussed in more detail in Chapter 4.

Points for reflective practice

1. What do you think is meant by the term 'personalised learning'?

2. How can you ensure that you personalise the learning for children in your setting?

3. What do you think are the benefits of a personalised learning approach?

Equal opportunities

Every early years programme and curriculum must offer all young children high-quality experiences that reflect their individual needs and abilities. Meeting the individual needs of all children is a key principle of the Early Years Foundation Stage. Early years practitioners should ensure their assessment and planning focuses on delivering a personal approach so that children get the best possible start in life.

It is the responsibility of the early years manager to ensure that the team actively promotes equal opportunities in the setting, in all aspects of their work. Equality of opportunity cannot be left to chance; it has to be carefully planned so that it becomes fully integrated into every aspect of the setting.

The way young children see themselves and the way others see them is crucial to their development. A child's positive self-image can be achieved only through a policy of equal opportunities that actively sets out to promote anti-bias and anti-discriminatory practice, with positive attitudes to diversity and differences consistently being demonstrated. In order to achieve this, practitioners should:

- actively involve parents and carers in the planning process
- research unfamiliar topics and issues
- keep up to date with related research and changes in practice
- make use of support and information available from specialist organisations.

In addition, the setting should:

- have in place a special needs policy that is regularly reviewed and updated
- have a designated special educational needs coordinator (SENCO), who is responsible for ensuring good practice and guiding and supporting colleagues.

Providing positive role models

Equal opportunities messages are best reinforced by the provision of positive role models. The following are examples of good practice.

- inviting both male and female visitors to the setting

- inviting people who are generally not well represented in a particular role – for example a female firefighter, a male nurse

- encouraging mothers and fathers, grandmothers and grandfathers to help in the setting

- always avoiding dividing the children by gender, for example 'Girls line up first' or 'Can I have two strong boys to help me?'

- representing different cultures in your resources, books, dressing-up clothes, cooking activities and experiences

- demonstrating positive attitudes to different races and cultures

- encouraging people from different ethnic backgrounds to become involved in the setting

- respecting the restrictions and choices of different cultures and religions

- collecting items and resources from a range of cultures to be used for display or to stimulate discussion

- having a welcome notice in different languages and dual-text books, and referring to them in talks with the children

- emphasising the value of diversity through learning about different cultures, festivals and celebrations.

Invite both male and female visitors to the setting.

In addition to promoting equal opportunities, practitioners are also responsible for modelling a range of behaviours. Children learn a great deal from adults around them. They learn how to communicate appropriately, how to apply social rules and how to interact with others. Early years practitioners model these skills through interaction with children, each other and the parents and carers. Other positive behaviour that can be modelled includes:

- active learning, exploring, problem-solving and questioning
- respect and courtesy
- active listening
- negotiation skills
- care for the environment
- social and emotional skills.

Many of these skills can also be encouraged through play, which is discussed below.

Young children learn a great deal from those around them, about themselves and others. Early years practitioners should offer children guidance and support in developing positive attitudes towards all people. In order to achieve this, all adults in the setting need to have an understanding and awareness of what equality of opportunities really involves and how to facilitate it. Inclusive practice helps to provide an environment rich in diversity that enables children to develop interpersonal skills and understand and appreciate differences, and this is considered next.

Inclusion

Inclusion is based on the belief that young children with particular or special needs are more similar to than different from their peers, and that all young children benefit from learning together as members of a diverse community. Children with particular needs are more likely to develop positive social skills when they are integrated with their typical peers.

Key Term

Inclusion – the process of ensuring equality of learning opportunities for all children irrespective of their diversity.

Children with special needs

Case Study

During an introductory visit to her new placement, Masuma, a student on a Diploma in Child Care and Education course, sat with Andrew, aged 4, who was struggling with a cutting activity. Masuma thought that he appeared younger than the other children and noticed that he was less able to use the scissors effectively. Masuma offered to help Andrew by holding the picture as he attempted to cut it out. Andrew enjoyed the attention and began to talk about what he was doing. Masuma praised him for working hard and encouraged him to continue to the end. After a short while, a member of the nursery staff interrupted them and suggested that Masuma might enjoy helping a more able child.

- What effect do you think the attitude of the member of the nursery staff might have on this child?
- What message is being given to the student?
- Why do you think the member of staff feels this way?
- As an early years manager how would you deal with this situation?

Enhancing self-esteem

Children appear to develop their level of self-esteem from early experiences; these build up for the children a picture of their own ability, competence and social acceptance in a range of activities. Such experiences will be gained in the family and in the early years setting, and can either build a strong foundation from which self-esteem will grow or cause a child to feel incompetent and insecure. It is the role of the early years practitioner to ensure children can develop their self-image through helping children to feel:

- competent and able
- confident in their physical skills and abilities
- socially accepted
- that they belong.

Children who have high self-esteem can recognise that they are not good at everything and may find some things difficult. They understand that they are not less worthy because they struggle with some tasks. They are not inhibited in trying out ideas and are not frightened of making mistakes.

Children who develop low self-esteem are less likely to develop to their full potential, either academically or socially. Children with low self-esteem:

- may dislike themselves and have few feelings of self-worth
- may appear over-confident, which is a common strategy to cover a fragile self-image
- may have difficulties in forming and maintaining relationships.

It is the role of the early years practitioner to support children with low self-esteem through consistent praise and encouragement. Such a positive approach can lead children to begin to develop the skills they need to learn and socialise.

Think it over

Children with a poor self-image are less likely to achieve their full potential. How can a setting actively promote a good self-image? Use the following questions to help you to evaluate practice in your setting. Try to think of examples for each question.

- Are children genuinely praised regularly, not only for achievement but also for effort?
- How much time do adults actually give to individual children during the session?
- How many children receive high-quality, meaningful, one-to-one interaction with an adult during the session?
- How do adults demonstrate that they value the contributions made by children and their families?
- How does the setting demonstrate that the children's families are welcomed and valued?

Share your findings with someone from another setting. Are there any common approaches to how a good self-image is promoted?

Play as a vehicle for learning

Play is regarded as the primary vehicle for children's development and learning and should be used as an opportunity for children to question, try out, test and explore ideas. A high-quality setting values the importance of play as a vehicle for high-quality learning. It is a fundamental principle that children learn through play, and high-quality play can provide children with the motivation for self-directed learning. In addition, play is essential to a child's healthy growth and development. Through purposeful play, children are able to develop a range of skills at their own individual level and pace (see Figure 2.1).

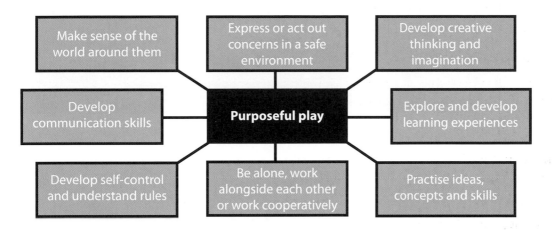

Figure 2.1. The skills children can learn through purposeful play

Points for reflective practice

Take some time to observe the children in your setting playing. Using the skills that children can develop or learn through purposeful play as a checklist (in Figure 2.1), identify the learning you see taking place. Can you identify and make a list of any gaps in their learning? If so, how can you ensure this area of learning is provided for?

The role of the adult in supporting play

The early years manager should ensure that the team understands its important role in both facilitating and supporting all varieties of play. Without well-planned, purposeful play opportunities, resources and sensitive support from adults, learning opportunities are not maximised. Sensitive support requires early years practitioners to know:

- how to offer physical support, for example holding a piece of paper being cut out by a child who is struggling with the task
- when to offer encouragement in order for children to complete tasks by themselves
- when to ask questions in order to support problem-solving
- when to make suggestions
- when their involvement, help or support is not needed.

It could be argued that the most important point is the last one. Early years practitioners should always resist the temptation to add to or complete children's work, as this takes away the children's ownership of it and minimises the value of the experience. They should also be prepared to have their offers of involvement rejected by children, who have the right to choose to play without adult input.

Think it over

Observe a colleague giving a group of children a creative activity to do.

- What level of adult interaction or support did the children require during the activity?

- Did the children receive uninvited adult support and attention?

- Were opportunities taken to extend the activity and the children's learning?

- What factors may have prevented your colleagues from providing the children with support during the activity?

Share your findings with the group.

2.2 Identifying quality indicators

Quality indicators should be evident in all areas of practice. They are specific areas of practice that can be assessed and, if necessary, improved. They can therefore demonstrate whether or not high standards of learning provision and care are being consistently met in the setting. An important role of the early years manager in assuring quality is regularly to review and evaluate all aspects of the setting. For that evaluation to be effective, it must lead to any necessary changes being made to practice.

Childcare currently has a high profile nationally and is the focus of new policies, accreditations and initiatives that aim to increase the quality of provision for young children. *Practice Guidance for the Early Years Foundation Stage* emphasises the importance of high-quality early childhood education and care and highlights the importance of all providers considering how to create, maintain and improve a setting so that it meets the highest standards and offers the best experience for young children. The guidance defines high-quality early years provision as provision that:

- improves all children's outcomes

- provides increased appropriate support for children at risk of exclusion or poor outcomes

- builds the foundations of future attainment for Key Stage 1 and beyond.

Practice Guidance for the Early Years Foundation Stage also outlines a range of quality indicator for early years settings, including:

- a safe and stimulating environment

- challenging and appropriate play-based content reflecting individual needs

- well-qualified and experienced staff

- access to effective practice and professional development for staff by recognising the importance of continuing professional development for all staff

- effective challenge and support by designing and maintaining systems of management which encourage continuous quality improvement and embed effective practice

- sustained shared thinking where adults are aware of children's interests and understandings

- monitoring information and data.

These quality indicators apply to all settings with young children and can be used as a guide for good practice. High-quality practice that is developmentally appropriate can be achieved only when all practitioners in the setting share the same professional principles and values. As an early years manager it is important to ensure that all of your team are familiar with the quality indicators so they can be consistently incorporated into practice. Practical ways of achieving this include:

- providing a list of quality indicators in staff induction packs

- displaying the list of quality indicators on the staff notice board

- regularly selecting different points to evaluate during team meetings to assess how well each is being met.

Below, more detailed consideration is given to the use of quality indicators in one of the areas listed above – a safe and stimulating physical environment – to illustrate how practice can be evaluated.

A safe and stimulating environment

A safe and stimulating physical environment, with high-quality equipment and resources inside and outside, is central to providing a quality learning experience for young children. The range of resources provided by a setting will greatly depend on budget, storage and availability; however, there are some basics that all settings should provide. These are listed in Table 2.1. By evaluating this aspect of the setting you can identify any areas that need to be added to or improved.

Table 2.1. Equipment and resources: basic provision checklist

Type of equipment/ resource	Check points
Sand	Wet and dry sand, plus tools and equipment that are changed frequently to maintain interest. Freedom to add other toys (e.g. cars, animals and people) to stimulate imaginative play
Water	Changed daily. Add colour, bubbles, warm water, ice cubes, snow to stimulate and extend learning
Imaginative play area	Changed regularly with the help of the children to encourage role play and provide a range of learning experiences (e.g. vet's surgery, post office, home, café)

Type of equipment/resource	Check points
Book corner	Frequently changed books as well as a stock of old favourites. Both information and storybooks available and books made by the children
Art and craft activities	A large range of materials and resources for children to access freely, without the support of an adult. Space for work and models to dry, be displayed and opportunities to return to finish work
Large construction blocks	Placed in a suitable area, which allows the children to be freely creative without disturbing other children at play
Small construction materials	Freely accessible
Table-top activities	'Small world' play, jigsaws, threading beads, etc., available for children to choose from and work with
Music area	Displaying both bought and child-made instruments, which can be freely used (i.e. not just with adult supervision)
Cooking facilities	A regularly provided range of cooking experiences, including a variety of sweet and savoury foods from different cultures. Cooking activities can be used to extend learning experience
Live animals and plants	Those that do not pose a health risk
Investigative area	Regularly changed resources and equipment that are interesting and stimulating
Space and time for physical activity	Including dance, drama, movement activity
Quiet area/baby sleep-room	For younger children to rest or sleep
Well-equipped outside area	With a range of equipment to encourage physical development
Staffroom	Space away from the children where staff can have meetings and take breaks
Toilets	Minimum of one toilet and washbasin with hot and cold water available per ten children over the age of 2; separate toilet facilities for adults

Think it over

Use Table 2.1 to assess the environment in your setting.

■ Does it provide all the equipment and resources listed?

■ If not, can you say why not?

■ How are these areas organised in your setting?

■ How might these areas be developed to maximise their potential?

When evaluating the equipment and resources in your setting it can be helpful to consider the following points:

■ Are all resources, equipment and furniture appropriate to the age and developmental stage of the children?

■ Are all the resources and equipment easily accessible and attractively presented?

■ Is all equipment maintained properly and checked regularly for safety?

In addition to the basics of equipment, the following is a useful list of key principles in relation to the early years environment.

■ All areas both inside and out should be interesting and inviting, with the flexibility to cater for the children's individual stages of learning.

■ The atmosphere should be warm, happy and relaxed, with a familiar routine and structure.

■ Accommodation should have a good-quality light source where children work and play.

■ Access should be adult controlled by means of a security system.

■ Display areas for children's work and interactive experiences should be offered at a variety of levels.

■ Furniture and fittings should be appropriate to the children's ages.

■ Toys and materials should be stored attractively, and be readily accessible and clearly labelled.

Equipment used by children should be checked regularly for signs of wear or damage.

- There should be a carpeted area for floor play and an easily washed floor for messy and creative play.

- The layout should give children the opportunity to mix freely and work individually, in pairs and in groups of varying sizes.

- There should be at least one quiet area.

- There should be separate, defined areas appropriate to various activities.

- The children should have enough clear space to use their energy safely, and in this regard they should be provided with stimulation and challenge.

- The staff need to plan a space for confidential listening and talking to children and parents.

Points for reflective practice

Think about the list of key principles for providing a high-quality environment.

- How many of these principles are already met by your setting?

- Are there any areas you feel need addressing?

- Do you monitor the layout of your setting and discuss with your team any changes identified as a result of observation?

Organisation of equipment and resources

Careful thought needs to be given to how equipment and resources are presented. Children need space to work individually, in pairs and in groups, according to age and preference. They need the freedom to make choices, select materials and be freely creative. The way in which equipment and resources are presented will greatly affect their use by children. In order to encourage children to use their natural curiosity and freely explore the range of equipment on offer, it needs to be easily accessible and attractive to them.

Many of the resources used in early years settings are consumable, particularly those linked to art and craft activities, for example paint, pencils, paper and glue. As these types of resources do not last long they can easily be neglected. In order to avoid this they need to be taken into account when each term's budget is set. How art consumables are managed is very important, as children who persistently have to work with resources and materials that are worn out or in short supply are unlikely to gain much from the experience. Poor management of these types of resources gives a strong message to children and parents that creative work is not valued.

Think it over

- How does your setting ensure that there is an adequate supply of consumable art materials and resources?

- How are these materials presented to the children?

- Are the children encouraged to be responsible for the care of consumable items, for example replacing lids on felt pens?

Renewing resources

Pip and Carol have recently taken over the running of their local playgroup. They have inherited a vast range of equipment and resources, some of which date back to when the playgroup was first established, 15 years ago. Part of their reorganisation strategy involves evaluating which pieces of equipment are no longer required, are out of date or are no longer suitable. They start by observing the children at play and recording which pieces of equipment are used regularly. From their observations they note that few of the children play with the very large range of jigsaws available. The jigsaws are stacked on low shelves in a quiet area of the room. Some are still in their original box while others are stored in plastic boxes with lids.

- Why do you think the children were not choosing to play with the jigsaws?

- Consider how equipment and resources are presented in your setting and whether this has an effect on their use.

Organisation of space

The organisation of space is another important aspect of providing a high-quality environment and should focus on the children as much as possible. The room arrangement should encourage spontaneous play and support play, not restrict or limit it. A sound knowledge of child development and an understanding of how children play should inform how a room layout is planned. Play underpins the delivery of the Early Years Foundation Stage and children should have the opportunity to play both indoors and outdoors. The outdoor provides children with the opportunity to develop a range of skills as well as raise children's activity levels. With growing concerns about childhood obesity there is much emphasis on encouraging young children to become more active. By creating a safe and stimulating outdoor environment it is possible to encourage children to spend more time playing outside. It is now common for some settings to implement much of their curriculum outside as there is nothing that cannot be covered in an outdoor classroom. Moving outside can complement and reinforce any work that is going on in the indoor classroom.

The way the indoor rooms are organised will have an impact on children and how they behave. You might consider:

- how well the resources are used by children
- how accessible resources are
- how active children can be
- how welcoming the setting appears
- the overall atmosphere
- the choices children make
- their relationships with adults and peers
- their behaviour
- their ability to play freely.

Nursery play

In the nursery class of a primary school a group of 3- and 4-year-olds regularly play a game which involves loading up trolleys and pushchairs with dolls and blankets and filling up bags and boxes with food and equipment from the home corner. These are then transported around the room where 'camps' or picnics are set up. The room arrangement supports this form of play and allows children unrestricted access to equipment and to move freely about the room without disturbing others. The early years practitioners regularly monitor and review the room arrangement in their team meetings. During a recent meeting Siobhan, a newly qualified early years practitioner, suggests that the room be rearranged to discourage this type of play as it causes too much tidying up at the end of the session.

- What skills are children developing through this type of play?

- Why is it important to allow children to play in this way?

- How can this type of play be supported and extended?

- What can the early years practitioners learn from observing children playing in this way?

Allow children to have unrestricted access to equipment in the home corner.

An evaluation of the layout and organisation of a setting's environment would cover the following points:

- Does the room look well organised?

- What are the first impressions when newcomers see the setting?

- Does the room look clean, bright and inviting?

- Are hazardous items clearly labelled, correctly stored and out of children's reach?

- Are resources used by the children clearly labelled, easily accessible and nicely presented?

- Are adult resources well organised, labelled and easily accessible?

- Is there suitable storage for equipment and resources?

- Is the outside environment used as an integral part of the children's learning, and do children have freedom to move between inside and outside for part of the session?

Think it over

Consider whether all of the spaces within your setting are used effectively.

- Is there space for children to engage in active learning?

- Do children have space to move around the room without disturbing others?

- Are all areas valuable for young learners?

Draw a floor plan of your setting, remembering to include access points and emergency exits, toilets, classroom sinks and non-movable items of furniture. Look at each area.

- Could they be organised more effectively?

- Are the resources required for each area stored nearby?

Throughout this chapter ways of achieving a high-quality provision have been discussed. Equally important as achieving it is maintaining it. Regular reviews of practice enable the manager to ensure that the very best service is provided for children and families in the setting. Therefore, to maintain quality, it is good practice to:

- review policies and procedures regularly

- monitor achievement

- review practice against quality indicators outlined in the *Practice Guidance for the Early Years Foundation Stage*

- include parents and carers in the assessment and evaluation process

- implement change as a result of assessment and review.

2.3 Identifying current good practice

Identifying current good practice can be achieved in many ways. Most approaches examine good practice by selecting characteristics of the setting, equipment or programme, and measuring them against key principles of good practice. There is no doubt that this is an important and valuable method of assessment; however, viewing good practice this way only gives a partial view of practice. Therefore it can be a worthwhile exercise to determine how those who use the setting experience the provision. Users will include children, parents and carers and the staff (Figure 2.2).

Reviewing the setting from different users' perspectives

The children's viewpoint

By evaluating the children's experience of the provision you can gain a valuable insight into its effectiveness. This evaluation requires answers to the central question 'What does it feel like to be a child in this environment?' You can use the following points as a guide to answering this question.

- Do the children appear to feel welcomed?

- Do they appear to feel that they belong as an individual or as just one of a group?

- Do they appear to feel accepted, understood and protected by the adults in the setting?

- Do they appear to feel accepted by each other?

Figure 2.2. Different users of a setting will have different points of view

- Do the adults in the setting address the children respectfully?
- Are the majority of the activities engaging, absorbing and challenging?
- Are the majority of the planned experiences meaningful?
- Are the activities and experiences age-appropriate?
- Do the children enjoy being in the setting?
- Are routines and procedures in place to meet the needs of the children and not for the convenience of the adults?

Each point represents a criterion of good practice derived from what is known about the influences on children's long-term growth, development and learning. If the answers to these questions are mostly positive you can assume that the setting is providing a high-quality service from the children's point of view. It will be one in which learning experiences are consistently intellectually and socially engaging. Research has shown that infrequent and isolated learning experiences are unlikely to have an effect on long-term development. In order to stimulate and satisfy curiosity, planned activities and experiences need to be frequent, and have clear aims and learning outcomes in order to be most effective. However, these activities and experiences do not have to be exceptionally dynamic or unusual to have an impact. Young children view the world with fresh eyes and it is easy to forget that what may seem mundane for adults is full of possibilities for children.

The parents' and carers' viewpoint

The assessment and evaluation of good practice will always take into account the viewpoint of parents and carers. You can use the following questions to help evaluate the relationship between parents and carers and the setting.

- Is information about the setting provided before children start?
- Are parents and carers encouraged to stay until their child has settled?
- Are they welcomed each day and are staff available to them?
- Are individual families' levels of involvement respected and understood by staff?
- Are parents and carers actively encouraged to discuss concerns, problems and changes involving the child or family as they occur?
- Does the setting celebrate achievements and milestones as they occur?
- Are experiences and activities shared through 'open' sessions, parents' workshops, outings, social events, publicity and fundraising?
- Are parents and carers invited to come in and talk about their own skills, hobbies and jobs with children or join in sessions to support children?
- Are themes, routines and 'happenings' shared via a noticeboard or newsletter?

Many of these questions form the foundation of work with parents and carers. However, it is good practice to review and evaluate what is done in order to maintain standards and to ensure that the needs of all the families in the setting are met.

The staff viewpoint

When assessing good practice in the setting, it is always useful for the manager to include an evaluation from the team's viewpoint. High-quality environments cannot be created unless they are also good for the adults who work in them. Experience shows that early years practitioners who feel good about themselves and their professional practice are more able to provide high-quality learning experiences for the children in their care. They are more likely to have time, confidence and energy to fulfil all aspects of their responsibilities with children and families.

There are three aspects to the quality of an early years setting from the practitioners' viewpoint:

- relationships with other team members
- relationships with parents
- relationships with managers, head teachers and/or owners of the setting.

The quality of the relationships between team members will affect the quality of the setting. It is difficult to be consistent and work towards shared aims when team members do not get on. It can be helpful for the manager to carry out a confidential assessment of the team's relationships with each other. An assessment of this aspect of quality would be based on how each team member answered the following question:

- Are your relationships with other team members mostly supportive, cooperative, accepting, trusting, respectful?

The answers can help you to organise your team. However, because skills and responsibilities also need to be taken into account, it is not always possible to separate team members. These answers will also highlight areas for staff development – by equipping individuals with the skills needed to work in teams in a professional manner you are able to work towards providing a more positive working environment.

The development of respectful and supportive relationships between staff and parents and carers from a diverse range of backgrounds requires staff professionalism based on a combination of experience, training and personal values. Parents and carers are more likely to approach staff when staff initiate positive relationships with them. Part of the process of assessing the quality of the setting would involve evaluating the characteristics of the relationship between the staff and the parents. The following question can help team members to evaluate their own relationship with parents.

- Are my relationships with parents mostly respectful and supporting, accepting, non-judgemental and non-biased, and ongoing, with frequent contact?

Parents and carers are more likely to feel part of the setting when the staff show that they value them.

Lastly, one potential indirect influence on identifying good practice is the nature of the relationships the team have with those to whom they are accountable. Research has shown that staff treat children in a similar way to how their managers treat them. If a team feels undervalued it can be hard for them to feel enthusiastic and positive about the work they are doing. They may not behave in an unprofessional manner, but their lack of enthusiasm will reduce the quality of their work. The following questions can help the early years manager to assess the team's relationships with him or her:

- Do the working conditions encourage the staff to develop their knowledge and skills, and take on more responsibility?
- Are staff usually treated with respect and understanding?

Some thought and consideration will need to be given to how these questions are presented to the team. Staff may feel that it is hard for them to answer these questions honestly and openly; therefore it can be good practice to present such questions on a form that can be completed anonymously.

Reviewing organisational systems and practice

Most early years practitioners recognise the value of regularly evaluating practice and procedures. As group dynamics change with each new intake, so do the needs of children and their families. Evaluation of practice ensures that these needs can be met. Regular review and assessment of organisational systems and practice enables you to identify achievements and areas for development. This enables the service to progress and meet the ever-changing needs of parents and children.

All organisational systems need to be evaluated frequently. Areas to be considered include the following.

- *The management of all team meetings*. Are there clear agendas?
- *Programme reviews*. Are there regular dates (termly) set for reviewing individual programmes in order to assess whether the needs of the children are being met?
- *Current research and ideas*. Are staff encouraged and given the opportunity to keep up to date with new ideas and current research?
- *Professional development*. Do all members of the team have the opportunity to attend regular training?
- *The management of policies, parental comments and concerns, and staff suggestions*. Are these being addressed appropriately? Are policies and procedures updated as necessary and always available to all staff and students for reference?

2.4 Maintaining quality

Research has found a correlation between high-quality provision and the level of staff training and continuing professional development (CPD). Early years practitioners in the UK are generally better trained than their counterparts in mainland Europe. *Practice Guidance for the Early Years Foundation Stage* highlights the importance of well-qualified and experienced staff, by:

- recognising the importance of CPD for all staff
- supporting staff undertaking CPD
- providing opportunities for staff to share good practice
- supporting other staff in the absence of staff undertaking CPD
- offering incentives for staff successfully completing CPD activities.

High-quality work in early years settings is possible only when staff are open to continuing professional practice. For this reason managers and mentors need to positively encourage their team to take part in regular training, challenging any reluctance to do so. Initial training is important, but continuous training and professional development are crucial (this is discussed further in Chapter 7). Early years practitioners need to continue to learn, and to be open to new ideas and approaches. As in any profession, early years practitioners can become stale and approach work always in the same way merely because that is how it has always

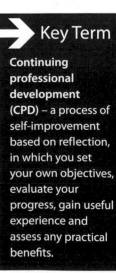

Key Term

Continuing professional development (CPD) – a process of self-improvement based on reflection, in which you set your own objectives, evaluate your progress, gain useful experience and assess any practical benefits.

been done. As an early years manager it is your role to ensure that your team receives ongoing training. This can include:

- in-house training
- update training for first aid and other renewable certificates
- short courses, seminars and talks provided by local networks
- college/university courses.

Training and updating should include the topics shown in Figure 2.3, as they are the subject of constant research and development:

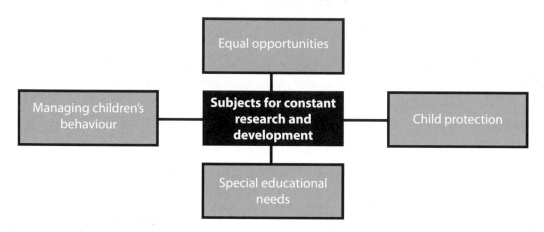

Figure 2.3. Some areas need constant updating

Early Years Professional Status (EYPS)

The Children's Workforce Development Council's (CWDC) vision is for the early years workforce to be led by well-skilled and highly motivated graduates. They describe these Early Years Professionals (EYPs) as 'practice leaders' whose role it is to develop, introduce, lead and supervise developmental work with children under the age of five.

Research has shown that one key indicator of the quality of childcare is the qualifications held by practitioners. Early Years Professional Status has been introduced in response to this evidence, to develop high-quality provision and services that will support the well-being, learning and development of all children.

The government recognises that access to high-quality childcare is important for all parents and their children. The move to a graduate-led profession represents a transformation of the early years workforce. To drive this transformation the government has stated that their aim is to have at least one Early Years Professional in every full-day care setting, and one in every children's centre.

The CWDC works with many training providers, local authorities and employers across the UK to train Early Years Professionals. A full list of these, along with their contact details, can be found on the CWDC website.

There are four pathways to completing full EYPS, depending on the existing skills and experience of the practitioner (see Table 2.2).

> **Key Term**

Early Years Professional Status (EYPS) – the new status for early years practitioners – a graduate leader in early years.

Table 2.2. Pathways to completing Early Years Professional Status

Pathway	Programme
Validation Pathway	Six days' preparation and assessment over 4 months (for candidates who are already working at the level of all the standards)
Short Extended Professional Development (EPD) Pathway	Part-time over 6 months (for candidates who are almost working at the level of all the standards)
Long Extended Professional Development Pathway	Part-time top-up over 15 months for those with a foundation degree
Full Training Pathway	Full-time over 12 months

Early years practitioners are assessed against a set of EYPS standards that set out expectations for professional leadership and personal practice. Practitioners are expected to demonstrate how they implement each of the standards in their setting.

Mentoring

It may also be your role as manager to either mentor your team or provide them with a suitable mentor. Mentoring is an important part of good practice. It can provide a framework of support for continuous personal and professional development and is integral to the development of high-quality early years provision. Alison Robins (2006) describes mentoring as a system of advice and support in the context of ongoing professional training and development which makes sense of reflective practice. The mentoring process enables practitioners to develop their skills of reflection, identifying areas of practice in need of further development. Mentors can also support practitioners by:

Key Term

Mentor – trusted and experienced professional person who can provide individual training, advice and support in an organisation or institution.

- focusing on the ability and potential of the practitioner
- identifying links between theory and practice
- sharing and role modelling good practice
- sharing professional values
- helping to solve professional challenges.

Think it over

Think about the people who have influenced you so far in your personal and professional development as an early years practitioner.

- Can you identify why they had such an impact on you?
- Make a list of all the qualities and skills you think a good mentor should have.

In order to ensure the mentoring process has a positive impact on the setting and those involved it is important that the relationship between a mentor and the practitioner is a positive one. Some consideration needs to be given to the pairing of the person who is mentoring (the mentor) and the person being mentored (the mentee), and whether they have similar expectations from the process.

Ideally a mentor would:

- be professionally competent and a positive role model
- be able to dedicate time to the mentoring process
- be aware of the need to maintain confidentiality
- believe in the potential of the practitioner they are mentoring.

Ideally a mentee should:

- have realistic expectations of their mentor
- be responsible for their own part in the process
- be receptive to guidance, advice and support
- view the process as a positive one.

Observation, assessment and record-keeping

In order to help ensure that your setting is implementing developmentally appropriate practice it is necessary to carry out regular observations of the children in the setting. These observations add to individual profiles built over time and inform planning. It is not possible to plan effectively without knowing exactly from where children are starting. Regular observation, assessment and record-keeping are considered to be the basis of good childcare practice (Figure 2.4).

- *Observation* allows you to maintain and update the profile of each child. It alerts you to any causes for concern and highlights advancement in development. Observation can be either formal or informal. Practitioners make frequent and regular informal observations of children, noting and sharing any significant points. Formal observations are most successful when there is a focus. Through formal observation practitioners are able to build a full picture of individual children's strengths and abilities and those areas that need support. Regular, focused observations are key to developmentally appropriate practice, as they inform all aspects of planning.

- *Assessment* is made of the results of observation and of information shared by parents and carers. Assessment results are used to inform planning and to identify areas in which children may need extending or supporting. Assessment of children's performance enables you to evaluate the effectiveness of educational strategies.

- *Record-keeping* is essential for good practice as it provides evidence for future reference. Records of observations, assessments and planning should always be kept.

High-quality provision combines observational evidence with a range of other techniques to provide a rich record of the achievements, interests and needs of children attending the setting. Early years practitioners constantly observe children and make formal records of observations according to a predetermined focus. Individual profiles containing samples of children's work and photographs of experiences can be shared with parents and carers.

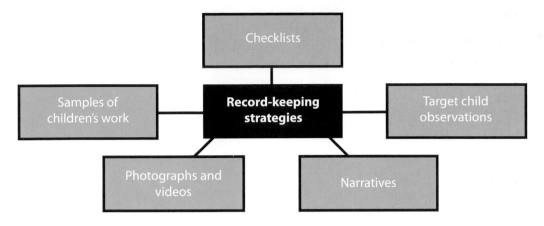

Figure 2.4. A variety of record-keeping strategies are commonly used in early years settings

Reflective practice

Another key aspect of maintaining quality is to be a reflective practitioner. Effective assessment and record-keeping support the process of reflecting on practice, as they provide evidence of past events. Reflecting on practice enables you to identify areas for improvement or change and highlight areas of success.

The curriculum content, procedures and routines that are offered to young children must match the content of their thinking, their development and understanding in order to extend their learning and understanding. The reflective practitioner may devise a variety of teaching approaches to support children's learning and needs to know which is most successful. For example, the practitioner may decide to change from a structured approach to one that allows children to select their own activities and wishes to know whether change has been beneficial.

Being a reflective practitioner requires you to:

- think about issues from more than one point of view
- review activities and approaches, and to find scope for improvement
- be open to new ideas, approaches and changes in practice
- acknowledge and recognise the feelings of children, parents and colleagues
- be actively involved and enthusiastic.

All early years managers are responsible for encouraging reflective practice within their team. Areas that benefit from reflective practice include:

- planning for children's learning
- organising developmentally appropriate learning opportunities
- supporting and extending learning
- recording children's progress
- meeting the individual needs of children
- working in partnership with parents, carers and colleagues.

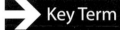
Key Term

Reflective practice – thinking about your role and practice with the aim of evaluating it and making any changes to improve its quality.

Teddy Bears day nursery

Diane is the manager at Teddy Bears day nursery. As part of the regular review of practice, Diane has asked each room supervisor to carry out a series of observations over a week, focusing on procedures and practice in order to identify any areas for development. The supervisor of the toddler room, Sarah, sees that the children frequently become distressed at lunchtime, when they are moved into the dining room to join an older group of children for their lunch. Further investigation shows that it is taking almost 15 minutes to complete hand-washing and that the children are becoming frustrated waiting for this to be completed.

- Why do you think the children are distressed at this time of day?

- What can be done to improve the situation?

- What procedures do you currently have in place for identifying areas for improvement in your setting? How effective are they?

Time management

Maintaining a high-quality service for the children and families using the setting is a time-consuming process. It is an ongoing process of review, evaluation, assessment and reflection, all of which have to be carefully planned and facilitated. Time needs to be managed carefully in order to achieve this. There are two elements to good time management: effectiveness and efficiency, or doing the right jobs and doing each job correctly.

As an early years manager you will find that your team is an essential resource to time management. Team members have a range of skills and abilities that should be utilised. Once these have been identified, related tasks can be delegated and redistributed, allowing you more time for other projects. By giving team members individual roles and responsibilities you are recognising their skills and demonstrating that their contribution to the setting is valued.

2.5 Welfare requirements of the Early Years Foundation Stage

The overarching aim of the Early Years Foundation Stage (EYFS) is to help young children achieve the five *Every Child Matters* outcomes (Figure 2.5).

It is intended that these outcomes will be achieved by:

- Setting the standards for the learning, development and care young children should experience when they are attending a setting outside their family home, ensuring that every child makes progress and that no child falls behind.

- Providing for equality of opportunity and anti-discriminatory practice and ensuring that every child is included and not disadvantaged because of ethnicity, culture or religion, home language, family background, learning difficulties or disabilities, gender or ability.

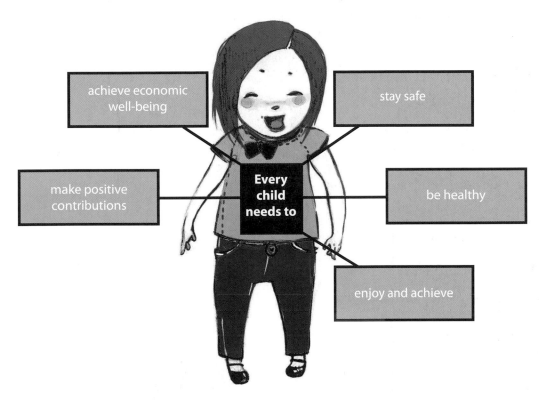

Figure 2.5. The five outcomes of *Every Child Matters*

- Creating the framework for partnership working between parents and professionals, and between all the settings that the child attends.

- Improving quality and consistency in the early years sector through a universal set of standards that apply to all settings, ending the distinction between care and learning in the existing frameworks, and providing the basis for the inspection and regulation process.

- Laying a secure foundation for future learning through learning and development that is planned around the individual needs and interests of the child, and informed by the use of ongoing observational assessment.

The EYFS framework outlines the welfare requirements that all early years providers must meet. The welfare requirements are designed to support providers in creating settings that are welcoming, safe, and stimulating, and where children are able to enjoy learning through play, to grow in confidence and to fulfil their potential. The following is a brief overview of the welfare requirements. A more in-depth version detailing the specific legal requirements can be found in the *Statutory Framework for the Early Years Foundation Stage* document (Department for Children, Schools and Families, 2008).

General welfare requirements

Safeguarding and promoting children's welfare

- The provider must take necessary steps to safeguard and promote the welfare of children.

- The provider must promote the good health of the children, taking necessary steps to prevent the spread of infection, and take appropriate action when they are ill.

- Children's behaviour must be managed effectively and in a manner appropriate to their stage of development and individual needs.

Providers should follow the guidance set out in the booklet 'What to do if you are worried a child is being abused' (Department of Health, 2003).

Key person

Each child in a group setting must be allocated to a key person. The key person is responsible for working closely with the child, parents and record-keeping.

Suitable person

Providers must ensure that adults looking after children are suitable to do so, with appropriate qualifications, training, skills and knowledge.

Suitable premises, environment and equipment

Outdoor and indoor spaces, furniture, equipment and toys must be safe and suitable for their purpose.

Organisation

Providers must plan and organise their systems to ensure that every child receives an enjoyable and challenging learning and development experience that is tailored to meet their individual needs.

Documentation

Providers must maintain records, policies and procedures required for the safe and efficient management of the settings and to meet the needs of the children.

Key Term

Safeguarding – the process of identifying children who have suffered or who are likely to suffer significant harm, and then taking appropriate action to keep them safe.

Meeting welfare requirements

The requirements are set out in three sections:

1 overarching general legal requirements

2 specific legal requirements

3 statutory guidance.

Early years settings must comply with all the legal requirements set out and should have regard to the statutory guidance. Ofsted will base its regulatory inspection judgements on whether a provider has met the general and specific legal requirements.

2.6 Meeting the requirements of *Every Child Matters* within the setting

Every Child Matters (ECM) makes a significant commitment to the nurturing and education of all children. It identifies that performance and well-being go hand in hand. Children cannot learn if they do not feel safe or if health problems create barriers. The five outcomes for children shown in Figure 2.5 are central to ensuring that effective joined-up children's services from education, health and social care provide 'wrap-around' care in settings, enabling children to achieve the outcomes.

Think it over

As a practitioner in an early years setting, what opportunities already exist for children in your care to make significant progress towards meeting the five outcomes of ECM successfully?

Other key aspects of the ECM framework include:

- early intervention and effective provision
- improving information sharing between agencies to speed up the process of obtaining help and support needed for children and families
- developing a Common Assessment Framework (CAF) across services
- identifying a 'lead professional' to coordinate services for children to meet their needs
- developing wrap-around care and multi-disciplinary services in and around schools and in children's centres
- safeguarding children partnerships
- integrating an inspection framework for children's services
- common occupational standards for all agencies working with children (workforce reform).

Think it over

In what way do you think each of the above aspects of ECM impacts on the adult's role in the setting?

Implications for the practitioner's role

The introduction of *Every Child Matters* has significant implications for the practitioner's role. In particular, the practitioner should strive to achieve the following goals shown in Figure 2.6.

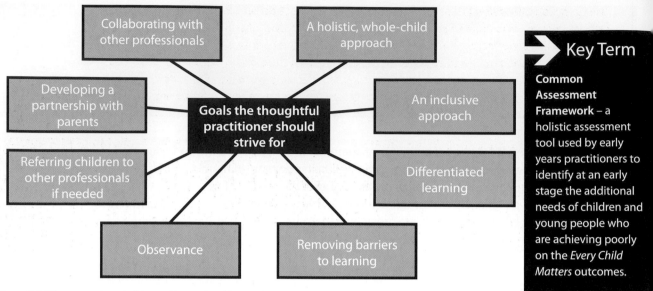

Figure 2.6. What every thoughtful practitioner should strive for

Key Term

Common Assessment Framework – a holistic assessment tool used by early years practitioners to identify at an early stage the additional needs of children and young people who are achieving poorly on the *Every Child Matters* outcomes.

Common Assessment Framework

The Common Assessment Framework (CAF) is a key feature of *Every Child Matters*. The CAF is a generic, standardised approach to assessment for children with additional needs that can be used by practitioners across all children's services. It aims to help early identification of need, promote coordinated services and reduce the number of assessments that some children go through. Practitioners are able to use the CAF to identify how best to support a child appropriately. It is intended that the CAF will also help to improve integrated working by providing a coordinated and consistent approach.

The Common Core of Skills and Knowledge for the Children's Workforce

The Department for Education and Skills (DfES) has worked in partnership with service providers and users to produce a common set of skills and knowledge. The Common Core of Skills and Knowledge for the Children's Workforce sets out the basic skills and knowledge needed by people, including volunteers, whose work brings them into regular contact with children. It aims to enable multidisciplinary teams to work together more consistently and effectively in the interests of the children.

The skills and knowledge are described under six main headings:

- Effective communication and engagement with children
- Child and young person development
- Safeguarding and promoting the welfare of the child
- Supporting transitions
- Multi-agency working
- Sharing information.

The Common Core reflects a set of common values for practitioners that promote equality, respect diversity and challenge stereotypes, helping to improve the life chances of all children and provide more effective and integrated services. It also recognises the important role parents, carers and families play in helping children achieve the outcomes identified in *Every Child Matters*. Over time there is an expectation that everyone working with children and their families will be able to demonstrate a basic level of competence in the six areas of the Common Core, and that this will be an integral part of training.

2.7 Leading and managing continuous improvement in the provision

Effective leaders in early years settings need to recognise that their role is more than management. They are responsible for nurturing shared values and beliefs and encouraging a collaborative work ethic among their team. Their role is to ensure that their team works productively towards continuous improvements in the provision. Key responsibilities are to:

- manage and develop self and workforce
- lead and manage a provision that respects, protects and promotes the rights and responsibilities of people
- develop and maintain systems, procedures and practices to manage risks and comply with health and safety requirements within the provision
- lead and manage positive communication that promotes positive outcomes for people.

Think it over

Think about the above list of key responsibilities. Identify links with:

- *Every Child Matters*
- Common Core of Skills and Knowledge for the Children's Workforce
- Early Years Foundation Stage Framework.

It is important that all providers consider how best to create, maintain and improve a setting so that it meets the highest standards and offers the best experience for children and their families. All managers of settings should continually think about how to improve their setting and what they are offering.

Conclusion

High-quality early years childcare and education have a significant impact on later academic achievement and social behaviour. Providing a high-quality service is not about taking on a whole new approach; it is about recognising and celebrating what you already do well and identifying areas that could be improved. Many, if not most, aspects of practice in your setting will be of a high standard, and it is this level that needs to be maintained. It is probably impossible to share a common definition of quality and therefore there is a need to work towards a common understanding of how staff, parents and children define the term.

There is no universal measure of quality, as it is relative and subjective. For example parents, staff and children will have different views on what they believe is a good-quality service. However, the key aspects of quality provision as outlined in this chapter include:

- regular review and assessment of practice, followed by change in practice where necessary

- a child-centred approach that is developmentally appropriate and values play as a primary vehicle for development and learning

- a programme that values and recognises the importance of diversity

- staff training and professional development

- reflective practice.

Early years practitioners generally share the same values and principles and work towards a set of nationally recognised quality indicators in order to facilitate developmentally appropriate practice. In practical terms this means that early years programmes take into account the child's level of development – social, cognitive, physical and emotional – and that practice is based on child-initiated activities and experiences. Early years practitioners widely accept that social, physical, cognitive and emotional learning are as important as academic learning. Programmes that incorporate these principles create a positive learning environment that is conducive to healthy emotional development and which motivates children to learn.

Regular review and changes to practice enable settings to ensure they are consistently meeting the needs of children and that the provision is developmentally appropriate. These changes need to be 'owned' by practitioners rather than imposed through inspection or accreditation frameworks in order to be most effective.

Check your understanding

1 'Quality encompasses all areas of the setting, not just those directly linked to the children.' To what areas do you think this statement is referring?

2 How is quality both subjective and relative?

3 What do you understand by the term 'developmentally appropriate practice'?

References and further reading

Department for Children, Schools and Families (2008) *Statutory Framework for the Early Years Foundation Stage*. Available at www.standards.dcsf.gov.uk.

Baldock, P. Fitzgerald, D. and Kay, J. (2005) *Understanding Early Years Policy*. London: Paul Chapman.

Bruce, T. (2004) *Developing Learning in Early Childhood*. London: Paul Chapman.

Cheminais, R. (2006) *Every Child Matters: A Practical Guide for Teachers*. Abingdon: Routledge.

Clarke, M. and Waller, T. (2007) *Early Childhood Education and Care: Policy and Practice*. London: Sage Publications.

Department for Education and Skills (2001) *Special Educational Need: Code of Practice*. London: DfES. Available at www.teachernet. gov.uk.

Department for Education and Skills (2007) *The Early Years Foundation Stage. Setting the Standards for Learning, Development and Care for Children from Birth to Five*. Available at www.teachernet.gov.uk.

Department of Health (2003) *'What to do if you are worried a child is being abused'*. Available from www.dh.gov.uk.

Dowling, M. (2000) *Young Children's Personal, Social and Emotional Development*. London: Paul Chapman.

Dury, R., Miller, L. and Campbell, R. (2000) *Looking at Early Years Education and Care*. London: David Fulton.

Early Childhood Education Forum (1998) *Quality in Diversity in Early Learning*. London: NCB.

Filer, J. (2008) *Healthy, Active and Outside! Running an Outdoors Programme in the Early Years*. Abingdon: Routledge.

Miller, L and Devereux, J. (2004) *Supporting Children's Learning in the Early Years*. London: David Fulton.

Moss, P. and Penn, H. (1996) *Transforming Nursery Education*. London: Paul Chapman.

Nurse. A. (2007) *The New Early Years Professional: Dilemmas and Debates*. Abingdon: Routledge.

Robins, A. (2006) *Mentoring in the Early Years*. London: Paul Chapman.

Rodd, J. (2007) *Leadership in Early Childhood*. Maidenhead: Open University Press.

Shimmin, S. and White, H. (2006) *Every Day a Good Day*. London: Paul Chapman.

Siraj-Blatchford, I. Clarke, K. and Needham, M. (2007) *The Team Around the Child*. Stoke-on-Trent: Trentham Books.

Tassoni, P. (2008) *Penny Tassoni's Practical EYFS Handbook*. Oxford: Heinemann,

Useful websites

Children's Workforce Development Council (CWDC): www.cwdcouncil.org.uk

Department for Children, Schools and Families: www.dcsf.gov.uk

Department of Health: www.dh.gov.uk

Every Child Matters: www.everychildmatters.gov.uk

Hertfordshire Early Years Development and Childcare Partnership: www.hertsdirect.org

National Standards: www.standards.dcsf.gov.uk

Qualifications and Curriculum Authority (QCA): www.qca.org.uk

3 Managing the Early Years Curriculum

There have been a lot of changes over the past few years in the way that we view childhood and more importance is now attached to the early years stage of development. There is a clear focus on practitioners providing a common framework for children's learning, with all children in Britain having access to high-quality provision in order to have the same opportunities to learn. An expression of this commonality is seen in the Early Years Foundation Stage (EYFS) for children aged from birth to five years. This has been developed by the Department for Children, Schools and Families and brings together *Curriculum Guidance for the Foundation Stage* (2000), the *Birth to Three Matters* (2002) framework and the *National Standards for Under 8s Day Care and Childminding* (2003). The EYFS aims to build a coherent and flexible approach to care and learning in which children receive a quality experience that supports their development and learning. All providers are required to use the EYFS to ensure that whatever setting parents choose, they can be confident that their child will receive a quality experience that supports their development and learning.

The Welsh Assembly Government has also made a strong commitment to early years provision and is developing the Foundation Phase from September 2008 for all children aged 3 to 7 years. To support its implementation, a statutory Framework for Children's Learning for 3- to 7-year-olds in Wales is available. This sets out the curriculum and outcomes under seven Areas of Learning. For each Area of Learning, the educational programme sets out what children should be taught and the outcomes set out the expected standards of children's performance.

The curriculum in Northern Ireland has also undergone some changes, and from 2007 there has been a Foundation Stage to meet the needs of younger children. This will provide an appropriate curriculum by developing skills and confidence and introducing children to formal learning when they are ready.

Scotland is currently undertaking a large reform of its curriculum which aims to provide:

- more freedom for teachers
- greater choice and opportunity for pupils
- a single coherent curriculum for all children and young people aged 3 to 18.

At the heart of the changes is the programme Curriculum for Excellence, which will challenge perceptions of the curriculum in Scotland and encourage practitioners to plan and act in different ways.

As an early years manager you will need to focus on interpreting the requirements of the appropriate curriculum in order to meet the needs of individual children and groups of children. You must consider the practical application of the curriculum and the relationship between planning and the relevant curriculum guidance and legislation. Your provision will be inspected and registered on this basis.

This chapter discusses the key issues involved in the management of the early years curriculum.

The chapter covers the following areas:

3.1 Defining the curriculum

3.2 Regulatory and legislative frameworks

3.3 Theories of how children learn and their influence on practice

3.4 The importance of play in learning

3.5 Planning, implementing and evaluating the curriculum

3.6 Assessment and assessment systems

3.1 Defining the curriculum

As a leader of an early years team you must have a clear vision and understanding of the term 'curriculum' to ensure that you provide your team with a focus for their work. The term can be defined in two ways:

- as a planned overview of activities that have specific learning outcomes

- as everything that children do, see, hear or feel in their setting.

With regard to the former, national guidance and legislation determine which activities the children should have access to, and should be taught, and the goals that should be met by a predefined stage. However, each setting will need to establish the stage of development of its children and the most appropriate way to meet their needs. Your own educational views, the national legislative framework and the strengths of your staff will influence the curriculum that you offer, in the second sense above, which is the focus of this chapter. The curriculum you can offer will also be influenced by your working environment, as well as commonly held views on how children learn (section 3.3).

Within an early years team people will hold different views on what a curriculum is and how it should be implemented. It will be necessary to spend time and energy on agreeing the fundamental principles behind an early years curriculum and how these can be implemented in your particular setting in order for all team members to share ownership of it. There may need to be a series of meetings to ensure continuity of approach and opportunity for reflection on the success of the curriculum.

In the UK the curriculum is generally based on a western approach towards education underpinned by the work of theorists such as Piaget (see section 3.3) and reflecting the thinking of modern-day practitioners and researchers, including Margy Whalley (2007), Tina Bruce (2005), Bernadette Duffy and Gillian Pugh (2006). The child is seen as the focus of the curriculum and is respected as a person with individual needs, not as a miniature adult.

Meeting curriculum requirements

Modern approaches require the curriculum to be:

- child-centred

- developmentally appropriate

- differentiated

- inclusive.

Child-centred

The starting point for the children is what they *can* do, rather than what they *cannot* do, and progression is encouraged through exploration and experimentation. The curriculum is carefully structured to ensure all areas of learning are explored while ensuring the interests of the children are maintained. This may be referred to as a child-centred curriculum, which will emphasise the child's development and relationships with others (see Chapter 2.1).

 **Key Terms**

Child-centred – an approach that has the child at its centre, with all aspects of the setting being informed and influenced by children's interests and needs.

Inclusion/ inclusive – the process of ensuring equality of learning opportunities for all children irrespective of their diversity.

Adults working with children in the early years will need to have a sound understanding of child development and a working knowledge of activities that promote development. To ensure the curriculum is balanced, practitioners will spend considerable time planning, reflecting on and evaluating the curriculum they offer. For the manager this process must be documented in order to meet Ofsted regulations.

Developmentally appropriate

The western approach to education acknowledges the need for a developmentally appropriate curriculum that recognises the child's age and stage of development. The curriculum will set out what activities and experiences will consolidate and enhance the child's learning. National guidance specifies a developmentally appropriate curriculum for children of given ages. The Early Years Foundation Stage, for example, gives clear goals for learning that are appropriate for children from birth to age 5 years and includes extension activities.

Differentiated

A differentiated curriculum enables individual children to learn in their own particular way. Children will progress through their educational life at their own pace and in their own style. Some children will learn to read at 4 years old while others will not do so until the age of 6. Counting might be easily mastered by a few children at pre-school, but others will not be able to count with understanding until they are in nursery. A differentiated curriculum recognises this fact and ensures that children have the opportunity to learn at their own pace.

Inclusive

Children who are challenged in their learning through disability or developmental delay will also need to have their learning needs accounted for within the curriculum. The modern approach is based on an inclusive education for all children. The challenge for early years providers is to integrate all children and meet the needs of individuals and the group as a whole. There is a need to incorporate the wishes of parents and to work together to provide the best possible curriculum. This may include the writing of individual educational plans (IEPs) – for children aged 3 and over – and it is good practice to include parents and all practitioners involved with the child in the planning process.

The Early Years Foundation Stage is based on the principle of inclusion and the commitment of early years professionals to work against discrimination in all its forms and to welcome all children and their families.

The modern curriculum aims to benefit all children and their families.

3.2 Regulatory and legislative frameworks

As a manager it is important to be fully aware of the regulatory and legal requirements of the appropriate curriculum frameworks and to put these into practice within your setting. You will need to show that your setting is meeting the relevant national regulatory and legislative requirements. You must also be able to plan with colleagues in order to provide the best possible structure for the children in your care and to give information to parents and carers.

The Early Years Foundation Stage (EYFS)

Setting the Standards for Learning, Development and Care for Children from Birth to Five in England

The EYFS is based around four themes, each linked to an important principle for the care and education of children:

- A Unique Child – Every child is a competent learner from birth who can be resilient, capable, confident and self-assured.

- Positive Relationships – Children learn to be strong and independent from a base of loving and secure relationships with parents and/or a key person.

- Enabling Environments – The environment plays a key role in supporting and extending children's development and learning.

- Learning and Development – children develop and learn in different ways and at different rates and all areas of Learning and Development are equally important and interconnected.

These are accompanied by 16 commitments that practitioners need to follow in order to put the EYFS principles into practice.

A package of resource materials accompanies the EYFS, consisting of:

- a Statutory Framework booklet which outlines the welfare, learning and development requirements that must be followed by all practitioners in delivering the EYFS

- a Practice Guidance booklet

- an A1 poster which shows the principles and commitments

- 24 Principle into Practice cards

- a CD-ROM.

The EYFS and accompanying materials provide practitioners with clear statutory requirements based on knowledge of child development. There is also an emphasis on the role of reflection and continuous development of professional practice. The CD-ROM allows practitioners to access information and video clips on effective practice and research.

The EYFS has six areas of learning:

- personal, social and emotional development

- communication, language and literacy

- problem-solving, reasoning and numeracy
- knowledge and understanding of the world
- physical development
- creative development.

Each area of learning is divided into six ages of development:

- birth to 11 months
- 8 to 20 months
- 16 to 26 months
- 22 to 36 months
- 30 to 50 months
- 40 to 60 months+.

There is an intentional overlap between the six ages of development as children develop at different rates. However, it is important for practitioners to be able to recognise the norms of development in order to establish when a child needs extra support

Early Years Foundation Stage Profile (EYFSP) 2008

This handbook and booklet contains the early learning goals and profile statements which are accurate descriptions of children's achievements in the EYFS. These are not assessment criteria but enable practitioners to identify the progress individual children have made. This provides a useful tool for collaboration with parents and colleagues, in particular when children are transferring to another setting.

Think it over

- Access the EYFS materials on www.standards.dcsf.gov.uk
- Choose the link to Positive Relationships.
- Select 2.1 Respecting each other.
- Watch the video clip – Greeting a friend.

Discuss the video clip with colleagues in your workplace:

- What does the clip show you about the stages of development of the children?
- Reflect on the importance of friendships to young children. Why is it important for children to make friends?
- How can you encourage children to establish friendships?

The EYFS has raised concerns from leading academics and childcare specialists that the statutory requirements based on the welfare and learning and development of young children are too formal in their approach and that this is not conducive with the way children under 5 learn. At the Open Eye Conference in February 2008 Steve Biddulph noted that if a child aged under 6 years old is forced to learn, or activities are planned in a regimented way, the child is likely to lose motivation, not to do so well, and may become averse to learning (Biddulph, 2008).

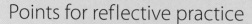
Points for reflective practice

- Access the Open Eye Campaign and consider the criticisms of the EYFS.
- Discuss these criticisms with your colleagues in the workplace.
- Reflect on the implications for your practice.
- Consider how you will present information to parents about the EYFS.

Key Stage 1 (KS1) teachers will need to be aware of the requirements of the EYFS in order to support and extend learning for individuals who have not met the early learning goals. For the early years manager it is essential to ensure that clear and detailed records accompany the child as they move into Key Stage 1. The Primary Framework for Literacy and Mathematics has been developed alongside EYFS and will help nursery, Reception and KS1 teachers to see how the six areas of the EYFS link to literacy and mathematics in KS1.

Foundation Phase Framework for Children's Learning for 3- to 7-year-olds in Wales

This curriculum has a staggered implementation phase and comes into effect on:

- 1 August 2008 for all 3- to 5-year-olds in the Foundation Phase
- 1 August 2009 for all 5- to 6-year-olds in the Foundation Phase
- 1 August 2010 for all 6- to 7-year-olds in the Foundation Phase.

The Foundation Phase contributes to the Curriculum Cymreig by developing children's understanding of the Welsh culture and promoting the Welsh language. The Welsh Assembly Government has a vision for education and lifelong learning. In the Foundation Phase this is based on seven core aims developed from the United Nations Convention on the Rights of the Child (UNCRC) 1989. The aim is to ensure that all children and young people:

- have a flying start in life and the best possible basis for their future growth and development
- have access to a comprehensive range of education, training and learning opportunities, including acquisition of essential personal and social skills
- enjoy the best possible physical and mental, social and emotional health, including freedom from abuse, victimisation and exploitation
- have access to play, leisure, sporting and cultural activities
- are listened to, treated with respect, and are able to have their race and cultural identity recognised
- have a safe home and a community that supports physical and emotional well-being
- are not disadvantaged by any type of poverty.

The Learning Country 2: Delivering the Promise

There are seven statutory Areas of Learning in the Foundation Phase:

- personal and social development, well-being and cultural diversity

> **Key Term**
>
> **Key Stage 1** – The first two years of primary school are known as Key Stage 1 (KS1) and cover children aged 5 to 7 years. Key stages are part of the National Curriculum in England and contain compulsory subjects. Children are formally assessed at the end of Key Stage 1 by their teachers.

- language, literacy and communication skills
- mathematical development
- Welsh language development
- knowledge and understanding of the world
- physical development
- creative development.

The educational programme sets out what children should be taught for each Area of Learning, and the outcomes determine the expected standards of children's performance. There are six outcomes for each Area of Learning, which incorporate Baseline Assessment Scales and Descriptions and the national curriculum level descriptions (Welsh Assembly Government, 2006).

Think it over

- Read through the Foundation Phase Framework for Children's Learning for 3- to 7-year-olds in Wales in detail.
- Reflect on the key messages from this document.
- Make comparisons between this approach to learning and the Early Years Foundation Stage in England.

The Foundation Stage in Northern Ireland

Children start formal education in Northern Ireland at four years of age, which is earlier than anywhere else in Europe. The Foundation Stage covers Years 1 and 2 in the primary education structure and offers a curriculum that aims to:

- promote children's personal development
- promote positive attitudes and dispositions to learning
- promote children's thinking skills and personal capabilities
- encourage creativity and imagination
- enable children to develop physical confidence and competence
- develop children's curiosity and interest in the world around them
- enable children to communicate in a variety of ways
- motivate children to develop literacy and numeracy skills in meaningful contexts.

There are seven Areas of Learning:

- religious education
- language and literacy
- mathematics and numeracy
- the arts
- the world around us
- personal development and mutual understanding
- physical development and movement.

Delivery of the curriculum recognises the importance of play and encourages a holistic approach towards children's learning.

Think it over

- Reflect on the differences between the Foundation Stage in Northern Ireland and other comparable curriculum structures.

- Consider the benefits and disadvantages of starting the Foundation Stage in Northern Ireland at 4 years of age.

Curriculum for Excellence in Scotland

In 2004 the Scottish Government, following a reform of education, formulated A Curriculum for Excellence. This programme, designed in partnership with Learning and Teaching Scotland, the Scottish Qualifications Authority (SQA) and HM Inspectorate of Education, is based on principles for curriculum design that will ensure children from 3 to 18 years have access to:

- challenge and enjoyment
- breadth
- progression
- depth
- personalisation and choice
- coherence
- relevance.

Curriculum for Excellence aims to challenge existing attitudes towards learning and teaching and has implications for the teaching profession and staff in Scotland as well as the organisation of the curriculum. The purpose of the curriculum 3–18 is to provide successful learners, confident individuals, responsible citizens and effective contributors.

At present the pre-school years of 3–5 have the Curriculum Framework for Children in their pre-school year (1997) guidance, which is based on principles of equality of opportunity and focuses on:

- the best interests of children
- the central importance of relationships
- the need for all children to feel included
- an understanding of the ways in which children learn.

Think it over

Consider the principles that underpin Scotland's Curriculum for Excellence and reflect on how your provision and practice recognises the importance of children's relationships.

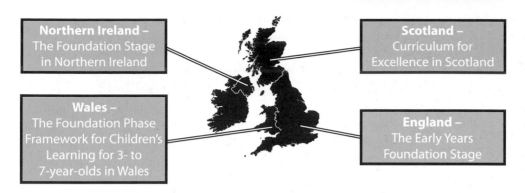

Figure 3.1. National early years curricula in the UK

3.3 Theories of how children learn and their influence on practice

Children have an innate ability to learn and this should be fostered by the environment around them and the experiences they have. The way in which children learn is therefore important to practitioners. It forms a basis for their work. Understanding how children learn and how to support this learning requires knowledge of child development, which in turn can be used to implement the curriculum.

Theorists and educators differ in the emphasis they put on the importance of 'nature' and 'nurture'. Biological theorists believe that there are biological or genetic explanations for the way children develop. Learning theorists hold that children develop as they do because they have contact with other people and learn from them. Psychoanalytical theories are in some ways a mixture of biological and learning theories: they describe children as being born with a set of needs that must be met if children are to develop healthily. Whatever your own views on genes versus environment, it is important to recognise the value of early experiences and how to build upon these within the educational setting.

Many theorists have been influential in the development of the curriculum in the UK today. The two who have perhaps been most influential on modern practice are discussed in detail below, as is a recent study that had important findings regarding the way in which children learn. The work of many other theorists is summarised in Table 3.1. Research continues into how children learn. You may wish to spend time looking in more depth at the work of various theorists and educators. You can then use this information to inform your planning. It is good to spend time reflecting on practice and why the curriculum is implemented in certain ways.

> ### Key Term
>
> **Nature v nurture** – This debate concerns the importance people put on the innate qualities possessed by an individual from birth and the significance of life experiences in moulding that individual.
>
> Parents find this debate particularly fascinating when observing their own children. Siblings in the same family, even twins, can be very different even though they have the same family background.

Find it out

Choose a theorist or educator from Table 3.1 and research their work, making notes on the key points.

- Reflect on that person's influence on modern-day practice in general.
- Discuss with a colleague the influence on your own approach to implementing the curriculum.

Table 3.1. Influential early years theorists and educators

Name	Area of study	Key points and influence on current practice
Chris Athey	Schemas	A schema is 'a pattern of repeatable behaviour into which experiences are assimilated and that are gradually coordinated' (Athey, 1990). Work has contributed to observation skills developed by early years practitioners. Building on Athey's work, Cathy Nutbrown (1994) suggested that children perform best if they have adults who are interested in self-development and who value children's rights and needs. Staff in early years settings are now encouraged to participate in continuous professional development.
Albert Bandura	Social learning theory	Children can learn through imitating others. The most influential people, for children, are those who are warm and loving towards the child or similar to them. In an experiment with a Bobo doll, children were shown a film in which an adult hits the doll and shouts at it. Three different endings were recorded, showing the adult rewarded, punished or nothing at all happening. When the children were later given their own Bobo doll they tended to hit the doll if they had seen the adult being rewarded for this behaviour. Conclusions were drawn that children will imitate behaviour they see rewarded, particularly if it is by someone they love. It was felt that children who were smacked or shouted at by adults would reflect this in their own behaviour. This emphasised the importance of positive role models.
John Bowlby	Attachment, separation, grief and loss	Work on how babies become attached to the mother figure and what happens when they are separated. Young children can experience feelings of loss and grief when they are separated from loved ones. Children need to develop strong bonds with parents or key carers for healthy development. Bowlby's work has influenced how children are settled into a new setting and the assignment of key workers to babies and children. Films by James and Joyce Robertson showed Bowlby's theory in action, in that they illustrated the stages that a child goes through when left by families in hospital. These include protest, despair and detachment in dealing with people. This has led to important work on how to deal with the hospitalisation of children, including the use of playworkers, and provision for parents to accompany their children.

Name	Area of study	Key points and influence on current practice
Tina Bruce	Early years education and play	Practical application of work of theorists. Reasserts in a modern way the principles of early childhood tradition (Bruce, 1997). Emphasises the holistic nature of children's learning, the value of play and the importance of the adult. Looked to the future by building on the past.
Jerome Bruner	Learning	Particularly interested in the role of the adult in children's learning. Adult provides the environment and the structure for learning. Scaffolding – the adult works with the child in a structured and supportive way. A skilled adult can enable the child to consolidate previous learning and move forward to the next step. Viewed language as central to children's thinking and learning. Believed a child could be taught any subject as long as it was in an appropriate way. Sequenced cognitive, or intellectual, development into three areas: enactive (learning through doing), iconic (imagining things they have done) and symbolic (e.g. talking, writing, reading). The impact has been to encourage practitioners to think carefully about the way they help children and to be aware that the adult role is significant in encouraging learning.
Friedrich Froebel	Learning	Founder of the kindergarten system in 1840, who devised activities for young children to learn through play. Saw the importance of children having 'real' experiences. Recognised importance of parents as first educators of their children. Considered that children's best thinking is done when they are playing. Saw importance of relationships with other children and adults. Very influential in the way we view children today; for example, considered children learn from the outdoor environment as well as indoors, invented finger rhymes and songs, and encouraged creativity.
Harry and Margaret Harlow	Attachment	Experiments on monkeys. Believed that contact and comfort are critical to emotional and social development. This work has given us greater understanding of this area of development, and the way in which children express emotions and build relationships.
Susan Isaacs	Emotional expression	Valued play as a means through which children can express their feelings. Also saw play as a child's work. Very significant input to the way we view play as a learning tool today. Considered that parents were the most important educators of their children.

Name	Area of study	Key points and influence on current practice
Mia Kellmer Pringle	Children's needs	Stressed the importance of intrinsic motivation based on the quality of a child's early social relationships. The social experiences children have had will affect the way they interact with other children in the setting. This has led settings to consider children's ability to make relationships based on previous experiences.
Lawrence Kohlberg	Moral reasoning	Identified six stages of moral reasoning in three levels. Interested in the way children reason and justify their moral judgements. The implication for the early years is in helping children to understand moral issues, or the right thing to do. This could be pertinent when trying to encourage children to share toys and equipment or to see another person's point of view.
Abraham Maslow	Children's needs	There is a hierarchy of needs through which individuals move. Early years practitioners consider the child's individual needs and consider ways to meet them, and to move the child onto the next stage of the hierarchy.
Margaret McMillan	Nursery schools	Keen for children to learn through first-hand experiences and active learning in order to understand the world. She believed that play helped children to apply and understand their existing knowledge. She pioneered nursery schools as an extension of the home and worked in close partnership with parents.
Maria Montessori	Learning	Designed 'didactic' materials that are structured to encourage children to learn particularly through use of senses. Observations of children led her to believe that children are particularly receptive to certain areas of learning during sensitive periods of development. Also believed that children learn best from self-chosen activity and by doing things independently (i.e. without adult interference). Adults need to be trained to give sensitive support. The learning environment was seen as being particularly important, with child-appropriate equipment and freedom to explore the environment. Some of these ideas are continued in mainstream provision today as well as in specific Montessori schools. Many parents see the benefits of the approach and choose to send their children to a Montessori nursery or school.

Name	Area of study	Key points and influence on current practice
Christine Pascal and Tony Bertram	Learning	Their Effective Early Learning project (1997) suggests that the child who is an involved learner is experiencing a quality curriculum. This project has been influential in encouraging practitioners to reflect on their practice as a team and has contributed to the modern approach of continual assessment of the effect of the curriculum. Some emphasis is placed on the quality of interactions between child and adult, child and child.
Ivan Pavlov	Classical conditioning	Experiments on dogs showed that some behaviour was a response to stimuli. Showed humans could learn through associations. Adults can get children to behave in the way that they want them to, by shaping their behaviour.
Michael Rutter	Nature/nurture debate; family break-up	Found a correlation between stress in a child's background and the likelihood of that child becoming deviant in later life. Considered learning is 60% nature and 40% nurture. Believed children can experience maternal deprivation within the family setting even when the mother is there. Defined deprivation as privation, disruption and distortion. There is a growing awareness in today's society of the effects of stress on children and how it affects their behaviour in group settings.
B.F. Skinner	Operant conditioning	Known for his work on rats, Skinner identified positive and negative reinforcers for behaviour. Behaviour can be manipulated through the use of reinforcements. This has encouraged early years practitioners to use positive reinforcement such as praise or rewards to encourage desirable behaviour.
Rudolf Steiner	Education	True purpose of education should be to allow children to develop. Believed in the importance of the community in sharing the educational experiences of the child. Children should stay with one teacher for as long as possible in order to build strong relationships. They should be encouraged to work together and help each other with activities and experiences. This is a particularly beneficial approach when considering the integration and inclusion of children with special needs.
Barbara Tizard	Attachment	Found that children can make attachments with 'new mothers'. Highlighted importance of key relationships between children and childcare workers.
D.W. Winnicott	Attachment	Showed, for example, how 'comforters' were important to children who were making a transition to a new setting. These were referred to as 'transitional objects' that comforted a child alone in a new situation. The object becomes a symbol of the mother/carer who will return. Winnicott's work has encouraged practitioners to be sensitive to young children's emotional needs.

Jean Piaget (1896–1980)

The key aspect of Piaget's work is the emphasis he put on children developing through stages. He believed that children were born with the ability to think as part of their genetic inheritance. He said that thinking develops in the same way in all human beings and through the same sequence of stages (see Table 3.2), each characterised by particular features identified through detailed observations of children.

Table 3.2. Piaget's stages of child development

Stage of development	Age of child	Key features
Sensory motor	Birth to 2 years	Reflexive behaviour in first weeks. Absorbs information through the senses as control of movement progresses. Learns from interaction with objects by seeing what they can do. Needs opportunity to explore. No concept of object permanence so that when an object disappears the child thinks it has gone forever. At a later stage the child will demonstrate object permanence by searching for the missing object. This is when peek-a-boo becomes an appropriate game to play.
Pre-operational	2–7 years	The age range of this stage is wide. A child of 2 will behave very differently from a 7-year-old, but Piaget identified this as the stage at which children are not yet able to think in an operational way – i.e. in an orderly, logical manner. Thought processes are developing but are not yet at the adult stage. Piaget considered that for full operational thought to take place children needed the ability to combine schemas – ideas or mental pictures established by a child through interaction with the environment. Schemas will exist for all aspects of life such as 'crossing the road' or 'picking up a book'. Operational thought allows children to combine schemas in a sensible way that gives them the means to think imaginatively and consider 'what may happen' if something else occurs. Egocentric behaviour is continued from the previous stage where the child is unable to see another person's viewpoint. Children are still unable to conceptualise abstractly but they do at this stage have an increasing ability to symbolise (e.g. writing, reading and imaginary play). They have strong respect for rules.
Concrete operations	7–11/12 years	More rational and 'adult-like' in thought processes. Able to think logically, although may still need concrete objects to assist with logical thought. Egocentricity declining. Less influenced by the appearance of objects. Ability to conserve (e.g. mass, number, length and area).
Formal operations	11/12–16 years	Cognitive structures are more like those of adults. Able to use own ideas to consider problems and to think abstractly. Presence of hypothetical thinking. Children also able to consider different arguments and points of view and to form their own opinions on moral and philosophical issues.

Piaget had a background of scientific discovery, initially in biology. He also developed an interest in psychology while working in laboratories in Zurich in 1919 and in a psychiatric clinic. In 1920 he conducted research for the intelligence test procedures developed by Alfred Binet. It was here that he became interested in the way that children absorbed information and used it to further their understanding. Using scientific interviewing techniques he began to investigate how children reason. His work convinced him that logical thought processes were used by children to solve problems and to give answers to specific questions.

Piaget devised a series of tests to gauge the level of thought children had reached. One such test involved providing a three-dimensional model of mountains and figures, and asking the children to describe the viewpoint of the different figures. If they were unable to do so, Piaget deemed them egocentric and therefore unable to see someone else's point of view. Another test involved counters set out in identical rows. Each child was asked to agree that the rows were identical in number. The position of the counters in one of the rows was then changed in front of the child. If the child had understanding of conservation, they would realise that the number of counters remained the same even though the appearance of the rows had changed. A child who was unable to conserve would think the longer row had more counters in it. Similar tests were devised to test conservation of volume and capacity.

Although these tests have been criticised subsequently, they have ensured that early years educators are aware that children may not see things in the same way as adults. This means that planned activities should consider the level of understanding a child has reached.

Influence on current practice

Despite criticisms of his work, Piaget remains a major contributor to the way we view children, and echoes of his theories are still seen in practice in early years settings. There is an emphasis on the importance of the environment and the quality of the children's interactions. There is also an acknowledgement that children develop through different stages and therefore the early years curriculum must reflect these individual differences.

Piaget's influence on modern practice can be summarised in the following points:

- Planning activities that are age- and stage-appropriate. It is necessary to consider the level of thought the child is capable of in relation to the stage he or she has reached, for example whether the child will be able to participate in an activity that requires cooperation if she or he is still at the stage of egocentricity.

- Planning activities that encourage abstract thought. These should include problem-solving and number work.

- Providing children with concrete materials to solve abstract problems. These could include bricks to help when building train tracks or number bars to help children calculate simple addition sums.

- Providing first-hand, practical experiences. These help children to continue to build mental processes and structures.

- Understanding children as individuals.

- Observing children and responding appropriately to them.

- Careful structuring of the curriculum to reflect the stage of development the child has reached.

- Providing a well-planned and organised learning environment that allows children to explore, experiment, plan and make their own decisions (see Chapter 2).

An example of learning by discovery.

Lev Vygotsky (1896–1934)

Like Piaget, Vygotsky firmly believed in the idea that children were active learners. He emphasised that children learn by exploring their world and by testing their ideas against reality. He believed that children were constantly seeking to expand their knowledge.

Vygotsky differed from Piaget in that he did not see the child as a solitary learner. He determined that a child's social environment was an active force in their development. Children need social interactions with other people who are more skilled than them in order to further their knowledge. These interactions promote cognitive development through instruction and assistance. He proposed the concept of the 'zone of proximal development', defined as the difference between what the child can do alone and the potential for what can be achieved with assistance from a more skilled adult or peer. Vygotsky did not specify how adults and children worked within the zone of proximal development but other researchers have developed this. In particular, Jerome Bruner (1977) termed this assistance 'scaffolding'. It is an interactive process in which adults adjust the support they offer to the child until the child has mastery of the skill being taught. The key to effective scaffolding is sensitivity to the child's level of development.

Vygotsky also emphasised the importance of mastery of language and its use as a communication tool. He considered that when children have developed the means to interact with other members of their social group they are able to transform their innate abilities into higher mental functions.

Another interesting aspect of Vygotsky's work concerns pretend play. He noted that children's pretend play tends to function at a level beyond their stage of life. They take on roles, such as parent or car driver, that are appropriate to adult life. Through pretend play children place themselves in the zone of proximal development. They are playing at a level that is beyond their true capabilities. Vygotsky believed that pretend play was important for children to learn about their world.

Influence on current practice

Vygotsky's work has had a major impact on our current educational approach. This is largely due to the emphasis on social development and the need for interaction between the child and more experienced people. For example, it is common practice to encourage paired reading between children of different ages or to enable children of mixed abilities to work together. This method of learning enables children to work beyond their capabilities but within their zone of proximal development.

Another important influence on modern practice is the emphasis put on the role of the adult in encouraging children to achieve their maximum potential. Practitioners consider carefully how they can sensitively respond to children in order to ensure they master new skills. They aim to enable children to work within their ability and provide scaffolding to facilitate development.

An example of scaffolding of learning.

Effective Pre-school and Primary Education 3–11 Project (EPPE)

This was funded by the Department for Education and Skills (1997–2003) and was the first major longitudinal study in the UK to focus specifically on the effectiveness of early years education. A key conclusion of the study is that the quality of interactions between children and staff is particularly important. It was found that the most effective arrangement was where two individuals work together to solve intellectual problems. This is termed 'sustained shared thinking' and is most beneficial when children interact on a one-to-one basis, either with an adult or with another child. The project supports the principles of the Foundation Stage and encourages practitioners, and government, to reflect on the issues of quality and the effectiveness of pre-school provision in the UK. Information on the study is available via the website www.ioe.ac.uk/schools/ecpe/eppe/index.htm.

Think it over

List three ways in which you and your team could increase the number of one-to-one interactions with children in your setting.

- How might more one-to-one interactions benefit the children's intellectual thought?

Key Elements of Effective Practice (KEEP)

KEEP has been developed for use by local authorities in their work with early years settings. It is consistent with the Common Core of Skills and Knowledge for the Children's Workforce Framework, which outlines the skills and knowledge needed by early years practitioners. KEEP reflects the Research into Effective Pedagogy in the Early Years (REPEY), Effective Provision of Pre-school Education (EPPE) and Study of Pedagogical Effectiveness in Early Learning (SPEEL) research projects. The REPEY and EPPE projects looked closely at the characteristics of effective practice in settings and carefully considered the components of successful early years practice. The researchers were particularly interested in the effects of good-quality pre-school provision and investigated practices in 14 Foundation Stage settings. They found evidence to suggest that high-quality pre-school provision improved children's thinking skills and provided:

- a balance between teacher-led and freely chosen activities
- effective differentiation to enable children to build on their own starting points
- opportunities to challenge children's thinking
- opportunities to sustain shared thinking.

It was also found that the quality of interactions between children and adults was highly important, with a need for sustained shared activity and feedback to learners a priority. The settings that involved parents and provided free movement for children within the indoor and outdoor environments were effective in improving children's learning. The use of open-ended questions to stimulate children, and consideration of the child's individual needs were also found to be contributory factors.

The SPEEL project identified 129 key statements which refer to the core competencies of a practitioner's role that underpin effective work with children. They are categorised under the headings of Practice, Principles and Professional Dimensions, and highlight that effective practitioners are reflective, self-evaluative and able to analyse their practice. Practitioners may find it useful to read the key statements and consider these in relation to their own practice.

International influences on current practice

The Reggio Emilia approach has influenced the perception of how children learn and has been influential in practice in early years settings in the United Kingdom today. This inspirational approach is based on the work of Loris Malaguzzi, who dedicated his life to working on his philosophy of education. This philosophy, influenced by Piaget, Vygotsky and Bruner, is linked with a strong sense of the importance of the community and the use of the expressive arts as a vehicle for learning.

The key features of the Reggio Emilia approach are as follows (Daly, Byers and Taylor, 2006, p. 32):

- The environment as an educator
- The importance of observing children and documenting their progress
- Partnerships with parents and the wider community
- The role of the adult
- Professional development
- Valuing and encouraging child-initiated activity
- Teachers have the time to reflect and discuss practice and children with colleagues
- The importance of the expressive arts.

The idea of Forest Schools originated in Sweden in the 1950s and has been adopted in the UK in acknowledgement of the importance of the outdoor environment in enabling children to develop and learn. The Forest Schools' belief is that children of all ages and abilities can benefit from outdoor activities through an opportunity to practise developing skills and by promoting confidence and a sense of achievement.

3.4 The importance of play in learning

Early years practitioners have fought long and hard to establish the importance of play as a learning tool for young children For many people, parents and politicians in particular, the role of play was undervalued in the curriculum. Many playgroups have changed their name to pre-schools in order to raise the public perception of their work. Indeed, the Pre-school Playgroup Association is now the Pre-school Learning Alliance. Until fairly recently there was no British research to support the value of play and to advocate play as an effective approach towards education and care. However, the EPPE research (2003) was able to confirm the central role of play in early learning. The project concluded that there must be a balance between adult-directed activities and a child's self-chosen play, and that there must be shared thinking and discussion for learning to take place.

The Early Years Foundation Stage (2007) acknowledges the benefits of a well-planned play environment and refers to the EPPE research in its resources. Play is identified as a key way for children to learn with enjoyment and challenge. With a planned and challenging environment and adults supporting children's learning, play can be used as a suitable vehicle for the Foundation Stage. Adults will need to ensure that play is challenging, and play needs to be planned if it is to be educational, but there must be a balance between child and adult input. An ill-equipped environment with little thought given to play is not likely to produce high-quality 'learning through play'. Similarly, children need time and opportunity to get involved in play that is not adult led. They will use this time to act out aspects of their own lives and of those around them, to help them make sense of their experiences. They will have opportunity to practise skills and refine their abilities. They will also have the chance to interact and communicate with peers. When children are truly stimulated by play they show great depths of concentration.

Think it over

Consider an early years setting in which you have worked.

- Did the children use play as a learning tool?
- Did the setting stimulate high-quality play in a challenging and inspiring environment?
- Were the children excited by their play?
- Did the children spend time and effort in one area of play?
- Did the children concentrate and become involved through their play?
- Were there areas of play that were ignored by the children?
- Were all areas of play accessible to all children?
- How much do you know about how children play and the value of play to learning?

It is useful to observe children playing. It can be very revealing about the amount of learning that is actually taking place. For example, two children of different ages spending a whole summer engaged in making tents and wigwams of different types and structures would develop tremendous skills of negotiation and team working. Other aspects of learning can be developed by the adult providing different materials and equipment or by participating in the fun. It is very important that play is enjoyable for children and always has that element of fun.

If all the elements of quality play are in place then the importance of play and exploration is that it provides children with the opportunity for:

- making choices and decisions
- using one's own ideas and imagination
- experimenting
- trying out new behaviours and practising old ones
- practising skills and learning new ones
- exercising, developing and coordinating body, mind and brain
- adapting or transforming knowledge, attitudes and skills
- negotiating
- following an interest or line of enquiry
- engaging in 'what if?' activity
- making up rules and changing them
- making mistakes
- demonstrating one's competence in many areas of development
- setting one's own goals
- trying to emulate someone else
- using symbols
- making sense of puzzling situations, events or equipment

- becoming and being confident and enjoying challenges
- having fun with friends and/or familiar adults
- learning how to be a 'player' fit for life in a high-tech, post-industrial society.

(Early Years Foundation Stage *Effective Practice: Play and Exploration*, 2007, pp. 3–4)

Practitioners have also found that play as a tool for learning can be most effective when they work closely with parents. By talking to parents and working together to observe children's play they are able to ascertain the interests children have and the schemas they are currently involved in (Nutbrown, 2006). They can then provide appropriate play equipment to stimulate and extend learning.

Jean Piaget (see section 3.3) highlighted the importance of children learning through play, and showed that play changes with the child's stage of development. At the sensory motor stage play gives an opportunity for the child to engage in experiences that activate the senses, particularly sight and touch. It also gives the opportunity for language to develop and for skills to be practised and repeated. Children may be engaged in playing with other children at this stage, but the expectation is that children will play alone. At the later pre-operational stage there is more likelihood of children participating in symbolic play and using language to reflect on their own experiences. Games begin to have simple rules and there is more play with other children.

Case Study

Extending Sidney's range of play

Sidney comes into the pre-school setting each morning with his mother and goes straight to the cars on the mat on the floor. He often plays with the cars for most of the morning, but sometimes he will do a jigsaw or sit and look at the books. Sidney is often very deeply involved in his play and shows he has developed skills of concentration.

Sidney seems to enjoy the pre-school but the practitioners have noticed that he is not happy getting dirty or involved in messy play and often plays alone. Sidney will be starting school in the next few months.

- How can practitioners extend the play opportunities for Sidney?
- What is the role of the adult in providing support for Sidney?
- Consider when and how practitioners should intervene in children's play.

Early years managers need to think carefully about the value of play as a vehicle for learning, and to consider the emphasis that staff in the setting place on it. They must also consider the quality of the play that is offered:

- Do children have the opportunity to develop their play and contribute ideas to it?
- Is play stimulating for them?
- Do they spend time concentrating and communicating with others in their play?
- Are all the children engaged in the play activities that you provide?
- Are there any children who need to be encouraged to play?

You should not underestimate the value that play has in encouraging and enhancing children's learning.

Children involved in play that is not led by an adult may act out aspects of their own lives and the lives of those around them.

3.5 Planning, implementing and evaluating the curriculum

Planning the early years curriculum

As a manager of an early years setting you will be responsible for curriculum planning. You may be asking yourself why you need to plan if the children come into the setting very happily, play contentedly during the session and go home smiling. What more could anybody want? However, early years practitioners can be guilty of setting activities that are purposeless in order to occupy children and keep them quiet. In order to provide a quality curriculum, activities must be purposeful and encourage the child to learn, and ultimately to achieve independence.

Good planning is essential because it:

- promotes equality of opportunity for all children
- ensures that each area of the curriculum is covered and that the associated standards are met
- raises professionalism, by encouraging early years practitioners to reflect on practice
- enables practitioners to build on what the children already know and can do
- helps to encourage a positive attitude to learning and prevent early failure
- helps parents and practitioners to work together on common themes
- ensures that the content of sessions is relevant and appropriate to children's needs
- ensures that each activity within every session is purposeful and provides opportunities for learning, both indoors and outside.

It is essential that the planning of the curriculum is led by the manager, who has an overview of the setting and is ultimately responsible for curriculum management. It is possible, however, to delegate responsibilities to colleagues, and in fact the whole team should be involved in the process. This empowers staff and gives them ownership of the curriculum.

Planning at the Fir Trees pre-school

Case Study

Kezi has recently taken over the leadership of the Fir Trees pre-school. The group had previously been run by Beryl, and the majority of the staff have worked at the pre-school for a long time. They are an established and experienced team who work well together. There had been no written curriculum plans – the group concentrated in the past on providing play activities for the children, and these were chosen each morning by the staff. Kezi has worked in other pre-schools and has a CACHE Diploma in Childcare and Education. She is very aware of the importance of planning in relation to the Early Years Foundation Stage curriculum and feels that there should be a more systematic approach to the activities offered to the children.

- Why is it important for the team to work together on the planning?
- What do they need to think about?

The planning cycle

Planning of the curriculum should be an ongoing process that is based on your knowledge of the children in your care. You need to match this knowledge to your understanding of child development and the way that children learn. The framework is provided by the Early Years Foundation Stage (page 70).

Planning takes the form of a cycle, as illustrated in Figure 3.2. The planning cycle begins with the needs of the child. These needs will be established through observations of the child's skills and abilities in the different areas of the curriculum. Parents' knowledge should also be considered, as should that of previous workers. For example, a child starting in a Year 1 class will already have a Foundation Stage profile. This will give the new staff information about that child to guide their planning. They will continue to make observations to build up their own knowledge and opinions of the child's capabilities based on the profile.

At the planning stage, early years practitioners will need to discuss and decide upon suitable activities to consolidate and enhance learning. Initial ideas will be developed to ensure all aspects of the curriculum are being met. During the implementation of the plan, children will be observed and the activities evaluated. Staff will then need the time and opportunity to discuss individuals and groups of children and their responses to the chosen activities. It is necessary to evaluate and reflect upon the success of the plan in order to continue the planning cycle in a productive way. If staff do not take time to assess the suitability of the activities and to consider the learning that has taken place for individuals and groups, the children may become 'stuck' and not show the progression they are capable of. Activities offered should have breadth and be balanced to match the children's abilities. They should be relevant to young children and varied in order to maintain interest.

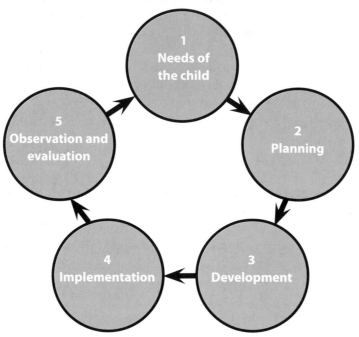

Figure 3.2. The planning cycle

The key person system

Early years practitioners often use group working and the key person system to ensure that children are meeting their potential (see also Chapter 2). The key person has a small group, usually of about 10 children, to focus on in observations and assessments. Differentiation of the curriculum, whereby practitioners adapt activities to enable children to consolidate and develop their learning, helps to ensure that individual needs are met (see also 'Individual education plans (IEPs)', below).

How do you approach planning?

There is no definitive approach to planning. Some people prefer to document planning by using charts, others by writing a piece of continuous prose. It does not really matter how you write your plans down as long as the resulting plan is accessible to all team members and benefits the children.

The main priority in any approach to planning is to ensure that you develop a clear overview of the child's time in the setting, whether that is for a year or for four or six terms. It is necessary to plan in order to promote the use of activities to support the children's learning. The planning must be carefully documented to show how the learning needs of the children

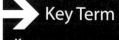 **Key Term**

Key person – a practitioner who is mainly responsible for providing lead support, contact and communication for a child and their family within the setting, with the aim of enabling and supporting close attachments between individual children and staff.

are met and extended. Each setting will devise its own workable plans over a period of time to fit individual circumstances and groups of children. Expectations held by Ofsted will also play a part in the creation of these plans and examples of good practice (for the 3–5-year-old range) can be found in the document *Planning for Learning in the Foundation Stage* (Qualifications and Curriculum Authority, 2001). The Early Years Foundation Stage places emphasis on using observations to inform planning for individual children.

Most people use long-, medium- and short-term plans. These are discussed below, and an example of each is given for a group of 3–4-year-old children. These examples are intended only to form the basis of discussion for settings and to illustrate possible approaches – they should not be viewed as models.

When considering the form that plans will take and the content of the curriculum, you must incorporate the individual needs of children as well as the group as a whole. Children with particular needs should be included in the overall plans, as well as having IEPs. Managers must give thought to the inclusion of children in their setting and also to the best ways in which to use extra help, such as learning support assistants. It is a good idea to keep copies of all plans, perhaps in a file, where IEPs and notes on differentiation and evaluation can be slotted in beside the planning documents.

Long-term plans

Staff teams use long-term plans to provide an overview of the learning opportunities that will be offered and to help keep the curriculum varied and challenging. They often follow a thematic approach initially, as young children enjoy the focus of a theme for their learning and staff find that an appropriate subject can motivate children. It is generally recognised that planning for the younger age group should cover all aspects of the child's development (physical, intellectual, emotional and social) and needs. There is an emphasis on individualised, personalised development, with children progressing at their own rate.

When using a thematic approach to learning it is important to remember that a theme is a starting point. The reactions of the children and their interests may well take you in unexpected directions.

Table 3.3 presents an example of a long-term plan for 3–4-year-old children. For children of this age the themes will need to be short and related to their immediate experiences. As children grow older they can sustain interest over a longer period and reflect on previous knowledge.

Table 3.3. Example of a long-term plan for 3–4-year-olds

Month	Topic
September	Ourselves
October	Babies
November	Fireworks and sound
December	Christmas preparations and traditions
January	Books
February	Cars
March	Homes
April	Gardens
May	Animals and 'mini-beasts'
June	Rainbows
July	Summer

When looking at this plan you may feel that it does not reflect sufficient breadth and balance of learning experience, or identify the learning that should take place over the year. In this case you will wish to add more detail at this stage of your planning, and include different themes, such as celebrations, that would enable children to develop awareness and enjoyment of other cultures and festivities. You may also wish to extend this plan to two years if the children are in the setting for that time. Some settings prefer to use areas of learning as a basis for their long-term plan and to include an indication of when to teach aspects of learning, and how regularly and frequently. Other settings prefer to spend longer than one month on each theme. Your choice will depend on a consensus of opinion among the staff and knowledge of the developmental stages of the children.

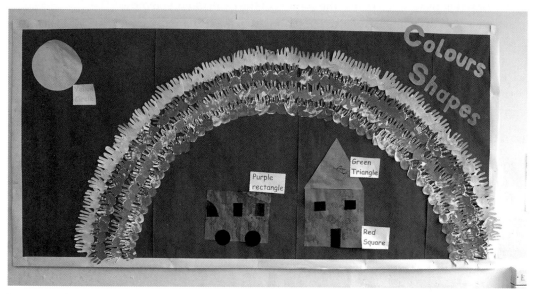

Incorporate themes into plans to help increase awareness and enjoyment.

Medium-term plans

These provide a framework for the themes identified in the long-term plan for all subjects or learning areas. They should highlight what resources will be needed and what trips or visitors have been planned. Medium-term plans are often used to bridge the gap between the broad outline of the long-term plan and the detail of the short-term plan. At this stage you could also include a rationale for the use of each type of resource area in the setting and for each routine, such as tidying away. You could also make the aims and objectives of the activities clear, and link these to individual learning outcomes for the children. This would be based on your own knowledge of the children in the setting.

Medium-term plans will need to be closely linked to the areas of learning outlined in the appropriate curriculum for your setting. These areas are not a curriculum in themselves, but establish a basis for planning. They help to lay strong foundations for future learning.

Short-term plans

The long- and medium-term plans provide the basis for the short-term plans which are developed using ongoing observations and assessment of the children. Short-term plans usually cover one week at most and are necessary for the team to know the focus of the sessions and their own responsibilities within the week. These plans should be used as a guide and not followed rigidly, as you will need to use your observations of children to adjust your plans in accordance with the children's needs and interests. Also, it is sometimes important to capitalise on unplanned events.

Managers and teams will want to devise their own particular form of plan, and it is important that all members of the team are part of this planning process. There will be certain times when children work in small groups with their key person, and as a large group for stories and rhymes. Many of the activities might be repeated during the week to consolidate learning and give children the time to practise skills.

You will also need to incorporate learning outcomes for individual children within your short-term plans. Many settings also highlight which activities will be child-initiated or adult-directed and how the children will be organised. A short-term plan can also be extended to include opportunities for observations, vocabulary to be focused on and opportunity for informal assessments of individuals or groups of children.

You could put the short-term plan on display so that staff and parents can share it, which might entail reproduction in other languages in order to ensure equality of opportunity. It is necessary to give staff time to:

- observe the children
- reflect on the success of the week's sessions
- discuss whether goals and targets have been reached.

Assessment and evaluation will enable practitioners to consider how to plan for the next week, bearing in mind the learning taking place and the interest shown by the children.

Individual education plans

Individual education plans (IEPs) are for children with an additional need. They are necessary when a child is identified as making little progress and when he or she is not responding to targeted teaching activities. The child may be working significantly below the level of classmates or have emotional or behavioural difficulties (Tassoni, 2003). IEPs will draw upon the experience of the whole team, particularly any staff with special educational needs coordinator (SENCO) responsibility, the parents and carers, and the child.

Ensuring Tasnim's development

Case Study

Tasnim has recently started with Emma, a local childminder. Tasnim is 3 years old and is currently staying with Emma for two days a week. Another child, also 3, attends at the same time. Emma is part of a childminding network group and often takes the children to visit other childminders and their children. Tasnim is exhibiting behaviour consistent with developmental delay and learning difficulties. Her developmental stage is comparable with a child of 18 months. Consider how Emma will ensure Tasnim's needs are met in a developmentally appropriate way.

- What will Emma need to think about in terms of planning?
- How will she evidence this?
- What support is available for Tasnim and her family?

A child with specific needs may benefit from play with materials that are at an appropriate developmental level and from some time spent playing with children of a similar developmental age. It is important, though, to ensure that you do not limit your expectations of children and that you plan the steps that will encourage progression. Managers need to consider carefully opportunities for repetition and practice, and how to take small steps towards learning new skills.

Implementing the early years curriculum

When implementing the early years curriculum, consider:

- the fundamentals of good practice
- the need for creativity and free choice.

The fundamentals of good practice

How you decide to implement the curriculum is to a certain extent influenced by your ideals and personal philosophy of education. This will be based on your understanding of child development and how children learn. It will also be influenced by your own attitudes to learning and experiences.

Leza's maths

Case Study

Leza is training for a childcare qualification at her local college. She is currently in her first term. She began her nursery placement two weeks ago and is working in a large class of 4-year-olds. The children and staff at the nursery welcomed her from the beginning and she has quickly found her way around and begun to interact with the children and staff. She has taken part in outdoor play and has read stories to small groups of children. Leza's placement supervisor, Adam, is pleased with her progress but is concerned about her attitude towards some aspects of the curriculum. She has a very negative attitude towards numeracy as a result of her own experiences at secondary school. This is proving to be difficult in the classroom. When Leza is asked to help small groups of children with their number work she avoids doing so and clearly lacks confidence. Adam is worried that this will influence the children's approach to numbers and he is anxious to encourage Leza to feel more confident.

- Decide how you could tackle the problem.
- Consider situations where your attitudes might interfere with children's learning.
- Analyse your own attitudes. Are there areas of learning where your approach encourages children or has a negative effect?

If you are honest about your influence on children's attitudes towards learning you can improve their opportunities. A practitioner who is enthusiastic about art activities can communicate this to the children and will see a similar enthusiasm reflected in the children's achievements. The staff member who loves to read stories will be the person who is surrounded by entranced children. The challenge for the manager is to recognise the strengths and weaknesses of staff members and to create a quality curriculum that meets the children's needs. It is important that this is a commonly agreed curriculum based on discussion and reflective practice by all staff members.

The Rumbold Report (*Starting with Quality*) stated that what children learn is not the only important factor; the way they are motivated to learn is equally as important. (Department for Education and Science, 1990, Part 1, para. 68) and Siraj-Blatchford (1998, p. 10) says that 'educators should guard against pressures, which might lead them to over-concentration on formal teaching and upon the attainment of a specific set of targets'.

In today's world of continuous assessment of children, you must not lose sight of the importance of *how* children learn and the pleasure that they get from knowledge. Who can forget the excitement and achievement of a child learning to ride a bicycle for the first time, or the pride of the child who makes their parents a cup of tea and brings it to them in bed?

The report *Start Right: The Importance of Early Learning* (Ball, 1994, pp. 51–3) sets out the principles of good practice that underpin early learning.

- Early childhood is the foundation on which children build the rest of their lives. But it is not just a preparation for adolescence and adulthood; it has an importance in itself.

- Children develop at different rates, and in different ways – emotionally, morally, socially, physically and spiritually. All are important; each is interwoven with others.

- All children have abilities, which can and should be identified and promoted.

- Young children learn from everything that happens to them and around them; they do not separate their learning into different subjects or disciplines.

- Children learn most effectively through actions, rather than from instruction.

- Children learn best when they are actively involved and interested.

- Children who are confident in themselves and their own ability have a head-start in learning.

- Children need time and space to produce work of quality and depth.

- What children can do (rather than what they cannot do) is the starting point in their learning.

- Play and conversation are the main ways in which young children learn about themselves, other people and the world around them.

- Children who are encouraged to think for themselves are more likely to act independently.

- The relationships which children have with other children and with adults are of central importance to their development.

Think it over

Working with a colleague, select two of Ball's principles and reflect on the influence they have on the curriculum.

- How can you put these principles into practice?

- Compare your answers with someone else's. Are there contrasting views? Can you reconcile any differences of opinion?

Allowing for creativity and free choice

According to Tina Bruce (2004) 'Creativity brings into existence new ideas, original ways of doing things and new creations of all kinds.' An interesting argument emerges when considering the implementation of the modern curriculum, and that concerns the place for creativity. Duffy (1998) states that creativity involves children in unique and unorthodox thinking and empowers them to create something original that breaks barriers of previously conceived ideas. They are able to use the learning from past experiences and relate this to new situations.

Suggestions have been made that the current curriculum offered to children does not give them enough breadth and stifles creativity. The Qualifications and Curriculum Authority (QCA) ran a 3-year project to investigate how to promote pupils' creativity in the national curriculum subjects and religious education (Figure 3.3).

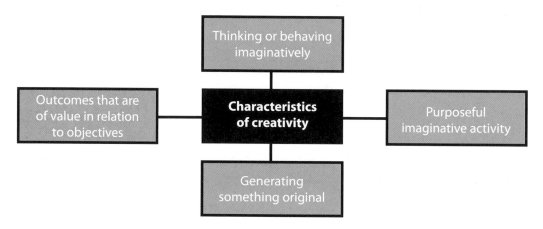

Figure 3.3. The QCA proposes four characteristics of creativity.

In addition to its characteristics of creativity the QCA also states that creative thinking can advance pupils' learning by taking thinking forward. It can enhance all-round development and raise educational standards by boosting self-confidence and self-esteem. Resources to encourage creativity can be found through links from the QCA website.

Think it over

For an excellent summary of creativity, see 'Common sense has much to learn from moonshine' (Philip Pullman, 2005) .

- What is your understanding of creativity?
- Where is the place for creativity in early years provision?
- Critically reflect on your own practice in relation to how you empower children to be creative.

Whatever your views on the place of creativity in the curriculum you must create exciting learning environments that inspire children to question, reason, solve problems and create. Adults can support and extend the learning and creative process. They can help children to communicate their thoughts, feelings and ideas. Some activities naturally allow more creativity than others, such as art, music and drama. With thought, other areas of the curriculum also lend themselves to a creative approach. Young children who are set the task of designing a new imaginative play area will respond with creative ideas. A group of children who have collected snails from the garden can be encouraged to design and make a suitable home for them. This activity will encourage problem-solving, leadership and innovative ideas.

The child's self-confidence is important to the learning process. A child's sense of self-worth is strongly influenced by the response to their activities of parents, carers, siblings, key people and peers. This is particularly relevant to the creative process. When anyone creates something – a drawing, a model or a cake – that person is at their most vulnerable. It is like baring the soul. Imagine the child who has spent all morning creating a model village from LEGO bricks, only to have it destroyed by the adult who is 'tidying up'. Early years practitioners can show that they value children's creative work by:

- showing respect for children's work, whatever their level of ability
- giving children the time to reflect and solve problems
- providing the opportunity for creativity
- responding to children's ideas in a positive way
- giving children the chance to be creative without adult interference
- giving children praise and encouragement
- appreciating the stages of creative development
- recognising creative talents.

It is important to value children's creative work, whatever their ability.

Think it over

- How comfortable do you feel with your own creativity?
- Can you remember a time when someone responded to your work with ridicule?
- What effect did this have on you?

Despite the importance to children of their self-belief, many adults often try to 'take over' their work. They tell them what to draw and how to draw it. They give them 'cut-outs' and tell them to fill them in with tissue paper. They provide resources to make a clown and a template – so 34 children all produce identical clowns. As the manager of an early years setting consider how you can encourage creativity.

Case Study

Use of cut-outs

A table was set out for a group of five 4-year-old children to make hedgehog models. There was one marker pen and five hedgehogs cut out on the table. The children were instructed individually by the adult to draw one eye on their hedgehog, to give the impression of a side view. The adult ensured they completed the task.

- Was this activity developmentally appropriate?
- What did the children learn?
- Was creativity encouraged?
- How could you encourage the adult to present this in a more meaningful way?

Too often practitioners are concerned with the end product and fail to realise that the process of learning is what is really important. Sylva (2000) found that children who were exposed to a balanced curriculum benefited most from their experiences. Balance in the curriculum was defined as being between free and guided choices. Benefits across the curriculum included:

- higher academic skills in reading and writing
- a high level of pretend play
- a low level of anxiety on entering school
- a high level of informal conversation
- a positive effect on children's perception of their own social acceptance and competence.

It is therefore important to give time and thought to the amount of free choice children are given within the delivery of the curriculum. The manager and staff do need to provide some sort of focus, of course, but children need the opportunity to make decisions and solve problems for themselves. They need to learn by doing and, if necessary, from their own mistakes. When adults learn to drive they have to *experience* doing a three-point turn or reversing round a corner. They have to learn practically, not by being told the theory of how to do it. Adults also need time to reflect on their efforts and to practise. How many times have you heard an adult say to a child 'but I have already shown you how to do that'?

There are two key issues for the manager and team.

- How much free choice should children have in their learning?
- How influential should the adult be in guiding the child?

Careful thought must be given to the quality and form of adult interaction. High levels of adult–child interaction can optimise learning. A high level of contribution from both the child and the adult can lead to open and interactive learning. The education tends to be of a high quality, with the child achieving maximum potential. In contrast, where the child has autonomy and the adult contribution is low, the quality of education tends to be lower, with the child achieving less success. However, where the adult approach is didactic, with little value placed on the child's contribution, opportunities for learning are often lost.

Research by Schweinhart and Weikart (1997) into the High/Scope pre-school curriculum produced some astonishing findings regarding the approach to learning that values the contribution of children in making choices and contributing to their education. Their study showed that children exposed to this approach benefited in the long term through more confidence and pro-social behaviour. Conclusions were drawn that this play-based programme of learning enabled children to learn to direct and control their own behaviour. The social skills they developed were also useful later on, and the children grew up to lead more fulfilled lives. They were more likely to be married, in well-paid employment and less likely to commit a crime.

Pascal and Bertram (1997) confirmed the importance of adult interaction in learning. Their work looked at three aspects of the interaction between children and adults: sensitivity, stimulation and autonomy.

- *Sensitivity*. The sensitivity of the adult to the feelings and emotional well-being of the child – includes elements of sincerity, empathy, responsiveness and affection.
- *Stimulation*. The way in which an adult intervenes in the learning process and the content of such interventions.
- *Autonomy*. The degree of freedom that the adult gives the child to experiment, make judgements, choose activities and express ideas. It also encompasses how the adult handles conflict, rules and behavioural issues.

To put this into the context of the learning environment, you need to consider the amount of interaction that takes place and the quality of that interaction. Some interactions with children can be meaningless. By close observation you can determine the interaction that enhances learning and improves the learning experience for the child.

Think it over

Consider the three aspects of the interaction between children and adults: sensitivity, stimulation and autonomy.

- How could a practitioner put these into practice?
- How can the child be more involved in the learning process?

Evaluating the early years curriculum

Evaluation of the curriculum is part of the planning cycle described earlier in this chapter. It is essential to reflect on the implementation of the curriculum and to use your conclusions to inform future planning. You must ensure that you are meeting the needs of all the children and that you are creating a learning environment in which adults and children work positively together.

How to evaluate the curriculum

Despite the importance of evaluating and reflecting on practice, often, for one reason or another, this is an area that is neglected. At the end of a session practitioners are often too tired, or too busy preparing for the next session, to record their thoughts.

It is imperative to work together as a team to devise practical methods of recording and assessing each session, either during the session or at an appropriate time afterwards. It is interesting to note that the Pen Green Early Excellence Centre at Corby sets aside time every Monday afternoon as a planning and assessment session, which all staff attend.

It may be necessary to change and adapt curriculum plans in the light of evaluation. As a manager you must be aware of the difficulties practitioners may experience in undergoing change.

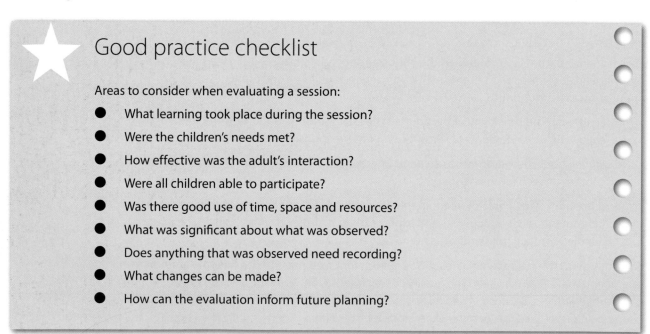

Good practice checklist

Areas to consider when evaluating a session:
- What learning took place during the session?
- Were the children's needs met?
- How effective was the adult's interaction?
- Were all children able to participate?
- Was there good use of time, space and resources?
- What was significant about what was observed?
- Does anything that was observed need recording?
- What changes can be made?
- How can the evaluation inform future planning?

3.6 Assessment and assessment systems

Why assess children?

It is essential that each child is given the opportunity to achieve success, to show what he or she knows, understands and can do. Assessment can be used to help children recognise the standards they are aiming for. It can inform parents about their child's progress and the next steps they need to take. It also provides feedback to the practitioner about children and enables planning to be more effective. It provides the setting with information to evaluate the staff's work. However, formal assessment is not required until the end of the Foundation Stage.

Vicky Hutchin in her book *Tracking Significant Achievement in the Early Years* (2000) suggests that a tracking record of significant achievements is beneficial to children and practitioners. This prevents recording becoming a burdensome task, yet allows progress to be identified and celebrated. In particular, Hutchin (p. 21) believes that a tracking record is able to show, at a glance:

- whether there are any children who appear to have shown no significant achievement, and therefore need to be focused on
- whether there are any children who have shown significant achievement in, say, reading, but not in writing, and therefore need to be observed
- whether none of the children has shown any significant achievement in, say, knowledge and understanding of the world, which indicates a need for the practitioner to rethink the curriculum on offer
- whether any bright children appear to have made no significant progress, which would indicate that they need to be given more challenging, open-ended tasks.

Hutchin also highlights the need to pass onto the next practitioner information that is relevant and can be read quickly and easily.

Observation and assessment

Case Study

A group of four children aged 3 to 4 years had been involved in a practical activity relating to the topic of the month, 'Animals and mini-beasts'. The children had been looking at snails in a plastic tank and observing how they moved across the surface of a plastic sheet. The children have now been asked to search in the garden to see if they can find any more snails. The objective of the activity is to encourage the children to show curiosity and have a positive approach to new activities. Marco is immediately interested in the activity and scuttles around the garden looking under bushes and up trees for snails. He responds positively to the task and soon has a collection of three snails. He takes them inside and starts showing them to other children in the classroom. Leroy is very interested in Marco's snails and goes outside to see if he can find any for himself. When he gets outside he sees that Robert has found one. He snatches it from Robert and runs to show it to Marco. In the meantime Robert gives up looking for snails and joins Eleanor and Sean on the slide.

- What is significant about this observation?
- How would you present this information?

The system for assessment

The *Foundation Stage Profile* (Qualifications and Curriculum Authority, 2003) was originally designed for use with the Curriculum Guidance for the Foundation Stage and continues to be relevant for the new Early Years Foundation Stage. The profile sets out how to record and summarise the progress and learning needs of young children, based on the information gathered by practitioners through observations and knowledge of the children. The profile is used during the final year of the Foundation Stage and is based on practitioners' own assessments of children's progress, and needs, based on the early learning goals.

The six early learning goals of the Foundation Stage curriculum were not intended to be used as assessment criteria. Rather, the Foundation Stage profile takes these goals and presents them as a set of 13 assessment scales, each of which has nine points. There are three or four assessment scales for the first three early learning areas, and one scale for each of the other three. The 13 assessment scales are therefore:

- *Personal, social and emotional development*
  - Dispositions and attitudes
  - Social development
  - Emotional development
- *Communication, language and literacy*
  - Language for communication and thinking
  - Linking sounds and letters
  - Reading
  - Writing
- *Problem Solving, Reasoning and Numeracy*
  - Numbers as labels and for counting
  - Calculating
  - Shape, space and measures
- *Knowledge and understanding of the world*
- *Physical development*
- *Creative development*

The profile booklet is designed to be completed as an ongoing task, to give a cumulative system of assessment. Parents, children and other settings are encouraged to contribute to the booklet, in order to have a full picture of the child. Professor Tina Bruce of the University of North London has said that: 'The foundation stage profile recognises the importance of parents as partners, including those with children with special education needs and disabilities, in the assessment process' (Bruce, 2003, p. 7). Parents have unique knowledge of their children. The summarisation of young children's achievements at the end of the Foundation Stage provides important information for parents and also for Year 1 teachers.

The practicalities of assessment

Any setting using the Foundation Stage profile must think about the practicalities of observing children. Some members of staff may need training in the different observation techniques and methods of evaluating results. All staff will need to consider how to make well-planned observations using a flexible approach. The success of the assessment scheme will depend on the:

- quality and continuity of practitioners' assessments
- standardisation of assessments
- practicality and ease of administering the scheme
- credibility of the scheme
- willingness of staff to undertake the assessments
- importance attached to the assessment at the next setting.

If staff within the setting are to participate in the assessment scheme, they must have sufficient training and experience to be able to recognise the achievements of individual children. They will need to have realistic expectations of the children, based on sound knowledge of child development. Time should be set aside for the completion of assessments and to discuss progress. It may also be necessary to discuss the standardisation of assessments with other settings.

It is important that the assessment scheme is practical and easy to use. There is never enough time when working with children. The use of assessments must not detract from the overall learning experience. There is no point in a practitioner walking around the classroom with a clipboard waiting to record Michelle's speech when she is too busy to talk to them!

Staff must perceive the assessment as valuable to the child and the learning process. They must not have the feeling that they are simply filling in boxes that no one will ever look at. Relevant information about individual progress and achievements must be readily accessible to parents and colleagues. There must also be respect between settings in order to ensure that notice is taken of assessments made by the previous setting. It is simply a waste of time and energy for nurseries to redo the assessments made by the previous pre-school setting because they do not value the professionalism of these colleagues.

The credibility of the assessment scheme is therefore essential. The Foundation Stage profile is drawn from the work of respected early education specialists and practitioners. This has ensured that the assessment criteria are based on sound understanding of children's development.

Think it over

- How would you encourage your staff to participate in the assessment process?
- How would you ensure the standardisation of assessment?
- What are the difficulties of sharing assessment data with parents?

Conclusion

This chapter has outlined the key features of the statutory curriculum structures for England, Scotland, Wales and Northern Ireland. The planning, implementation and evaluation of the curriculum for the under-8s have been considered in some detail, alongside the assessment of children's learning and the influence of researchers and theorists. Play as a vehicle for learning has also been discussed. It is vital that the manager and staff have sufficient time to think about what the setting offers, and that they continually adjust and improve the curriculum to meet the statutory expectations as well as the learning needs of individual children.

Check your understanding

1   What is your understanding of the term 'curriculum'?

2   What is your overall vision for the education you offer children?

3   How would you communicate this to staff?

4   How would you ensure that all the children have equal access to the educational opportunities offered?

5   How could you assess the learning that is taking place?

6   How could you use this assessment to inform your planning?

7   How much emphasis would you put on the value of play as a vehicle for learning?

8   How would you communicate to colleagues and parents and carers the value of play?

References and further reading

Athey, C. (2007) *Extending Thought in Young Children: A Parent–Teacher Partnership* (2nd edn). London: Paul Chapman.

Ball, C. (1994) *Start Right: The Importance of Early Learning*. London: RSA.

Barnes, P. (ed.) (1995) *Personal, Social and Emotional Development of Children*. Oxford: Blackwell.

Bee, H. (1992) *The Developing Child*. New York: HarperCollins.

Biddulph, S. (2008) *Open Eye Campaign*. Available at http://openeyecampaign. wordpress.com.

Bruce, T. (2001) *Learning Through Play: Babies, Toddlers and the Foundation Years*. London: Hodder and Stoughton.

Bruce, T. (2003) *Quoted in OnQ,* issue 13, p. 7. London: QCA. Available at www.qca.org.uk.

Bruce, T. (2004a) *Cultivating Creativity in Babies, Toddlers and Young Children*. London: Hodder and Stoughton.

Bruce, T. (2004b) *Developing Learning in Early Childhood*. London: Paul Chapman.

Bruce, T. (2005) *Early Childhood Education* (3rd edn). London: Hodder and Stoughton.

Bruce, T. and Spratt, J. (2008) *Essentials of Literacy from 0–7 Years: Children's Journeys in Literacy*. London: Sage Publications.

Bruner, J. (1977) *The Process of Education* (2nd edn). Cambridge, MA: Harvard University Press.

Bruner, J. (1990) *Acts of Meaning*. Cambridge, MA: Harvard University Press.

Daly, M., Byers, E. and Taylor, W. (2006) *Understanding Early Years Theory in Practice*. Oxford: Heinemann.

Davenport, G.C. (1988) *An Introduction to Child Development*. London: Collins Educational.

Department for Education and Science (1990) *Starting with Quality: The Report of the Committee of Inquiry into the Quality of Educational Experience Offered to 3 and 4 Year Olds (the Rumbold Report)*. London: HMSO.

Department for Education and Skills (2003) *National Standards for Under 8s Day Care and Childminding. Full Day Care*. London: DfES. Available at www.surestart.gov.uk.

Donaldson, M. (1986) *Children's Minds*. London: HarperCollins.

Dowling, M. (2000) *Young Children's Personal, Social and Emotional Development*. London: Paul Chapman.

Drake, J. (2001) *Planning Children's Play and Learning in the Foundation Stage*. London: David Fulton.

Duffy, B. (1998) *Early Childhood Education Forum Quality in Diversity in Early Learning. A Framework for Early Childhood Practitioners*. London: National Children's Bureau.

Duffy, B. (2006) *Supporting Creativity and Imagination in the Early Years*. Buckingham: Open University Press.

Early Years Foundation Stage (2007) *Effective Practice: Play and Exploration*. Available at www.standards.dcsf.gov.uk.

Elfer, P., Goldschmied, E. and Selleck, D. (2003) *Key Persons in the Nursery: Building Relationships for Quality Provision*. London: David Fulton.

Goldschmied, E. and Jackson, S. (1994) *People Under Three*. London: Routledge.

Hobart, C. and Frankel, J. (1994) *A Practical Guide to Child Observation*. Cheltenham: Stanley Thornes.

Hutchin, V. (2000) *Tracking Significant Achievement in the Early Years*. London: Hodder and Stoughton.

Lindon, J. (2005) *Understanding Child Development: Linking Theory and Practice*. London: Hodder Arnold.

Miller, L. Cable, C. and Devereux, J. (2005) *Developing Early Years Practice*. London: David Fulton.

Nutbrown, C. (2006) *Threads of Thinking: Young Children Learning and the Role of Early Education* (3rd edn). London: Sage Publications.

Pascal, C. and Bertram, T. (1997) *Effective Early Learning: Case Studies in Improvement*. London: Paul Chapman.

Pound, L. and Hughes, K. (2005) *How Children Learn: From Montessori to Vygotsky – Educational Theories and Approaches Made Easy Step*. Leamington Spa: Step Forward Publishing.

Pugh, G. and Duffy, B. (2006) *Contemporary Issues in the Early Years*. London: Sage Publications.

Pullman, Philip (2005) *'Common sense has much to learn from moonshine'*. The Guardian, 22 January.

Qualifications and Curriculum Authority (2001) *Planning for Learning in the Foundation Stage*.

Qualifications and Curriculum Authority (2003) *Foundation Stage Profile*.

Roberts, R. (1995) *Self-esteem and Successful Learning*. London: Hodder and Stoughton.

Schaffer, H.R. (1996) *Social Development*. Oxford: Blackwell.

Schweinhart, L.J. and Weikart, D.P. (1997) Lasting Differences. *The High/Scope Pre-school Curriculum Comparison Through Age 23*. Ypsilanti, MI: High/Scope Press.

Siraj-Blatchford, I. (ed.) (1998) *A Curriculum Development Handbook for Early Childhood Educators*. Stoke-on-Trent: Trentham Books.

Sylva, K. (2000) *'Early childhood education to ensure a "fair start" for all'*. In Cox, T. (ed.) *Combating Educational Disadvantage: Meeting the Needs of Vulnerable Children*, pp. 121–35. New York: Falmer.

Tassoni, P. (2002) *Planning for the Foundation Stage. Ideas for Themes and Activities*. Oxford: Heinemann.

Tassoni, P. (2003) *Supporting Special Needs. Understanding Inclusion in the Early Years*. Oxford: Heinemann.

Valentine, M. (1999) *The Reggio Emilia Approach to Early Years Education*. *Scottish Consultative Council on the Curriculum*.

Whalley, M. (1994) *Learning to be Strong: Integrating Education and Care in Early Childhood*. London: Hodder and Stoughton.

Whalley, M. (2007) *Involving Parents in their Children's Learning* (2nd edn). London: Paul Chapman.

Whalley, M. and Whitaker, P. (2005) *Leadership and Management in the Early Years*. Corby: Pen Green Base.

Whitehead, M. (1996) *The Development of Language and Literacy in the Early Years*. London: Hodder and Stoughton.

Wood, D. (1988) *How Children Think and Learn*. Oxford: Blackwell.

Useful websites

Curriculum for Excellence, Scotland: www.curriculumforexcellencescotland.gov.uk

Department for Children, Schools and Families: www.dcsf.gov.uk

Early Years Foundation Stage (EYFS): www.standards.dcsf.gov.uk

Effective Provision of Pre-school Education (EPPE): www.standards.dcsf.gov.uk

Foundation Phase in Wales: http://new.wales.gov.uk

Key elements of Effective Practice (KEEP): www.standards.dcsf.gov.uk

Northern Ireland Foundation Stage: www.nicurriculum.org.uk

Qualifications and Curriculum Authority (QCA): www.qca.org.uk

Researching the Effective Pedagogy in the Early Years (REPEY): www.standards.dcsf.gov.uk

Study of Pedagogical Effectiveness in Early Learning (SPEEL): www.dcsf.gov.uk

4 Managing the Needs of Children in Early Years Settings

This chapter looks at relationships between the setting and children and their families, and how these can be nurtured within early years settings. Children should remain the key focus of every aspect of the setting:

- the planning of suitable, age- and stage-appropriate activities that encourage and stimulate children to investigate their environment (this is covered in Chapter 3)

- suitable routines that enable children to feel safe and emotionally secure in their surroundings

- a warm, welcoming environment that is also child-centred, safe and stimulating.

Research suggests that children develop best in environments where adults are highly responsive. The role of the early years practitioner has changed dramatically over the years – partly as a result of legislation. They now have more responsibilities and more paperwork to manage, but this must not be at the cost of the children. Early years managers need to manage their time effectively so that they are able to remain highly responsive to the needs of the children. How the children are managed in the setting has an impact on their development and learning. The role of the early years practitioner is to ensure that the needs of each child are met in order to encourage independence and confidence. Children who feel confident about themselves are more able to have a positive learning experience, which will lay a strong foundation for later learning. The quality of the support children receive from the early years practitioners in the setting will have an effect on how valued they feel. When children feel part of the community within the setting they are able to develop their independence and confidence. By regularly reflecting on and reviewing practice, you will be able to maximise the opportunities for high-quality learning and minimise challenging behaviour.

This chapter looks at how early years practitioners manage the needs of children within the setting and thus provide a quality service.

The chapter covers the following areas:

4.1 Creating a welcoming and supportive environment for children and their families

4.2 Providing routines

4.3 Key person approach

4.4 Supporting transitions

4.5 Positive behaviour expectations

4.1 Creating a welcoming and supportive environment for children and their families

As an early years leader and manager you will be managing a range of people (Figure 4.1).

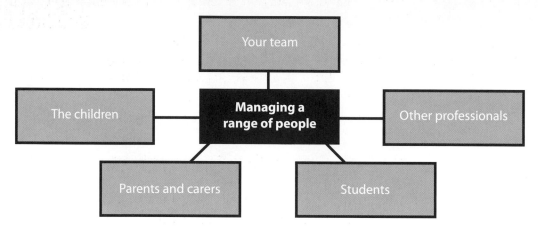

Figure 4.1. Some of the people you could be managing

It could be argued that the children are the most important people on this list. How you and your team manage the children's experiences will have an impact on their learning. The relationship with the children starts from their initial contact with the setting and ends with supporting their transition to the next setting. Between the two there is the important matter of settling the children in and welcoming them each day. This section looks at all these matters.

Initial contact

Children's initial contact with the early years setting comes in a variety of forms, all of which are equally important (see Table 4.1).

 **Key Term**

Transition – a move from one environment (setting) to another. This may be from home to a childminder, or from one year to another within a school or day care centre.

Table 4.1. The different forms of initial contact with children starting in an early years setting

Form of contact	What is involved
Home visiting	Members of the team offer home visits to meet the children and families in their own homes prior to starting at the setting. This gives families the opportunity to ask questions and start to develop contact with the setting and team.
Preliminary visits to the setting	Visits before the children start at the setting help the children, parents and carers to become familiar with its staff, routines and the organisational structure.
Letters home	Letters to the children, parents and carers before the children start help them to feel valued and included. A colourful card or decorative letter addressed to the child can be very welcoming.

Home visiting is becoming more commonplace as the benefits of building this initial rapport with families have been recognised as invaluable in building positive relationships with children and their families. However, home visits are only worthwhile when both the practitioner and the family feel comfortable with the arrangement.

Preliminary visits to the setting give children the opportunity to become familiar with the staff, children and the environment before starting. Ideally visits should be planned as close to the children's start date as possible, with the opportunity to visit more than once. Preliminary visits need to be carefully planned to minimise disruption to the established children and routines. Arrange for visiting children to arrive after the session has started and leave before the session ends. This should give them enough time to experience a range of activities as well as experience some aspects of the daily routine.

All young children enjoy receiving a letter through the post and this is an exciting way of introducing them to the setting. You can also prepare parents for the initial visit by providing them with a timetable of the session. This will help them to feel more comfortable and know what to expect and how to best support their child.

Shimmin and White (2006, p. 11) recommend the following pointers on how best practitioners can help parents support their child during a visit.

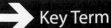

Key Term

Home visiting – practitioners from a setting visit the child and family in their own home with the aim of getting to know them before the child starts to attend the setting.

- Emphasise that the aim of the visit is for children to leave the setting with a collection of happy memories.

- Where a child wishes to stay with their parent for the entire duration of the visit, reassure the adult that this is absolutely fine. If necessary, explain to a parent that their child is in a new setting and it is perfectly natural for them to be 'clingy'.

- Some children may not want to participate in any activity. Reassure parents that simply observing what is going on is a valuable experience in itself and quite normal behaviour for young children in a strange environment.

- Some children are happy to operate quite independently of their parents. If necessary, suggest to the parent that they step back and let their child explore the setting themselves.

- Occasionally, parents find it difficult to accept that their child does not appear to want them. If this is the case, compliment them on their child's confidence and independence and remind them that it bodes well for the future.

- Let parents choose whether or not to join in with snack time and group activities. If a child is happy to sit in the group by themselves, suggest that their parent sits behind them or at the side of the room. If the child wants reassurance, encourage the parent to sit inside the circle with the child on their knee.

Attending nursery, school or a childminder for the first time is often a child's first contact with a care environment outside the home. It can be a daunting and stressful experience for both the child and family, especially if there has been a bad experience in the past for the parent. The way in which children and families are welcomed has a huge impact on their relationship with the setting. If handled well at this early stage it can also have a positive impact as the child progresses through the whole education system.

Settling in

The routines and processes in place that support the smooth transition from home to the setting must be flexible and take into account the needs of individual children and their families. The settling-in process allows children to become familiar with their new surroundings at their own pace, with the support of the early years practitioners caring for them. For some children this will be gradual and require consistent support, while for others it will be a much shorter process with less support.

For many children, leaving parents and carers for the first time can be a stressful experience. The sensitive support and reassurance received from the early years practitioners caring for them will contribute to their emotional well-being. For some children it will be the first time they have been left by their parent or carer, and others may have had a poorly managed previous experience of separation. It is widely agreed among early years practitioners that encouraging parents or carers to stay with their child while they settle in is good practice. They should be encouraged to stay for as long as it takes their child to settle. This could be a few minutes each day or the whole session. It can take up to half a term to settle children, especially those who have not spent time away from home before.

In order to ensure a successful settling process the early years practitioner needs to be sensitive to the needs of both children and parents. The majority of parents are willing to support their children by gradually introducing them to the setting and staying with them if required; however, there are those who feel that leaving promptly is a better strategy for their own child. Explaining the benefits of parental involvement here may encourage more parents to participate. Some benefits are that:

- it lessens distress for the child
- it facilitates the development of a trusting relationship between the child and the early years practitioner
- the child is likely to settle much more quickly.

However, early years practitioners need to respect the wishes of families who prefer the setting to be solely responsible.

Good practice checklist
Settling children in

- Keep parents informed. Tell parents and carers about the routines and processes in place to support them and their children during the settling-in period before children start.
- Ask parents and carers to be brave. Children easily pick up on how their parents are feeling and will respond accordingly. If the parents and carers are outwardly confident in coming into the setting then the children will also feel more positive about it.
- Ask parents and carers to try to arrive on time. Children want to conform and being late can be very unsettling.
- Ask them to return on time, as being the last to be picked up can be very distressing for the child.
- Invite parents and carers to stay with their child for as long as necessary.
- Reassure them that any crying or distress is a normal reaction to separation.

Welcoming children each day

In order to cope with such a momentous experience as starting nursery, children need to feel that the setting they are entering welcomes and values them. Unfortunately this is not always given the thought and planning it deserves. The aim is to create a warm and welcoming first experience and thereafter every day. If this point of the day is not treated with sensitivity it is possible to damage the newly established relationship between the setting, the parents and carers and the children.

Children need to feel the setting welcomes them.

Different welcoming strategies

Welcoming strategies include the following:

- Whole-group welcome time. As children arrive they sit either in small groups or all together and are greeted by an adult as a group rather than individually.

- Singing a welcome song. Once the children have started their chosen activity at the start of the session a welcome song is sung.

- Individual contact at some point early in the session. Adults make a conscious effort to speak to each child individually during the first part of the session.

These strategies, however, are not personal or immediate, and do not meet the children's need for emotional support as they arrive. Research has shown that whole-group activities can be stressful, especially for new children. These children found it less threatening to be involved in self-directed activity for the first part of the session. Therefore there is a strong argument for individual and personal greetings.

However, a few children may not wish to be acknowledged as they arrive, and prefer to arrive discreetly and just get on with an activity without any fuss. You need to recognise this and respect the unsaid wishes of individual children. This does not mean that you ignore the child, but rather replace a greeting with a more subtle form of acknowledgement.

Think it over

Consider the arrival routine in your setting.

- How are the children greeted as they arrive?
- Is this done in a well-organised manner?
- Is there anything that prevents you from greeting each child individually?
- List the advantages and disadvantages of various greeting strategies.

Elements of a warm welcome

Individual greetings provide the ideal basis for developing good relationships. In order to promote children's self-esteem Dowling (2000) suggests that early years practitioners use:

- eye contact
- a genuine smile
- a warm, friendly, approachable manner.

Although Dowling meant for these strategies to be used when interacting with the children throughout the day, they are also elements of a warm welcome. Other valuable strategies include:

- making physical contact (such as holding a hand)
- using the child's name
- making a personal comment
- sustaining a conversation if possible.

It is also helpful to ensure that each child has a named peg for a coat and a named drawer, as this will reinforce the feeling of belonging. These should be ready on the child's first day.

A practical approach to personal greetings

It is not always possible to greet every child every day. For example, a setting may have only two members of staff, you may be in an informal meeting with parents, or a particular child may need extra support. However, it is possible to plan effectively so that these events have minimum effect.

Good practice checklist

Early morning routines

- Ensure that all necessary preparations are complete before the children arrive so that you are free to greet the children and their parents and carers.
- Ensure that the initial activities do not require large amounts of adult support. Other activities will be more inclusive for the children and will allow you to be available for them.
- Ensure that the parents are familiar with the arrival routine and know what they can expect from the setting.

- Have a system for parents to leave messages for you. However, it is important that this is not a substitute for your personal availability. Remember that not all parents are comfortable with written communication.

- If a particular child gets distressed at being left and needs extra support on arrival, ask the parents to arrive a little later. This will enable you to give the necessary support to both the child and parent, as well as to reduce the stress in the room as the other children arrive.

- Take time to observe the children as they arrive. You are aiming for an atmosphere that is relaxed, happy and productive.

- New problems are inevitable as group dynamics change. Involve the whole team in resolving any new problems as they arise.

Find it out

Arrange to visit an early years setting that is similar to your own and observe the arrival routine. Note how the team manages this part of the session, including contact with parents and carers, room preparation and welcoming the children.

Why welcome each child?

Greeting the children provides the early years practitioner with the opportunity to assess how each child is feeling and to respond with appropriate support. Young children especially benefit from having routines in their lives (see section 4.2). They thrive on the regularity of familiar events and gain an immense sense of security from them. Greeting children as part of the regular routine enhances their feelings of security and belonging. This in turn has a positive effect on their emotional development and their success as learners.

Open-door policy

Many settings have an open-door policy whereby parents and carers are free to access the setting and a member of the team at any time during the session. Some settings actively encourage this form of contact as they recognise its value and importance to the relationship with the family. However it may not always be practical, especially in settings with small numbers of staff. Encouraging parental participation is discussed in detail in Chapter 5.

Other practical ways to help parents and families feel welcome include:

- a clearly signed reception
- a staff photo board with names and roles of each practitioner
- examples of children's work
- photographs of activities and events
- information packs about the setting
- parents' noticeboard.

Think it over

Many of the strategies identified above are common practice; however some settings, for a variety of reasons, do not actively encourage parents and carers into the setting. How would the following statements make you feel if you were a parent visiting a setting and these were displayed at the entrance?

- No pushchairs beyond this point
- No parents beyond this point

How could these be managed differently?

Figure 4.2. Some settings may not actively welcome parents and carers

Find it out

Arrange to visit another early years setting and focus on your first impressions.

- How welcoming does the setting feel?
- Is the reception or entrance clearly signposted?
- Are you greeted by a member of staff?
- Are there examples of children's work displayed?
- Is there a parents' noticeboard?

4.2 Providing routines

Daily routines

The daily routine within the setting is a central part of the management of children within the setting. Suitable routines that enable children to feel emotionally safe and secure therefore warrant careful thought and management. All settings are bound by the requirement to meet the physical needs of young children, such as regular nappy changes, sleep and food (including snacks). These have an impact on the routine, as activities and experiences are planned around them.

It may be helpful to turn this around and fit nappy checks, for example, around activities, or changing children when needed rather than all together (although snacks and mealtimes are less flexible). Experience has shown that children who are changed when needed receive more individual care and higher-quality one-to-one interaction. More time is spent communicating with children and the experience becomes less hurried and more pleasurable. This, however, would require careful record-keeping to ensure no one was forgotten. Children who are engrossed in play can be left until a natural conclusion is reached, rather than be disturbed for a nappy change, causing less disruption and fewer changes.

The daily routine can affect the behaviour of young children. In some cases a child's behaviour will improve if daily routines are simplified. Some young children have difficulty coping with frequent or rapid changes in environments where they are expected to be cooperative, have self-control and be self-sufficient. For these children, a simpler routine with fewer changes can be beneficial. Others cope very well with unexpected changes to the routine.

Within a setting's daily routine there are several smaller routines that are established such as putting your coat on your peg, walking when indoors, hand-washing, clearing away an activity when you have finished with it. The list is endless and young children soon develop ownership of these and do them automatically, gaining comfort from these types of expectations and boundaries.

Benefits of a daily routine

Daily, consistent routines are considered good practice as the predictability of what is going to happen next enables children to feel emotionally secure and safe. Early years practitioners can use opportunities that arise during daily routines to help children explore their own feelings and emotions.

It is important to create a daily routine that supports children's development, as this can help avoid many of the frustrations that lead to challenging behaviour. This is explored in greater detail further on in this chapter, however avoiding too many disruptions to the daily routine can be helpful.

Disruption to daily routines

Most children will demonstrate an awareness of time as a result of suitable routines long before they can actually tell the time. They understand that story time follows snack time which follows outside play, and can find it stressful or upsetting when there are unexpected changes.

There are often times when routines need to be changed, for example when a member of staff is off sick or when children need to be collected by someone else. Early years practitioners can support children in a number of ways (Figure 4.3).

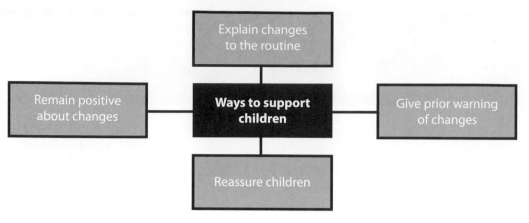

Figure 4.3. Ways of supporting children through disruption

Think it over

Think about the last time your regular routine was disrupted, maybe due to the weather, an incident or unexpected visitor.

- How was this communicated to the children?

- What impact did it have on the children?

- Did you notice any changes in their behaviour?

4.3 Key person approach

What is the key person approach?

John Bowlby's work on attachment and loss pioneered the idea that children need a secure base from which to develop social interactions (see also Chapter 2). The importance of attachment to a key carer and having a secure base are major issues in considering what supports or constrains children as they develop their learning in a range of settings, including the home, childminders or day nursery (Bruce, 2004). Babies and young children show attachment behaviour when they make sure their special adult remains nearby, crying for them, smiling when close, moving towards them when feeling worried and moving away and exploring when feeling safe (Miller and Devereux, 2004).

The key person approach is a system often used in settings working with very young children where the focus is to establish a close, reciprocal relationship between a member of staff, child and their family.

Key Terms

Key person – a practitioner who is mainly responsible for providing lead support, contact and communication for a child and their family within the setting, with the aim of enabling and supporting close attachments between individual children and staff.

Attachment – a stable and secure relationship between a child and their primary carer. John Bowlby is the best-known theorist on children's need to be with their primary carers.

The key person's role involves:

- developing a strong emotional bond with the child allocated to them
- welcoming the child at the start of the day
- handing the child over at the end of the day
- liaising with parents and carers – sharing highlights of the day and any concerns
- maintaining a home contact book
- maintaining observations and assessments
- meeting physical care needs
- meeting social and emotional needs.

Benefits of the key person approach

Elfer, Goldschmied and Selleck (2003) identify it as an approach that has clear benefits for all involved:

For babies and young children: The key person takes care of their allocated children's physical and emotional needs ensuring they feel cherished and valued while away from home.

For parents and carers: The key person approach ensures parents have the opportunity to build a relationship with an individual member of staff who is familiar with their baby or child.

For the key person: For the practitioner the key person approach can make their job much more satisfying. The role can be very demanding, however the pleasure gained from working closely with a baby or young child and their family can outweigh any disadvantages. It is a huge responsibility being a key person in a child's formative years but one that is very rewarding.

For the setting: The key person approach leads to a greater staff involvement, improved quality of care and learning for children. Relationships with parents are more positive and mutually respectful and there is a greater commitment to the setting with less staff sickness.

Disadvantages of the key person approach

The key person approach, many aspects of which have been highlighted above, is considered good practice among early years practitioners in general. However, there can be disadvantages to this approach that need careful consideration:

- Only the key person tends to the physical care needs of their allocated children.
- A child may find it difficult to relate to another member of staff if their key person is away.
- Some children are at the setting longer each day than their key person, so they are not always available to greet them or send them home.
- Some parents worry about a special relationship forming between their child and the key person.
- It can be a difficult skill for a practitioner to acquire to be a key person to more than one child.

Think it over

- What do you think are the main advantages and disadvantages of the key person approach?

- How could the disadvantages be minimised?

4.4 Supporting transitions

Identifying transitions

The *Every Child Matters* (ECM) government strategy is one of the most significant programmes of changes aimed at improving the lives of young children today (see Chapter 2). The ECM standards provide settings with a clear and consistent baseline to measure and judge their progress towards meeting the ECM outcomes. Standard 11: Transitions and Transfers highlights the value of settings recognising the importance of supporting transitions in line with achieving the ECM well-being outcomes.

Transitions are the move from one environment to another. Adults have numerous strategies to cope with transitions such as starting a new job, moving to a different part of the country, getting married or becoming parents. However, young children have not had the opportunity to develop these strategies. They can experience a range of reactions to transitions, including feeling vulnerable and frightened, which in turn has an effect on their ability to integrate and learn. For these reasons it is important to support children during times of transition. It is the role of the early years practitioner to be sympathetic to any anxieties and to be sensitively supportive.

Transitions are not only a move to a new phase of life, but can also be:

- the daily move from one environment to another

- a new experience

- a sudden change in routine

- an unexpected event.

The most common form of early transition is the daily separation from a parent or carer when children attend day care, a childminder or nursery school.

All forms of transition can be stressful for young children and the levels of stress can be influenced by many factors. For example, children may be less able to deal with transitions at times when they are dealing with other events. Children's reactions to transitions can therefore change over time, as can their need for support. In order to provide appropriate support, think about the types of events the children in your care may experience (Figure 4.4). Even something adults may consider to be a small or insignificant event can be quite traumatic for children.

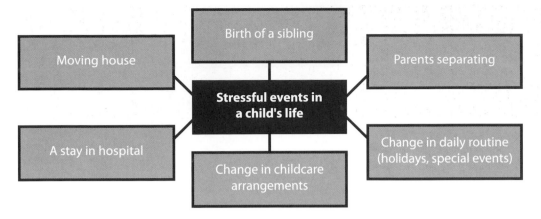

Figure 4.4. Some stressful events in a child's life

Think it over

Think back to the last time you experienced a major transition in your life (for example a new job or moving house).

- How did you feel?
- How did you prepare yourself for this new phase in your life?
- How could this transition have been made easier for you?

Supporting transitions through understanding

In order to provide children with effective support it is necessary to understand why transitions need to be incorporated into the setting's daily planning. The transition from home to nursery can be a difficult time for young children, and any negative experience here can have a detrimental effect on the subsequent transition to school (Blatchford et al., 1982). Familiar people, things, places and routines become even more important, and the more they can be maintained during transitions, the better. Continuity and consistency are key elements for enabling babies and young children to feel emotionally safe and secure, yet these are at most risk of being broken during transitions.

It is your role as an early years practitioner to provide effective support to ensure that transitions are as positive as possible.

- Try to get to know each child as quickly as possible so that you are aware of individual needs and can act on them.
- Actively foster warm and positive relationships with parents – if children see that their parents are welcome in and trust the setting, they will too.
- Implement an effective settling-in policy which involves lots of contact with the setting and staff prior to starting.

Figure 4.5. A child may form a strong bond with their key person

The impact of poor transitions

Bronfenbrenner (1979) considered the environment in which children develop to be a major influence on their ability to be successful learners. Just as adults do, children apply previous experiences, both negative and positive, to new situations. Children who have been traumatised by poorly managed transitions will naturally presume all transitions to be traumatic, whereas if young children have had positive experiences of being left by their parents or carers they are more likely to be able to make successful transitions. When children enter a new environment they apply previously learned skills and behaviour and continue to use this strategy throughout life.

Bronfenbrenner believed that at times of transition a positive partnership between home and setting makes the event less stressful. It is reassuring that something so simple can have such a major impact. However, it is because it is so simple that it can sometimes be overlooked and left to chance. Chapter 5 looks at ways of developing positive partnerships with parents and carers and how they can affect children's early years experience.

Think it over

Think about the transitions made by the children in your setting.

- How were these transitions accommodated?
- What preparations were made for children leaving the setting?
- What strategies were used to involve parents at times of transition?

Compare your answers with someone else's. Are there any notable differences?

Sideq starts day care

Sideq is 3 years old. He has just started attending day care for four mornings per week. Before he started, the early years manager invited Sideq and his mother to attend two introductory sessions. During these, he was shown around the nursery and given a peg and drawer for his belongings. Sideq started to attend the following week and initially settled well and began to make friends. However, he is now becoming distressed when left by his mother, and staff are unable to comfort or distract him. He is unwilling to participate in activities and wants to sit by the door and wait for his mother to return. During the next team meeting staff discuss their concerns about Sideq. A senior practitioner suggests that they ignore his behaviour. Another member of the team suggests that his mother should leave him as quickly as possible, as her 'fussing' is making the situation worse.

■ How do you think Sideq and his mother can be best supported at this time?

■ What do you think may be the cause of Sideq's change in behaviour?

Good practice checklist
Smoothing transitions

- Ensure that there is a clear transition and transfer policy.
- Start planning transitions early.
- Match transition planning to children's individual needs.
- Share class activities, assemblies and events.
- Work closely with colleagues and provide them with information they need and will use.
- Make change slowly.
- Involve the children.
- Involve the parents.
- If age appropriate, use a peer buddy system to support the induction process.
- Develop a positive relationship between the setting and home.

4.5 Positive behaviour expectations

Some of the more direct ways of managing behaviour are considered below. First, however, two prerequisites to good behaviour within a setting are considered:

- showing that the adults value young children and promote their self-respect
- good communication between adults and children.

Valuing young children and promoting self-respect

Experience has shown that the quality of the relationship between the early years practitioner and the children is a crucial element to how well they do both socially and academically. When children see that they are supported and respected it leads to positive attitudes and feelings of being valued, and in turn these help children to develop self-respect. Self-respect is one of the most important qualities needed to be a good learner. Children who do not feel valued or respected often demonstrate this through inappropriate behaviour.

Positive relationships with carers can have a beneficial effect on behaviour. The child who has a secure relationship initiates positive interactions with others and responds positively. It is not unusual for children who have insecure relationships with their carers to use various negative strategies, such as ignoring instructions given to them.

Communicating with young children

It is the role of the early years practitioner to enable young children to develop effective communication skills. These skills are influenced by the adults around children and how responsive they are. Children who have little experience of enjoyable conversations reflect this in their own communication with others. By providing children with consistent support and opportunities to communicate, they will develop the skills needed to be effective communicators. They will also be much less likely to engage in inappropriate behaviour.

Communication can be both verbal and non-verbal. The latter includes body language, facial expressions and gestures. Early years practitioners need to be sensitive to what message they are giving through their own non-verbal communication. 'Closed' body language – for example folded arms and little eye contact – and negative facial expressions give the message that you are unapproachable and unavailable. Early years practitioners should therefore:

- be aware of their own non-verbal communication and that of the children
- be responsive to the children and other adults in the setting
- initiate conversation and take time to respond appropriately to conversations children begin
- extend and encourage children's use of language
- show a genuine interest in what the children have to say, so that they will be encouraged to communicate

- encourage curiosity and exploration
- answer children's questions
- be active listeners.

You can show children that you are actively listening to them by:

- maintaining eye contact
- getting on the same physical level as them
- responding appropriately to what they say to you
- concentrating on what they are saying.

It is important to show a child that you are actively listening.

It is not always easy to follow all these points at busy moments, but you can probably think of a time when you have not paid full attention to what a child was telling you and have answered with the throwaway comment 'That's nice'. I never made this mistake again when the child replied 'Well, we were very sad that he died.'

Think it over

Think about the daily routine in your setting.

- At what times were the children able to initiate a conversation with an adult or be listened to by a group of children?
- Which communication skills did the children have the opportunity to develop?

Compare your answers with those of someone from another setting.

Expectations of behaviour

In order to meet the needs of children in the setting and minimise challenging behaviour it is useful to identify what behaviours are unacceptable.

Think it over

- What do you consider to be challenging behaviour?
- What aspects of challenging behaviour have you experienced professionally in a setting?
- What were the expectations in that setting?
- How did the children know what the expectations were?

One of the first steps to managing challenging behaviour within the setting is to look at the expectations and decide whether or not they are realistic. This is not about lowering standards, but about giving the children achievable and realistic targets. Children are at risk of behaving badly in response to unrealistic expectations imposed on them by the adults in the setting. Such expectations can often reflect the adults' lack of understanding about young children's development. Early years practitioners need to bear in mind the social and emotional stages of development, as these will affect how children behave in different situations (see Table 4.2). Linking stages of development to age can be unreliable, however, and therefore only by getting to know each child well can expectations be realistic.

It is important to remember that there is a vast range within the norms indicated in Table 4.2. There are also additional influences on behaviour that must be taken into account, including:

- the birth of a sibling
- the death of a family member
- relationship breakdown between parents
- moving house
- parental absence (short- or long-term)
- a change of routine
- any event that traumatises the child to a lesser or greater extent.

In addition to these social influences, research has also identified the following emotional triggers.

- The need for attention. Some children believe that they belong only when they are noticed. This belief is so strong that they do not mind whether it is negative or positive attention they receive. The early years practitioner can respond by giving positive attention and reinforcement at other times, by ignoring inappropriate behaviour if it is safe to do so and by using redirecting and distraction strategies. Distraction strategies require the early years practitioner to be able to pre-empt inappropriate behaviour and subtly intervene by redirecting children away from the situation.

- The need for power. Some children believe they belong only when they are in control. The early years practitioner can respond with kind but firm respect, by giving limited choices, setting reasonable boundaries and, again, by using redirecting and distraction strategies.

■ Feelings of inadequacy. Some children feel the need to show to others through their behaviour that they are inadequate. Early years practitioners can respond by encouraging the child to try new things, focusing on the child's strengths, teaching new skills in small steps and by giving praise and encouragement.

Table 4.2. Children's development and the associated social and emotional influences on behaviour

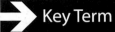 **Key Term**

Age of child	Stage of development
0–3 months	Feelings and relationships begin to develop. Children begin to recognise people they know well. They begin to smile and turn towards a familiar voice.
3–6 months	Children can differentiate their mother's voice from others. They like to be held by a familiar person. They may begin to enjoy peek-a-boo games and to be wary of strangers. They learn self-worth from the actions and reactions of others.
6–12 months	Children begin to develop a sense of self-image and become more aware of the feelings of others. They realise that objects and people are separate from them. They show fear of strangers. They understand the word 'no'.
1–2 years	Children begin to have a mind of their own and to develop a sense of identity. They begin to express their needs using words and gestures. Interpersonal relationships are based on taking rather than giving.
2–3 years	Children of this age can imitate others. They enjoy symbolic play. They begin to explain how they feel, to show autonomy, to do things for themselves and to show more patience. They will share and be more affectionate, although they can also be inflexible and demanding.
3–4 years	Children begin to be interested in having friends. They are influenced by each other. They can cooperate and negotiate. They can be easily frightened. Routines are less important.
4–8 years	Children establish a stable self-concept and take in and internalise social rules. They respond positively to explanations and reasons for things. They learn to be assertive without being aggressive. They are beginning to sort out real from make-believe and truth from untruths.

Positive reinforcement – Behaviour can be manipulated through the use of reinforcements. Children learn to repeat desired behaviour when they are given genuine praise and encouragement for positive behaviour.

It is also important to remember that the setting's dynamics change with each new intake and with each child's departure. You need to be sensitively aware of all these influences on behaviour and adjust expectations and goals accordingly.

Finally, there are also physical influences on behaviour. For example, a toddler aged 2–3 years is not yet physically developed to be able to sit still for more than a very short time, and therefore an expectation to do so would be unrealistic.

Pasta necklaces

Afia is a newly qualified nursery assistant working with 1–2-year-olds in a day care centre. She likes all aspects of her new job, but particularly enjoys planning and implementing activities. Today it is raining so the children will not be able to play outside in the garden after snack time. Afia has been asked to set up a short activity instead. She decides to make pasta necklaces with the children, and sets out all the necessary materials on the table. After snack time the other nursery staff encourage the children to choose what to play with. Once all the children are busy, Afia encourages four of them to come and do the activity. When the children are seated at the table it quickly becomes obvious to Afia that the activity is going to be unsuccessful and of no value to the children – it is inappropriate for this age group.

◼ Think of all the possible causes of the activity being unsuccessful.

◼ How do you think the children reacted to this activity?

◼ How does this link to your knowledge and understanding of child development?

Knowing the expectations

Expectations need to be clear, consistent, realistic and supported by all the adults in the setting. But how do the children know what the expectations of their behaviour are? Sometimes this is overlooked and it is assumed that the children 'just know'. Some settings regularly involve the children in drawing up the classroom rules, and display a copy in the room as well as sending one home for the parents to reinforce. These rules are more likely to have an impact if they are based on a positive viewpoint. That is, they should focus on actions and behaviour to be encouraged. For example:

◼ We always try to be kind to others.

◼ We always try to speak nicely to each other.

◼ We look after our own and other people's things.

◼ We take care of our nursery.

◼ We put things back where they belong.

◼ We look after living things.

A behaviour policy

If the setting has realistic expectations and the practitioners know and understand each child well, the children are more likely to meet expectations (Figure 4.6).

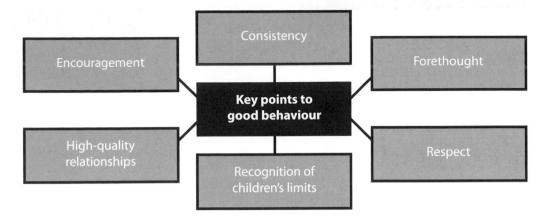

Figure 4.6. A positive behaviour policy

Realistic and consistent targets are likely to foster good behaviour. By creating and implementing a behaviour policy all adults know what is expected both of them and the children. Each setting should create its own behaviour policy, and this should reflect the specific needs of the children. Owing to the frequent change-over of children, parents and staff, it is essential to review the policy regularly. In order for the policy to be workable it should be created by all those who work with the children, with additional input from parents. It will need to set out realistic and achievable targets that are based on a sound understanding of child development.

Evaluating children's behaviour

When evaluating the children's behaviour, try to decide for whom the behaviour is a problem. Often natural curiosity and the desire to experiment can be mistaken for challenging behaviour.

Case Study

The wrong toys

A group of 3- and 4-year-olds are playing in the sand when one of them suggests they make a road. They use the spades and rakes to form paths in the sand. Emily brings a box of cars and some farm animals from the small-world play area and tips them into the sand tray. The children start a game with the cars and animals, playing cooperatively together. They create a road and farm, making up a story as they play. Andrew, a childcare student, intervenes and asks the children to return the cars and farm animals to where they belong. Oliver asks why they can't play with the cars and animals. Andrew explains that they are not sand toys and that they will get spoiled.

- As Andrew's supervisor, how would you deal with this situation?
- What justification would you give Andrew?

Alice and the glue

In the nursery class a group of children aged between 3 and 4 years are sitting at a table doing a craft activity. All the materials needed for the activity have been set up ready for the children to use. Alice picks up the glue and begins gently to pour it over the paper in front of her. She uses the glue spreader to spread the glue over the paper. She then presses both hands into the glue repeatedly. Alice is clearly enjoying this first experience of glue. Zeena, the early years worker supervising the group, points out Alice's action to her colleague, saying 'Look! She's doing it deliberately. She knows we don't allow them to do that. That's so naughty!' Zeena asks Alice to go and wash her hands.

- Is Alice's behaviour 'naughty'?
- Why do you think Alice is using the glue in this way?
- Why do you think Zeena responds in this way?
- How would you deal with this situation?

Encouraging positive behaviour

The most effective strategy in behaviour management is prevention. To this end, the setting should agree a team approach and represent an environment that:

- encourages independence
- builds self-esteem
- meets the individual needs of children
- takes into account the likes and dislikes of the children
- provides the children with a wide range of appropriate, stimulating activities and learning experiences that encourage exploration and problem-solving
- caters for the developmental needs of all the children
- is well organised and stimulating.

Positive reinforcement

Encouragement, smiles and genuine praise for cooperation produce positive results. These strategies lead to the repetition of the desired behaviour, as they build on the children's need for acceptance. Children who are shouted at and scolded do not change their challenging behaviour permanently.

The good practice checklists can help you to evaluate whether or not your setting is geared towards preventing challenging behaviour and encouraging good behaviour.

Good practice checklist

Encouraging good behaviour

- Ensure that children know and understand the setting's behaviour policy and class rules.
- Stick to the policy fairly and consistently.
- Praise good behaviour.
- Be a positive role model.
- Discuss right and wrong in appropriate contexts as the opportunity arises.
- Be well organised and plan effectively. This will help prevent the children getting bored.
- Ensure the routine supports the children's emotional needs.
- Encourage the children to find their own solutions to problems.
- Give plenty of opportunities for the children to develop their social skills.
- Encourage children to understand the consequences of their actions.

Good practice checklist

Discouraging challenging behaviour

- Provide enough resources and materials so that the children do not have to share too many items and wait too long for their turn.
- Provide sufficient play materials to allow the children choices.
- Check that activities are appropriate to the children's ages and stages of development.
- Remove barriers to success to prevent the children becoming frustrated.
- Keep waiting times to a minimum.
- When dealing with challenging behaviour explain why it cannot be tolerated. Remember to remain calm, speak quietly, slowly and firmly, ensuring that you maintain eye contact with the child.
- Give reasons for your judgements when conflict occurs.
- Always remember to let the child know that it is the behaviour that is unacceptable, not the child.

Conclusion

High-quality management of children's needs within the early years setting is central to their all-round development and learning. Positive early educational experiences lay a strong foundation for later learning.

Early years managers need to ensure that they provide a warm, welcoming environment in order to support positive early educational experiences. They also need to implement an agreed team approach and realistic behaviour policy; this in turn will be helped by establishing routines for the children.

Managers can ensure that they are providing the best possible service by implementing and regularly evaluating a range of child-focused strategies, including:

- home visiting
- consistent contact with the child's home
- the settling-in process
- actively providing a positive and supportive learning environment
- supporting transitions
- welcoming children
- demonstrating that children are valued and respected
- positive communication with young children
- expectations of good behaviour
- appropriate daily routines.

Check your understanding

1 What do you understand by the term 'transition'?

2 How can the early years practitioner provide effective support to ensure that transitions are as positive as possible?

3 Individual greetings provide the ideal basis from which positive relationships can develop. What practical steps can be taken in order to greet as many children as possible each day?

4 The environment can affect children's behaviour. Outline the practical steps necessary to ensure the environment encourages good behaviour.

References and further reading

Athey, C. (2007) *Extending Thought in Young Children. A Parent–Teacher Partnership*. London: Paul Chapman.

Blatchford, P., Battles, S. and Mays, J. (1982) *The First Transitions*. Slough: Nelson.

Bronfenbrenner, U. (1979) *The Ecology of Human Development*. Cambridge, MA: Harvard University Press.

Bruce, T. (2004) *Developing Learning in Early Childhood*. London: Paul Chapman.

Bruce, T. (2006) *Early Childhood*. London: Sage Publications.

Cheminais, R. (2006) *Every Child Matters: A Practical Guide for Teachers*. London: Paul Chapman.

Cheminais, R. (2007) *How to Achieve the Every Child Matters Standards: A Practical Guide*. London: Paul Chapman.

Dowling, M. (2000) *Young Children's Personal, Social and Emotional Development*. London: Paul Chapman.

Elfer, P., Goldschmied, E. and Selleck, D. (2003) *Key Persons in the Nursery: Building Relationships for Quality Provision*. London: David Fulton.

Lindon, J. (2005) *Understanding Child Development: Linking Theory and Practice*. London: Hodder Arnold.

Miller, L. and Devereux, J. (2004) *Supporting Children's Learning in the Early Years*. London: David Fulton.

Moyles, J. (2007) *Effective Leadership and Management in the Early Years*. Maidenhead: Open University Press.

Pugh, G. and Duffy, B. (2006) *Contemporary Issues in the Early Years* (4th edn). London: Sage Publications.

Riddall Leech, S. (2003) *Managing Children's Behaviour*. Oxford: Heinemann.

Robert, R. (2006) *Self-esteem and Early Learning* (3rd edn). London: Paul Chapman.

Rodd, J. (2006) *Leadership in Early Childhood* (3rd edn). Maidenhead: Open University Press.

Shimmin, S. and White, H. (2006) *Every Day a Good Day*. London: Paul Chapman.

Smidt, S. (2007) *A Guide to Early Years Practice* (3rd edn). Abingdon: Routledge.

Whitebread, D. and Coltman P. (2008) *Teaching and Learning in the Early Years*. Abingdon: Routledge.

5 Supporting Children and Families

This chapter explores the relationship between the setting and the parents and carers of the children who attend. From the first day a child attends your setting you are building a valuable and important relationship with the child, their parents and carers and any other significant people in the child's life. Through sensitive and thoughtful communication with them, the early years practitioner is able to gain an insight into each child's likes and dislikes, abilities, experiences and home life. This information enables practitioners to support the child in the best possible way, as well as to provide an appropriate environment that will meet the children's individual needs.

High-quality relationships with the parents and carers of the children in the setting have a positive effect on children and their subsequent learning. This positive first contact can also have a positive impact on future transitions made by the child and their family. Early years practitioners who understand these principles also recognise the importance of encouraging parents and carers to participate in all areas of the setting's work.

However, not all early years settings appreciate the full value of high-quality relationships between themselves and the parents and carers they work with. Some value the parents and carers as contributors to decision-making and policy-making, while others still permit parents and carers only to supervise snack time or wash the paint pots. This could be seen as not working in true partnership with parents and carers. There is no doubt that these are necessary tasks, but this approach can give a clear message that parents and carers are valued only for such mundane tasks. Parents and carers have a wealth of knowledge and experience with their own children or from the workplace, in addition to their own personal skills. It is these skills that can be used to the benefit of the setting. For example, those parents and carers who are keen gardeners might like to be responsible for maintaining the garden area. Likewise, those who enjoy cooking might like to have input into the planning and implementing of cooking activities.

This chapter explores why relationships with parents and families should be valued and the benefits of positive interactions with them.

The chapter covers the following areas:

5.1 The principles and practice of working with parents and families

It is widely agreed among professionals working with children of all ages that a close, positive relationship with families has a significant long-term impact on the child's school experience.

The need to develop partnerships with parents and carers was highlighted by Ball (1994, p. 43): 'Parents are the most important people in their children's lives. It is from parents that children learn most, particularly in the early months and years … the closer the links between parents and nursery the more effective that learning becomes.'

Yet, while the principles of closer working partnerships with parents and carers have been generally accepted within early years settings, practice has often fallen somewhat short. Many settings offer what Wolfendale (1989) describes as 'moderate' involvement. He recognised that early years practitioners work closely with parents and carers but do not always involve them in all aspects of the setting.

The partnership with parent and carers can be promoted in a number of ways. These can include:

■ practitioners carrying out home visits

■ parents working in the setting

■ parents on the management committee or governing body

■ parents attending workshops and courses

■ parents running services.

Partnership with parents should be regarded as a key aspect of provision. Parents should be recognised as children's first and enduring educators and as key partners in supporting children's learning and development through school years and beyond. Much has been written about the positive impact close relationships with parents has on children's development and learning, and there are many ways of developing partnerships with parents; the common features of these are shown in the good practice checklist. Table 5.1 summarises three models of parent involvement in early years settings. Aspects of both the transplant and consumer model are practised widely.

Good practice checklist
Supporting children and families

● Parents' fundamental role in their children's education is acknowledged by staff in the setting and a partnership is developed with them, based on shared responsibility, understanding, mutual respect and dialogue.

● There is recognition of the role the family has already played in the early education of their child and that their continued involvement is crucial to the child's learning.

● Families feel welcome and there are opportunities for their collaboration with staff.

- There is recognition of the expertise of parents and other adults in the family, and this expertise is used to support children's learning within the setting (see the case study 'Tailoring involvement', page 152).

- Adults working in the setting give families access to information about the curriculum in a variety of ways, such as open days, meetings, social events, brochures and video presentations (in a range of languages where appropriate).

- Families are fully informed of their children's progress and achievements.

- The starting times of sessions are flexible in order to allow for discussion with parents and carers, and for children to feel secure in the new setting.

- Opportunities for learning provided in the setting are sometimes continued at home (for example reading and sharing books) and experiences initiated at home are sometimes used as stimuli for learning in the setting.

Table 5.1. Three models of parental involvement in early years settings

Model	What happens	Implications for practice
The expert model	The early years practitioner assumes the 'expert' role, takes overall control and makes all of the decisions. There is little encouragement for parents and carers to become actively involved.	This approach disempowers parents and carers, and makes them dependent on early years practitioners.
The transplant model	The early years practitioner sees parents and carers as a resource, and so hands over some responsibilities but retains control over decision-making.	Parents and carers are involved in a limited range of activities, under the direction of practitioners. Parents' and carers' wealth of knowledge, experience and skills are not fully used.
The consumer model	Parents and carers have the right to decide and select what they believe is appropriate and are fully involved in all decision-making.	The early years practitioner involves the parents and carers in all aspects of provision; however, this needs to be managed well, as not all parents and carers share the same values and beliefs.

Legislation

Developing positive relationships with families is not a new concept. At the beginning of the twentieth century Margaret McMillan recognised the value of working closely with parents and provided a programme of lectures for parents alongside her nursery provision. However, by the 1960s parental involvement focused mainy on parents whose children were underachieving. Today, growing recognition of the value and importance of staff, parents and carers working together is reflected in legislation. The Children Act 1989 emphasised the importance of professionals working in partnership with parents and carers to enable them to care for their children to the best of their ability, by enhancing their knowledge and understanding of childcare and development. Similarly, the Education Reform Act 1988 highlighted the need for parents and carers to be given access to information about the curriculum and their children's progress. The Early Years Development and Childcare partnerships are required to provide children's information services that enable parents to access information on a range of matters. It is also the responsibility of early years practitioners and teachers to provide support, guidance and encouragement to parents as educators. Working closely with families is also reflected in the Early Years Foundation Stage (EYFS), as well as the five *Every Child Matters* (ECM) outcomes for children, which will be better supported when parents, practitioners and settings work in partnership.

Supporting and encouraging parents and carers

The foundation of a successful partnership is mutual respect and a sharing of purpose, information, responsibility and decision-making. It is good practice to involve parents and carers in the setting. The more involved parents and carers are in what goes on in the setting, the more guidance and support early years practitioners can provide. This level of interaction increases the availability of the early years practitioner to answer questions on parenting and child development on an informal basis. This can sometimes be more appealing to those parents and carers who have built trusting relationships with the early years practitioners in their child's setting.

Traditionally parents have had limited involvement – home and school were seen as separate. This reflected the attitude that 'schools know best' (the expert model in Table 5.1). However, research has shown that working with parents has a positive effect on the child's early learning. A key function of any early years setting is to develop a two-way relationship which helps families to increase their understanding and knowledge of their children's development and education. This in turn will help to build the self-esteem and confidence of parents, and enable them to support their child's learning at home.

Early years workers need to value and respect all contributions, no matter how big or small. One of the key reasons early years practitioners work so closely with parents and carers is to ensure inclusion opportunities for all families. It is important not to forget about families who may usually choose not to be actively involved with the setting – they can still gain a valuable sense of belonging by feeling included. They do not have to make a practical contribution to be part of the setting. They are part of the setting because their children attend. By ensuring all families feel included and by widening participation, more parents and carers can have access to the best possible service available.

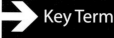 Key Term

Two-way relationship – a genuine relationship (in this context between families and the setting) that takes into account and values the viewpoints of families and the contributions families make to the setting. Practitioners are available to families and actively seek their opinions and viewpoints.

Billy's mother

Billy's mother enjoys cooking and gardening and in the past she has helped with the toddler group doing craft activities under the guidance of the leaders. She has expressed an interest in helping in the nursery but feels embarrassed about her lack of literacy and numeracy skills.

- What are her skills and strengths?
- How could these be used to benefit the nursery?
- How might Billy's mother benefit from helping in the nursery?

The 'working with parents' policy

It is good practice to have in place a 'working with parents' policy. The aim of the policy is to ensure that staff, and the setting, more widely:

- respect and value the contribution parents and carers make towards their children's learning
- support the development of the children
- provide ongoing support and encouragement for parents
- work in partnership with parents and carers
- provide opportunities for parents to discuss their child's progress
- provide guidance, advice and resources to support home learning.

The policy should briefly outline the general principles held by the setting in relation to working with parents, such as:

- the value of working together
- how the setting works with parents
- how the setting meets the needs of individual parents
- how all parents are welcomed and valued.

The fact that the setting has such a policy will show that work with parents and carers is a key element of the setting's overall ethos. The policy will also allow staff to have a consistent approach to practice with parents and carers, and demonstrate to new families that they are respected and that their contributions are valued.

The policy should be included in an information pack provided to parents and carers before their children start at the setting. In order to raise its profile, it can be referred to during the pre-entry meeting, when the key points can be highlighted.

All staff should also have access to the policy, so that their approach can be consistent. Regular assessment and reviews of the policy as a team helps to maintain its importance and keep it up to date.

It is good practice to involve parents and carers in the setting.

A flexible approach

The practice guidelines, policies and procedures in place in your setting aim to ensure a quality service for all families. However, when these procedures are followed too closely they can actually prevent you from delivering a high-quality service. It is essential for early years practitioners to be flexible in their approach.

Find it out

Ask the families using your setting what they expect from the setting and the staff. It can also be helpful to consider what you expect from the families in relation to supporting their children's learning and well-being. Are your expectations the same as your colleagues'?

A flexible approach

Case Study

Jack attends a day care setting which works alongside an on-site nursery school. His mother informs Alex, an early years practitioner, that Jack will be going home with his friend Pria, who attends the nursery school, after lunch. However, Alex reminds Jack's mother that the two children have their lunch at different times, as it is not possible to accommodate both the day care and nursery children in the dining room at the same time. By leaving with Pria after her lunch, Jack would not have had his. Jack's mother expresses concern about her son going without his lunch and suggests that he joins the first group for lunch. Alex is unsure whether this would be possible.

■ Was Jack's mother's request reasonable?

■ How do you think the nursery could accommodate this request?

Key principles for working with parents and carers

In her book *Every Child Matters. A Practical Guide for Teachers*, Rita Cheminais (2006, p. 102) outlines a set of key principles for practitioners to consider when working with families.

- Deal with any parental queries promptly.
- Utilise the parents' preferred means of communication to relay good news or express concerns.
- Ensure that any written information to parents on aspects of school life and activities or curriculum is produced in jargon-free, parent-friendly, alternative formats, especially for those whose home first language is not English.
- Always listen carefully to what parents say about their children in relation to their learning, behaviour, well-being and additional educational needs, and use this information to guide the child's personalised learning.
- Remember that the insights and opinions parents have about their child are just as valuable and important as those of teachers and other professionals.
- Find out if the parents of children in your class have any particular talents or interests that could be utilised as part of supervised out-of-hours learning activities.
- Reassure parents of the benefits of helping their child with their learning and encourage networking with other parents.

Sandra Smidt (2007) also discusses the importance of establishing strong positive partnerships between parents and the setting. The most important factor is the need for practitioners to recognise and value each parent's role as a primary educator (p. 169).

Respect for children as individuals and for the different ways that parents choose to bring up their children is fundamental to good practice. Early years practitioners are responsible for:

- ensuring that children are not discriminated against, either by adults or by other children in the setting
- promoting a positive environment for young children, where activities reflect other cultures and religions and resources portray a range of positive images.

The key principles outlined above aim to improve the quality of service provided, yet have a very different focus. The first set focuses on how early years practitioners can best work with and support families. The second set focuses on the need for practitioners to value and respect the diversity and differences that exist in families and parenting. By involving and valuing the contribution of parents and carers from all cultural and social backgrounds you can enrich the children's experience of society.

Encouraging staff to work with parents and carers

As an early years manager you should raise the principles set out above in staff meetings or use them as the basis for staff training. This would allow you to find out how your team feels about working with parents and carers and what support they will need. By identifying your team's individual skills and preferences you can allocate responsibilities accordingly. This can help your team to be more positive, efficient and productive.

Find it out

Investigate what opportunities other settings provide for parents – for example parenting classes, support groups, activity groups.

- What opportunities could you implement for the parents in your setting?

- How could you ensure you were meeting the needs and interests of the families in your setting?

Good practice checklist

Training your team to work with parents and carers

- Provide staff with extra time to organise, support and train parents and carers, set aside from their contact time with the children.

- Provide a range of suitable resources that will aid in supporting and training parents and carers.

- Provide staff with suitable training and support to develop their skills in working with parents and carers.

- Provide staff with opportunities to observe good practice in other settings.

- Provide regular opportunities to discuss progress and review practice.

5.2 How strong partnerships can have a positive effect on children and their learning

As parents are the most influential people during a child's formative years it makes sense to involve them in their own child's education as much as possible. It is widely agreed among practitioners that there is a need to recognise the role parents have already played in the early education of their child, and that their continued involvement has a positive impact on their future learning. Early years practitioners can learn a lot about an individual child from the child's parents. It is good practice to reflect on information gathered from parents when planning:

- the classroom curriculum

- activities

- room arrangement and organisation

- routine and daily structure

- staffing.

Home visiting

One of the essential elements of parental involvement and partnership is the sharing of knowledge about the children before they join the setting. This can be achieved via visits to the home by the early years practitioners or through visits to the setting by the child and parent (see Chapter 4).

Home visits can build strong partnerships from the outset.

Home visiting has become common practice and is valued as one of the best ways for early years practitioners and families to get to know each other (see Figure 5.1 on the next page). Home visiting has several benefits for the child, family and setting.

- It enables the early years practitioner to start to build a relationship with the child and family.
- It provides the child and family with a familiar person to relate to right from the beginning.
- It gives the parents the opportunity to ask questions.
- It enables parents and carers to find out about the setting's policies and procedures.
- It enables parents to find out about the practical things such as coat pegs, the required children's footwear and mealtimes.
- It allows parents to express any concerns or anxieties they may have.
- It is an opportunity for personal information to be shared, which can then be used to meet the child's individual needs when an appropriate curriculum is planned (see Chapter 3).

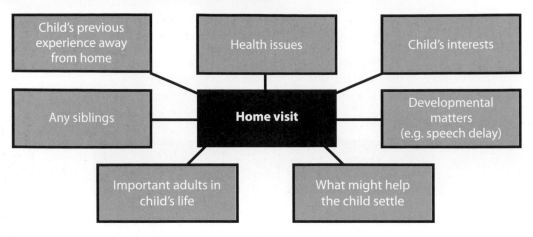

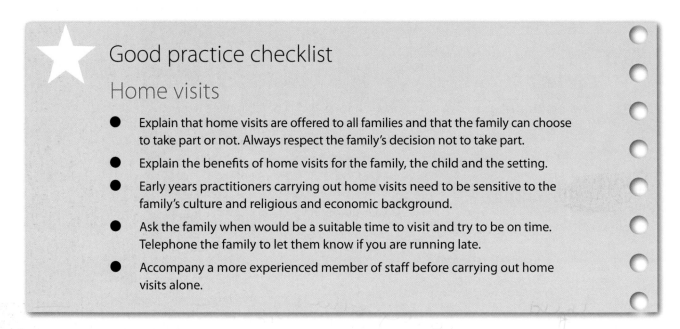

Figure 5.1. The range of information that can be obtained during home visiting

⭐ ## Good practice checklist

Home visits

- Explain that home visits are offered to all families and that the family can choose to take part or not. Always respect the family's decision not to take part.

- Explain the benefits of home visits for the family, the child and the setting.

- Early years practitioners carrying out home visits need to be sensitive to the family's culture and religious and economic background.

- Ask the family when would be a suitable time to visit and try to be on time. Telephone the family to let them know if you are running late.

- Accompany a more experienced member of staff before carrying out home visits alone.

Finding time to carry out home visiting can be challenging and there will be time constraints that are particular to your own setting. You may need to be resourceful and think creatively about how you are going to manage your time, but the relationships formed at this point are helpful in smoothing the transition from home to the setting.

The effects of partnerships with parents and carers on children and learning

Vygotsky believed that children operated at a higher level when an adult sensitively supported their play. He used the term 'zone of proximal development' to describe tasks that children might be unable to perform alone but could do with help (see Chapter 3). Adult support can help children:

- extend and introduce new language

- clarify and develop concepts

- maintain concentration and interest.

If parents and carers play an active role in the setting and support children, this will increase learning opportunities. Both social interaction and communication are essential tools for intellectual development.

Points for reflective practice

Involving parents in their child's learning

Discuss with your colleagues how parents in your setting are currently involved in their child's learning. Can you think of any other ways you could engage parents in their child's learning?

Can you identify any parents who would benefit from additional support and encouragement? How could you do this?

Investigate how other settings involve parents in their child's learning. Are there any strategies that you could implement in your own setting?

Parental involvement increases the child:adult ratio, which is crucial if children are to be supported at different levels across different activities. It is important that children are offered rich, powerful, first-hand experiences and that they are actively supported by adults to make full use of these experiences and to extend them. Children need access to adults who will behave in ways that will stimulate and encourage language. The adults do not need to be professionally trained – there will be early years practitioners on hand who are. However, research has shown the importance of the adult's own confidence in supporting young children. It is therefore essential that early years practitioners provide parents with the necessary guidance and support in order to enrich children's learning within the setting.

5.3 Communicating with parents and families

One of the many essential skills needed in order to work effectively as an early years practitioner is the ability to communicate. This is especially true for the manager. You are required to communicate not only with the children and other professionals, but also with parents and families. Throughout your career you will be working with parents and families from a wide range of cultural, social and economic backgrounds, who have varying skills and abilities. It is therefore important that:

- each parent is treated with respect and consideration
- there is a genuine two-way relationship between families and the setting
- information goes from setting to home and from home to setting.

Key principles

When working to establish a two-way partnership with families it can be helpful to consider the following key principles.

- All parents are made welcome and can see evidence of their culture and language being reflected in the setting.
- Parents and carers and early years practitioners are equal partners.
- Parents usually know their child best of all.
- It is the role of the early years practitioner to involve parents and carers in the work of the setting.
- Early years practitioners should treat each parent with respect and consideration.
- Parents have a right to be consulted on changes and issues that may affect their children.
- Early years practitioners should recognise the need for confidentiality in dealing with parents and carers.
- Parents have the opportunity to contribute to the assessments made of their own child.

These principles lay a foundation on which to build firm relationships with parents and carers.

Arrival and departure times

At these times it is especially important that staff are accessible, approachable and welcoming. In most settings this will be when you would have the most contact with parents and carers.

It is important to be approachable, even at busy times.

Think it over

Think about the arrival and departure times in a setting and consider how you may have been perceived by parents and carers.

- Where were you, generally?
- How did you appear?
- Were you always busy?
- Did you engage eye contact with the parents and carers?
- Were you approachable and welcoming?

It can be helpful to ask parents and carers how they feel about these times at the setting, and use the results of the survey to inform staff training.

In order to ensure that staff are accessible, the following guidelines are common practice (see also Chapter 4).

- Ensure that all room preparation is complete before the arrival of the children so that the staff are free to welcome them.
- Have a 15-minute arrival time so that not all of the children arrive at the same time. This also accommodates parents and carers who drop off siblings at other settings.
- Start the session with free play rather than an adult-led activity. This allows staff to be available for parents and carers as they arrive.
- Have members of the team standing near the entrance of the room to welcome the children and parents and carers as they arrive.
- Be available to discuss smaller issues with parents and carers (for example changes in pick-up arrangements) or to make an appointment for later the same day for issues that need more time.

Staff involvement

It is not appropriate for one member of staff to be solely responsible for liaising with parents and carers. Traditionally this has been seen as the role of either the class teacher or the nursery manager. With accessibility being a key element to building positive and constructive two-way relationships with parents and carers, it is no longer practical for one member of staff to take on the role. Parents and carers are individuals and may well relate better to one person than another. To ensure that all parents and carers are reached, staff need to be accessible and approachable. However, it is not always appropriate for students and other parents to deal with confidential matters concerning other families. They should be encouraged to redirect any concerns or queries that are beyond their role to the relevant member of the team. This is not about excluding parents or devaluing helpers, but about maintaining confidentiality.

Letters home

Beth works as an early years practitioner in the nursery class of a school that accommodates children from a variety of backgrounds. Letters are sent home via the children that remind parents and carers of the forthcoming summer fair. Beth gives one of the letters to Pria's mother and says 'This letter is about the fair next Saturday. It starts at 2 p.m. and we are asking the nursery parents and carers if they would like to help with the refreshments. Would you like to help?'

■ Why do you think Beth has used this approach with this mother?

■ When else would this strategy be helpful?

■ How do you ensure that you access all parents and carers in your setting?

In the case study 'Letters home' Beth, the early years practitioner, is implementing many of the recommendations in this chapter. She is being welcoming, including and valuing the contributions made by this parent without being patronising or judgemental. She is valuing the individual child and family by ensuring that communication is being maintained. But above all she is ensuring that this parent has equal access to written material, as this mother is unable to read. It is not important whether the mother attends the fair or not. What is important is that her needs have been accommodated and she has been sensitively included.

Steps should be taken to ensure that all parents and carers know how to contact members of staff and who is the best person to contact about a range of issues. Some methods that will help to ensure you remain in close contact with parents and carers are described in Table 5.2.

Table 5.2. Methods of contact with parents and families

Method of contact	How it works
Open-door policy	An open invitation for parents and carers to meet with staff or access the setting at any time. Parents and carers would be informed of this policy during introduction meetings and in their welcome packs. The practicalities of this policy can be hard to manage, so simple guidelines may need to be issued. For example: ■ Small matters can be discussed with an early years practitioner at any time; however, larger issues will need an appointment, which will be made for the same day if mutually convenient. ■ Picking children up outside the normal times is permitted, but parents and carers need to report to reception first.

Method of contact	How it works
Meetings with parents and carers	Meeting with parents and carers regularly is a great way to keep in touch and maintain good relationships. Meetings may involve the whole setting, individual groups or individual parents and carers. It is hard to arrange meetings that suit everybody. By being flexible and holding meetings at a variety of times, or by giving parents and carers a choice of times, you can become more accessible and increase parents' and carers' involvement. Early years teams will hold regular parents' and carers' meetings and conferences. When meeting with parents and carers it is helpful to create a comfortable environment in which they feel free to share information, ask questions and make recommendations. Be careful not to make assumptions about the level of knowledge, understanding or interest parents and carers have. Explain any terminology so that they can develop their understanding of the subject.
Letters home	Regular newsletters home are as important as the daily contact parents and carers have with the setting. They are a means of keeping parents and carers up to date with current events, issues or staff changes which may affect their children. Letters need to be informative and user-friendly if they are going to be read. Small boxes or columns of information, as in a newspaper, can help to achieve this. For more formal occasions and events it can be helpful to follow up any written invitation with personal contact to make parents and carers feel more welcome.
Parents' room	A parents' room provides space for parents and carers to meet with each other or with staff. It can be used to store resources for families to use. It is not always possible to provide a separate room, but a shared room or area is a good start. By creating a space to be used by parents and carers you are demonstrating that they are a valued part of the setting.
Staff photograph board	Displays of photographs of members of the team with their name, qualifications, role and any special responsibilities will help parents and carers to find the person they need to talk to. Remember to update this as staff join or leave the team.

Good communication skills

As an early years practitioner you are required to communicate effectively with colleagues, parents and carers and other professionals, as well as the children. You are expected to communicate in a manner which conveys respect and consideration at all times (Figure 5.2). It is helpful for the early years manager regularly to review the team's communication skills. This can be done as part of a staff development programme (see Chapter 7).

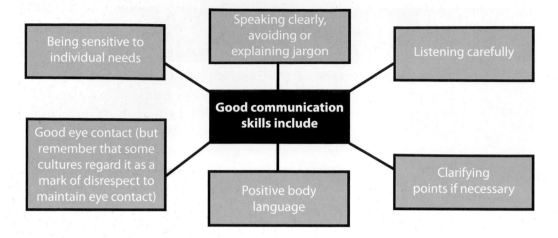

Figure 5.2. Elements of good communication skills

Good listening skills

Good listening skills go hand in hand with good communication skills. Early years practitioners need to take time to listen to what is being said by everyone they have contact with, not only the children. It is a useful strategy to paraphrase and repeat what has been said in order to make sure you understand and have heard correctly.

Dealing with concerns

On occasions parents and carers will raise concerns about their child or the running of the setting. No matter how big or small these concerns may seem, they need to be addressed in a professional manner. It is impossible to anticipate all potential concerns, but one of the best ways of dealing with them is to have strategies in place that help to minimise their occurrence. These include:

- promptly reporting accidents and incidents to parents and carers
- sharing information with your team, where appropriate
- keeping your team up to date and well informed of any changes in circumstances that may affect how they work with the children and their families
- participating in regular training to maintain and update communication skills.

Find it out

Following a discussion with colleagues write a checklist on how you think concerns can be dealt with in a professional manner. Share your list with your colleagues and discuss any changes that may need to be made to it.

Points for reflective practice

Think of a time when you had to deal with a concern raised by a parent. Using the information in this chapter, evaluate how well you dealt with the situation.

Do you think you could have dealt with the situation more effectively? If so how?

5.4 Valuing parents' and carers' contributions

If parents and carers are going to have a real sense of being valued by the setting they need to be able to contribute their personal skills and see that they are making a difference to the running of the setting. All parents and carers should be encouraged to feel part of the setting and their contributions, no matter how small, need to be appreciated. However, remember that not all parents and carers are able to contribute to life in the setting. You must respect this and not pressure them to do so or criticise them if they feel they cannot.

Today's society requires many parents to work, which does not enable them to spend time in their child's classroom. Nonetheless, firm partnerships can still be built with these parents by involving them in activities which take place out of hours, and by keeping them informed of current issues and their child's progress. Parents' and carers' practical contribution to a setting will greatly depend on their time constraints and other commitments. It will also depend on the type of setting you are working in. Parents with children in day care, for example, are often working and will need to be encouraged to feel part of the setting in other ways. Regular newsletters, information on changes within the setting and invitations to social events are examples. In contrast, parents of children in state-funded pre-school settings may have more opportunity to get involved by volunteering their time and skills.

Parents of children in early years settings may have younger siblings to care for and this needs to be accommodated. In the past, parents and carers with younger children were not always encouraged to help, as it was felt that having younger children in the setting might be disruptive. However, this has generally proved not to be the case. Experience has shown that younger siblings can actually have a positive effect. For instance, children with challenging behaviour can become nurturing and caring towards the younger children, perhaps by showing them around. These are skills that early years practitioners should be encouraging all the children to develop. Welcoming younger siblings into the setting should be seen as another advantage to working with parents and carers.

Aside from time and opportunity, other factors may inhibit some parents and carers from becoming more involved in the setting. It is important that these are recognised and accommodated so that they can be provided with an equal chance to access a quality service. The factors include:

- the parents' experience of their own school environment
- their lack of basic skills
- their having English as a second language.

Think it over

Think about the parents and carers in your setting.

- ■ Can you think of some who are not involved in any way?

- ■ Other than personal choice, what factors prevent individual parents and carers from contributing regularly?

- ■ How can you support these parents?

Points for reflective practice

Think about the different ways your setting actively involves parents, carers and families. Make a list and contrast it with another setting.

Are there any ways you had not thought of that you could use in your setting?

Encouraging parents, carers and families into the setting

Working in partnership is not just about the two very different environments of home and early years setting working together. It is also about people from different cultures learning to work together for the good of the child. The stronger the relationship between the parent and practitioner, the happier the child is likely to be. However, it can be difficult to persuade some parents and carers to spend time in the setting, as traditionally they have seen school as being completely separate from home and believe that education is the responsibility of the teacher. Their active participation and contributions are valuable because children begin to form attitudes about themselves and others from what they see and hear around them at a very young age. By involving all parents and carers in some way you can give a clear message to children that everyone is welcome, valued and respected.

Tailoring involvement

Case Study

Fiona is a new mum at the day care centre and has just recently moved into the area. Before having her two daughters, Sophie and Paige, she worked in a large bookshop. She has expressed an interest in helping at the nursery; however, she is not able to do so regularly during nursery hours because of her work commitments. She is invited to discuss her involvement informally with the nursery staff and comes up with the idea of providing a birthday book for each child. Fiona becomes responsible for purchasing suitable books for the nursery children, which are presented to them at their birthday celebration in the setting. She works closely with the fundraising committee in order to support this project financially. Fiona's involvement in the setting has been tailor-made to take into account her skills, interests and time constraints.

- ■ How have Fiona and the setting benefited from this arrangement?

5.5 Multi-agency working

Whether you work in a small team of four or five early years practitioners or a much larger team with professionals representing a range of services, you will need to be receptive to working as part of a multi-agency team. Working closely together to ensure the best outcome for children and their families is the focus of current legislation and a key feature of *Every Child Matters* and the Early Years Foundation Stage.

In order to deliver the best outcomes for children and their families it is vital that professionals work closely together. Professionals can be from a wide range of agencies or services, some of which are shown in Figure 5.3.

> ### Key Term
>
> **Multi-agency working** involves different services, agencies and teams of professionals working together to provide support that meets the needs of children and their families.

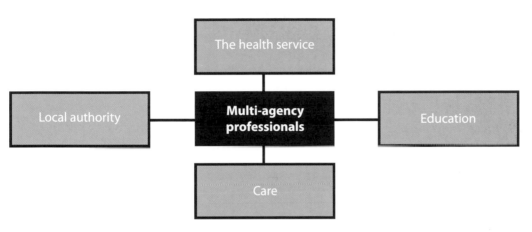

Figure 5.3. Some sectors involved in multi-agency working

In order to work effectively in a multi-agency team it is vital that you understand your own roles and responsibilities as well as those of others. You need to understand and respect the aims and objectives of each service and actively seek ways of working together. The key to this is a genuine understanding of how partner services operate and their roles and responsibilities.

Find it out

The aim of this activity is to explore your team's understanding of the roles and responsibilities of their colleagues. These can be either professionals who work closely with the setting or those who work *within* the setting.

Provide your team with a large piece of paper cut into the shape of a person (either one each or in small groups depending on the size of your team). On each 'person' write the job title of someone in your team – for example health visitor, education psychologist, teaching assistant, community nursery nurse – making sure everyone has a different job role from their own. Encourage each team member to write down what they think their 'person's' roles and responsibilities are.

Using their ideas as a discussion point, explore any preconceived ideas, misunderstandings and fill any gaps. If you work in a large team with a variety of services represented you should use the job titles of those on your team for this activity and get them to check the group's ideas and feed back at the end of the activity.

Conclusion

This chapter has explored why it is so valuable to actively encourage positive two-way relationships between the setting and families, and to encourage families to be involved in their children's early education. In the past parents have had limited involvement, but with changes in policy and growing awareness of the value of high-quality partnerships there has been a shift towards greater involvement. Partnerships between parents and professionals are not only good practice, but also the focus of legislation and key features of *Every Child Matters* and the Early Years Foundation Stage.

Research confirms that young children tend to do better when their parents have a greater understanding of their children's learning. A key function of any early years setting is to share good practice by helping parents to increase their knowledge and understanding of child development and early education. Research has also shown that families who receive frequent, sensitive and positive communication from early years practitioners tend to become more involved in their children's education. It is therefore essential that families are welcomed into the setting and their involvement encouraged. The partnership is not just about the two very different environments of home and educational setting working together. It is also about people from different cultures and backgrounds learning to work together for the good of the children. By reflecting the outside community within the setting you can enrich children's experience of society.

The foundation of a successful partnership is a two-way process. It is one of mutual respect, sharing the same purpose, information and high levels of communication. High-quality partnerships with parents and carers can be developed when there is a balance between practical help and active involvement in decision-making.

Good relationships between families and the setting are too important to be left to chance or regarded as an optional extra. They are fundamental to the functioning and success of the setting and should be evaluated and reviewed regularly. As with all areas of provision, it is vital that you reflect on current practice to improve services.

Check your understanding

1   Outline the aims and objectives of a 'working with parents' policy.

2   Why is it important to regularly review and evaluate how you work with parents and carers?

3   As an early years manager you are responsible for training your team to work with parents and carers in a sensitive and thoughtful manner. Outline the key principles to remember when supporting your team.

References and further reading

Aubrey, C. (2007) *Leading and Managing in the Early Years*. London: Sage Publications.

Ball, C. (1994) *Start Right: The Importance of Early Learning*. London: RSA.

Cheminais, R. (2006) *Every Child Matters: A Practical Guide for Teachers*. Abingdon; David Fulton.

Early Childhood Education Forum (1998) *Quality in Diversity in Early Childhood*. London: NCB.

Moss, P. and Penn, H. (1996) *Transforming Nursery Education*. London: Paul Chapman.

Moyles, J. (2007) *Effective Leadership and Management in the Early Years*. Maidenhead: Open University Press.

Nurse, A. (2007) *The New Early Years Professional*, Abingdon: Routledge.

Pugh, G. and Duffy, B. (2006) *Contemporary Issues in the Early Years*. London: Sage Publications.

Pugh, G., De'Ath, C. and Smith, C. (1994) *Confident Parents, Confident Children*. London: NCB.

Shimmin, S. and White, H. (2006) *Every Day a Good Day*. London: Paul Chapman.

Siraj-Blatchford, I. (1994) *The Early Years: Laying the Foundation for Racial Equality*. Stoke-on-Trent: Trentham Books.

Smidt, S. (2007) *A Guide to Early Years Practice*, (3rd edn). Abingdon: Routledge.

Whalley, M. (1997) *Working with Parents*, London: Hodder and Stoughton.

Willan, J., Parker-Rees, R. and Savage, J. (2007) *Early Childhood Studies* (2nd edn). Exeter: Learning Matters.

Wolfendale, S. (1989) *Parental Involvement*. London: Cassell.

6 Managing and Developing a Team

The quality of provision for the care and education of children in their early years is hotly debated throughout society, from politicians to the layperson in the street. As a result of this national awareness, competition is fierce and the success of a setting can rely very heavily on its 'word of mouth' reputation. This reputation will depend to an extent on the curriculum offered, the experience of the children at the setting and the perceived success of the establishment. Parents and carers are very aware of the pressures faced by their children and rightly expect the best for them. They appreciate the value of play and are keen for their children to have access to high-quality experiences that reflect the appropriate curriculum stage.

A key element to the provision of quality, and the patronage of parents and carers, is the staff employed by a setting. The staff are the best asset that a setting has. A well-trained, motivated and committed staff team who enjoy their job and work well together will raise the standards and provide quality care and education.

The recruitment of staff can be the most challenging aspect of the manager's job. Well-qualified, mature, enthusiastic and caring staff are a tremendous selling point, but in today's climate can be very difficult to find. It is necessary to plan the recruitment and retention process carefully and sometimes provide perks and bonuses to attract suitable staff.

The aim of this chapter is to outline the key elements of managing staff and working together in a strong cohesive team.

The chapter covers the following areas:

6.1 The theory of organisational culture and team roles

6.2 Effective teams

6.3 Recruitment, selection and retention of staff

6.4 Legal obligations

6.5 Management of team working

6.6 The manager as a communicator

6.7 The manager as a motivator

6.8 The role of the manager in managing change

6.1 The theory of organisational culture and team roles

Before the more specific and practical aspects of team development are dealt with below, it is helpful first to consider the wider picture of the sorts of organisations in which teams work.

Organisational culture

Different organisations have different atmospheres, ways of doing things, levels of energy and vitality, personalities and cultures. They have different norms, values and beliefs – all of which are reflected in their systems and structures. For early years settings the culture is usually formed by a common goal – to meet the needs of the individual children in the setting. Although a great deal has been written about organisational culture, only a brief overview of some theories is given here. You will need to take note of the suggestions for further reading to deepen your knowledge of this area. This section examines one model by way of illustration.

The model considered here is of four types of organisational culture, which are based on ideas about:

- the way in which work is done
- the degree of control to be exercised
- how people should be rewarded
- what loyalty and obedience are expected
- what hours should be worked
- how people are expected to dress.

These four cultures are termed:

- power
- role
- task
- person.

Table 6.1 gives a brief explanation and examples of each.

Table 6.1. Models of organisational culture

Name	Power culture	Role culture	Task culture	Person culture
Description	Best pictured as a web. It is dependent on a central power source; rays emanate out from this and are connected by functional or specialist 'strings', but the power rings are the hub of activity and influence. The organisation works on precedent and the anticipation of the wishes and decisions of the central power source. Rules and procedures are few; there is little bureaucracy. Control is exercised through key individuals. It is a political organisation, decisions being taken on the outcome of balance of influence rather than logical or procedural grounds. These organisations are proud and strong – they move quickly and react well to threat and danger. Success depends on the quality of decisions of the person in power. Such organisations are power-orientated and politically minded. They take risks, have faith in individuals and are tough and abrasive. Control of resources is a major power source, plus some elements of personal power at the centre. Judgement is by results.	Bureaucracy – thought of as a Greek temple. Logic and rationality are its strengths; its pillars are functions of specialism that are strong in their own right. Work and interaction are controlled by procedures, definition of jobs and tasks, delegation of authority and rules for operation and settlement of disputes. Coordination is by a senior management team. All persons are expected to be loyal and obedient and carry out instructions. Concentration is on the description of the job, not the incumbent. Selection is by satisfactory qualifications and performance, and over-performance is not always encouraged as it can be considered disruptive. Bestowed authority or position is the main power source; personal power is discouraged. Influence is through methods and procedures. The culture is dependent on rationality and success of work allocation and meeting responsibilities rather than individualisation.	Job and project orientated. The organisation can be visualised as a net, a grid or a matrix. Some strands of the net or grid are stronger than others. Much power lies at the interstices of the net or grid. The emphasis is on doing the task – thus appropriate resources are deployed and redeployed to this end. Influence stems from expert power and is more widely dispersed than in other cultures – it is a team culture – individual objectives are obliterated, as are differences in status or style. It is the unifying power of the group that creates efficiency and absorbs the individual into the organisation. It is an adaptable culture – groups or teams are formed for a specific purpose or task, and abandoned once this is fulfilled and resources are reallocated. Individuals have a high degree of control over their work and relationships are easy and informal. Judgement is by results – respect is for capacity rather than age or status. Control is difficult and is retained by the overall top management in the allocation of resources to tasks/projects. Reporting on progress and justification of team action is the job of the task/team leaders. Resources need to be readily available. It is a culture in tune with modern management style/thinking and with innovation and development. It is appropriate when flexibility and sensitivity to the market are important.	A cluster or galaxy of individual stars. Such organisations are rare. The individual is the focal point. The organisational structure exists only to serve the individual within it.
Examples	Small entrepreneurial organisations, occasionally trade unions, property and finance companies, some trading organisations, family firms and founder organisations.	Civil service, automobile industry, life insurance, banking, retailing	Product groups of marketing departments, consultancies, take-over ventures, advertising agencies, merchant banks, management service functions.	Barristers' chambers, consultancies, communes and other special groups, as well as academic university departments.
Possible negative aspects	Size is a problem for power cultures as the web can break if too many activities need linking – it can grow only by spawning other web-like organisations. Maximum independence needs to be given to each web-head. Finance binds the web together.	Role cultures are slow to perceive change and slow to react if faced with problems. These organisations need stable environments – monopoly or market stability – as product life cycles are long. They often try a number of alternative measures to redesign their structure. Collapse can ensue. There is insufficient development of individuals, which can be frustrating for the ambitious.	It is hard to achieve 'economies of scale' in this culture, or growth or depth of expertise.	It is difficult to form this culture as organisational goals are subordinate to individual goals. Control can be only by mutual consent. The organisation seldom has power over individuals. The individuals are difficult to manage as it is rarely possible to influence them; only a strong and similarly interesting individual would warrant attention and individuals tend to be 'wrapped up' in themselves.

These organisational cultures are obviously generic and, although you may not recognise one of these as being totally descriptive of your setting, you should find that there are aspects of each which do apply. Management theorists have said that an effective organisation will demonstrate facets of some or all of these cultures. People working in early years teams will recognise some facets of these cultures when working with other agencies through a multi-disciplinary approach. This could cause challenges for professionals working in smaller settings as they may become frustrated that other systems and approaches can be different and slow.

Figure 6.1 shows the factors that influence organisations in their adoption of a certain culture.

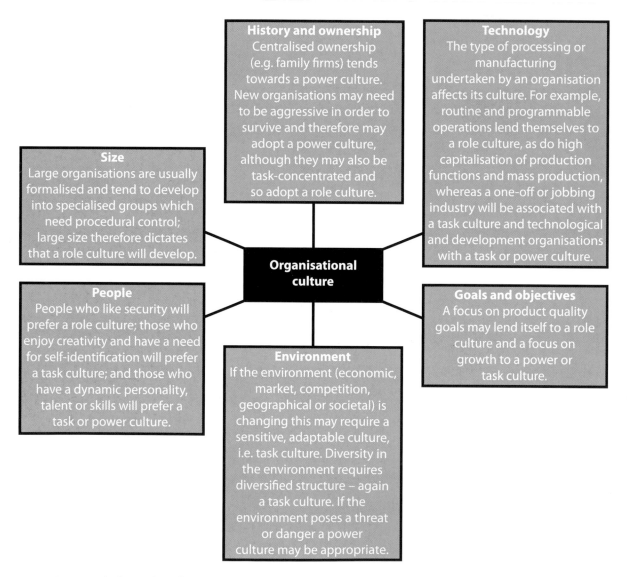

History and ownership
Centralised ownership (e.g. family firms) tends towards a power culture. New organisations may need to be aggressive in order to survive and therefore may adopt a power culture, although they may also be task-concentrated and so adopt a role culture.

Technology
The type of processing or manufacturing undertaken by an organisation affects its culture. For example, routine and programmable operations lend themselves to a role culture, as do high capitalisation of production functions and mass production, whereas a one-off or jobbing industry will be associated with a task culture and technological and development organisations with a task or power culture.

Size
Large organisations are usually formalised and tend to develop into specialised groups which need procedural control; large size therefore dictates that a role culture will develop.

Organisational culture

People
People who like security will prefer a role culture; those who enjoy creativity and have a need for self-identification will prefer a task culture; and those who have a dynamic personality, talent or skills will prefer a task or power culture.

Goals and objectives
A focus on product quality goals may lend itself to a role culture and a focus on growth to a power or task culture.

Environment
If the environment (economic, market, competition, geographical or societal) is changing this may require a sensitive, adaptable culture, i.e. task culture. Diversity in the environment requires diversified structure – again a task culture. If the environment poses a threat or danger a power culture may be appropriate.

Figure 6.1. The factors that influence which culture is adopted by an organisation

Organisations may change their culture, and they may even have more than one culture; a somewhat complex organisational pattern can then emerge. Having looked at the four-culture model of organisations, you might feel that you can now link at least one of them to a particular early years setting.

Aspects of the early years culture

The four-culture model outlined applies in principle to any organisation. Within the early years sector specific questions arise that can be directly linked to the issue of organisational culture. These follow the list of ideas on which the four-culture model draws (see Table 6.1).

Why do things work the way they do?

For new staff joining a setting there can sometimes be confusion about why things work the way they do. There might be historic reasons for the way in which things are done, as some practices may have been passed down from former staff teams or, where there is a long-established team, some of the practices could have stayed the same because 'that is the way we have always done it'. Because of this resistance to change the setting can appear to be solely task-orientated and the staff will lack motivation.

What degree of control has to be exercised?

Early years managers are expected to exercise control within the setting, but most of this control will be set around policies and procedures and will have been explained to the staff so that they appreciate the need for it. Many early years managers will not feel the need to exercise control in an aggressive way and will earn the respect of the team by being a good role model. That is not to say that all early years staff are easily controlled and compliant but that, in the main, if they feel they are valued and working towards a common set of goals, they will be happy to comply. This will depend very much on how the manager communicates with the staff and handles any conflicts or disputes (see section 6.6).

How are people rewarded?

Obviously there is a monetary award (if small!), but for most people working with children this is not the primary motivator. They work with children because it is a vocation and they find it rewarding in terms of the sense of achievement that is gained from seeing children develop as a result of their care, and being valued for that contribution.

What loyalty and obedience should be expected?

Although you will encounter many different personalities within any team, loyalty should not be an issue if there is a cohesive atmosphere and staff are proud of what is being achieved.

What hours should be worked?

This will of course vary from setting to setting. The hours of work become an issue only when there is lack of understanding, too many changes to routine and too high an expectation of staff.

How are people expected to dress?

Many early years settings have dress codes, and these are usually decided by the owner or manager. Some will adopt a uniform and others a code of dress (for example a 'no jeans' policy). It is perfectly acceptable to have these expectations as long as it is explained to staff before they start work and that cost is taken into account.

Team roles

Before assigning a particular team member to a task or responsibility within the setting it is worth investigating the individual's personal qualities and how they interact with the rest of the team. This could be done in a team-building exercise or by a trial period within all areas of the setting. Some people are keen to work in a team and benefit from the associated support and security, whereas some will find the same security stifling and are uncomfortable interacting closely with others.

There is no doubt that teams can be complex and getting a team to work effectively can take time, but the use of teams taps a greater range of experiences and abilities. Teams can produce sound ideas when given the opportunity, and being able to work together motivates members to do better and work in unity ('team spirit').

Meredith Belbin identified eight different roles which were present in the most successful teams. They are described in Table 6.2.

Table 6.2. Belbin's team role descriptions

Team Role	Contribution	Allowable Weakness
Plant	Creative, imaginative, unorthodox. Solves difficult problems.	Ignores incidentals. Too pre-occupied to communicate effectively.
Resource Investigator	Extrovert, enthusiastic, communicative. Explores opportunities. Develops contacts.	Over-optimistic. Loses interest once initial enthusiasm has passed.
Coordinator	Mature, confident, a good chairperson. Clarifies goals, promotes decision-making, delegates well.	Can be seen as manipulative. Offloads personal work.
Shaper	Challenging, dynamic, thrives on pressure. The drive and courage to overcome obstacles.	Prone to provocation. Offends people's feelings.
Monitor Evaluator	Sober, strategic and discerning. Sees all options. Judges accurately.	Lacks drive and ability to inspire others.
Teamworker	Cooperative, mild, perceptive and diplomatic. Listens, builds, averts friction.	Indecisive in crunch situations.
Implementer	Disciplined, reliable, conservative and efficient. Turns ideas into practical actions.	Somewhat inflexible. Slow to respond to new possibilities.
Completer Finisher	Painstaking, conscientious, anxious. Searches out errors and omissions. Delivers on time.	Inclined to worry unduly. Reluctant to delegate.
Specialist	Single-minded, self-starting, dedicated. Provides knowledge and skills in rare supply.	Contributes on only a narrow front. Dwells on technicalities.

Belbin's self-perception test comprises a set of questions with corresponding scores which indicate which role or roles suit the respondent. There are other tests and analyses of team roles, for example the Myers and Briggs Type Indicator (MBTI), built on the work of C.G. Jung (1875–1961). The MBTI looks at ways in which people behave in certain situations. The results depend on whether they are introvert or extrovert, and other factors such as thinking and judgement. These role tests primarily indicate personality styles. To do the test the participant answers a series of questions and is given a score. If you are taking part in a real test the team's results will be analysed and the results fed back to you and your team. However, such tests are generally run by professional psychology consultancies, so there is a cost involved. In any case, there is no need to take part in such a test to become a more cohesive team.

Early years managers may or may not have the opportunity for their staff to take part in some form of personality test. The important thing is that the manager is aware of the role each member of staff plays as part of the team (in Table 6.2 you are likely to see some of the traits of people you work with). If you are aware, for example, that someone displays many of the qualities of a resource investigator you will be able to make use of their skills. If that particular member of staff also lacks confidence and has low self-esteem your recognition of those skills will boost that person's self-esteem and make them feel valued and appreciated.

Team-building exercises

Team-building exercises can give members of the team the opportunity to stand back and look at their own ways of working so that they can then search for ways of improving them. Many establishments use consultants to run a one-day exercise, when all staff dress casually and leave all hierarchy behind. The day can be memorable and fun and raise awareness among the staff of their personal skills. With a little imagination it is also possible for a manager to raise this awareness in a team-building exercise that is planned as an inset training day. These opportunities can help managers to distinguish different viewpoints and identify people who may work well together. However, it will be after the team-building day that the real work will need to take place; the knowledge gained should be used to form a more cohesive operational team.

Team-building exercises can help improve working practices.

Team development

A manager can use a variety of ways to look at how a team has come to a certain point in its development. A group of people working together can take some time to form a team; some groups never become cohesive teams, although they may want to be known as such. Tuckman and Jensen (1977) came up with a five-stage theory on how groups form into teams. This theory is quite well known and demonstrates the process teams have to go through in order to achieve cohesiveness (see Figure 6.2).

All early years teams need to provide stability of care and are required to work within a complex network of early childhood provision. This indicates that a wide range of skills is needed to overcome some of the barriers faced when working through multi-disciplinary collaboration.

Stage 1: Forming
This stage is when members of the group are getting to know more about each other. They may be given initial information on the group's objectives.

Stage 2: Storming
This is a time when there may be some initial group conflict. Members will challenge some of the group's objectives and there can be brief or prolonged inner power struggles.

Stage 3: Norming
The group now starts to establish some group norms. These may not be explicitly expressed but have become expected ways of behaving. Individual roles have been cast and this is often a difficult time for new members to join the group.

Stage 4: Performing
This is now full communication. Everyone is collaborating in a team effort. Everyone is now aware of the goals and objectives of the team and understands what their contribution is.

Stage 5: Adjourning
This is the stage at which the group may disband or go their separate ways.

Figure 6.2. Tuckman and Jensen's (1977) five-stage theory of team formation

6.2 Effective teams

One of the key responsibilities of a manager is to organise people with different personalities and strengths into an effective and cohesive team that delivers high-quality services for children and parents.

A team is a group of two or more people working towards a common goal – whether professionally or socially. Teams can offer a sense of security and relationships that make work satisfying, rewarding and often enjoyable.

Think it over

- First, think of a group you have been in that left you feeling good about the group or yourself. It could be a work, social or friendship group. List the things that made the experience a good one.

- Now think about a group you have been in that left you feeling negative about the group or yourself. Again, it could be a work, social or friendship group. List what things made your experience of the group negative.

- When you have done this you will have formed a list of things both positive and negative about working in groups.

To make a team more effective, it is necessary to consider what stage of development the team is at (see Figure 6.2). This will of course be influenced by how long the group has been established. Some typical events in the life of a team that might be the stimulus for some sort of team-working activities are when:

- the members of the team are being selected
- the team begins to work together and needs to establish its purpose and how it will try to achieve this
- a team has been working together for some time and wants to review its effectiveness
- team members begin to experience problems working together (this is possible at the earlier stages, when things do not seem to be settling down, or at some later stage, when working relationships deteriorate or if the leadership falters)
- new members join the team and need to be integrated
- team members also have line management responsibilities and are finding it difficult to reconcile their dual roles
- a new challenge arises, and the team has to adapt its ways of working to cope with the change.

Alternatively, a team might not wait until a particular need emerges. Instead, the members may regularly devote time to looking at the way in which they work together and see this sort of activity as a means of maintaining cohesion and preventing small issues from growing into major threats (see below).

The advantages of effective teamwork

Effective teams can lead to greater creativity, improved job satisfaction and increased energy and excitement. Working as part of a cohesive team can make going to work something to look forward to so that you are going to work not just for monetary gain, but for the feeling from working in collaboration with a group of like-minded people. But what does working as part of a team mean to early years workers?

Qualitative data from unpublished research has clarified childcare and family day care coordinators' understanding of teamwork in early years settings. The perceived advantages of teamwork were looked at by asking the question 'Why do we work in teams in early childhood services?' The following advantages were consistently recorded (Rodd, 1998, p. 100):

- support and stimulation
- a sense of belonging and equality
- opportunity for growth and development
- stress reduction
- facilitation of a pleasant working environment
- opportunity to work through issues
- the minimisation of conflicts
- the provision of a role model for children and parents
- the opportunities for staff members to assume leadership in the short term
- assistance in the efficient achievement of goals
- shared workload

- shared human resources and ideas
- acknowledgement of staff members' professional capabilities
- increased motivation and commitment to the task or decision.

What makes an effective team?

Figure 6.3. The four key characteristics of an effective team

A sense of purpose and clear objectives

Working towards a common vision or aim can ensure a team's cohesiveness and cooperation. If the staff share common values and beliefs this makes working together easier. Although it cannot be assumed that everyone holds the same values and beliefs generally, it *can* be assumed that most people working in early years settings will be working to the same sets of guidance and principles as set down by legislation relating to early years settings (see Chapter 3).

An effective team must:

- consist of members who feel they are working towards the same results
- maintain a sense of purpose.

Aims and objectives can be written down in a formal mission statement, but this will be tokenistic unless the team can see them evolving in their everyday practice. Although early years settings have the needs of the children at the heart of their practice, they may have quite different ways of achieving this end.

Case Study

A family atmosphere

Toad Hall Nursery is a privately run 50-place sessional nursery for children aged 2 years 11 months to 4 years 11 months. It has an excellent reputation and always has a waiting list. The nursery manager is also the owner and there are established, well-qualified staff. The nursery has a mission statement based on Christian ethics, but religion is not a key feature of the curriculum offered – children are not indoctrinated. The staff are told about the nursery's aims and mission at interview and are very proud of the family atmosphere. As the nursery was formerly a house there is a warm and familiar feel about the place. Children's needs are paramount and it is evident that they take total precedent. The children are courteous and caring and are allowed to move about the nursery fairly freely. The manager is a very professional person who guides prospective parents around but always asks staff members to help explain what goes on at the nursery. Parents are introduced to everyone, including the caretaker and the kitchen staff. The manager does not need to be present for the nursery to run smoothly and has two very efficient deputy managers, who job share. The staff team makes cooperative decisions about the running of the nursery but take them to the manager to make the final decision, when her final word is binding. She listens to her staff's ideas and goes away to investigate them before returning to staff with a decision.

- What is the secret of this setting's success?
- What style of management has the manager adopted?
- Would you say the staff were valued?

A balance of roles within the team

Childcare teams need a balance of individuals to provide different skills, attitudes and personal qualities. It is important to ensure harmonious working relationships are created and maintained and that the team works together. The manager will need to build an understanding of the personality traits of the team in order to promote effective team working. It may also be necessary to establish where there are gaps in the skills of the team. A team is not going to operate effectively if all its members wish to be the leader, or indeed if no one does. A balance of the roles as described in Table 6.2 is necessary.

In order to build such a team you also need to take account of the development of teams, as outlined in Figure 6.2. First, the leader needs to create a vision and a set of values within the team (see above), and to generate commitment and involvement from team members.

In building effective teams it is important to note that one person can belong to different teams and adopt different team roles. For example, there are many team-leading roles within the typical early years setting – it is therefore not appropriate for the manager of the setting to be seen as the sole person with any sort of leadership responsibilities (see Table 6.3). Some settings will not allocate so many responsibilities to members of staff, and some of these duties will be part of the deputy manager's duties. The list also suggests ways in which team members can be allocated specific responsibilities.

Table 6.3. Sample leadership roles in an early years setting

Leadership role	Responsibilities
Team leader	Head of room, head of foundation stage, room supervisor – any one person with responsibility for a particular area or stage of development
Special educational needs coordinator	All settings are required to have a named person who coordinates the management of special needs within the setting
Coordinator of gifted and talented children	Must identify and support children in the setting who are recognised as gifted or talented so that they can fulfil their potential
Head of kitchen	Important member of staff responsible for providing nutritious meals and snacks for the children, and who may be in charge of other employees, depending on the size of the setting
Training and development coordinator	Must keep abreast of current trends and requirements to ensure the team's training and development needs are met
Project or fundraising coordinator	A difficult role but vital for the setting to remain financially stable
Parent liaison	A person who deals with all parent and carer activities, such as newsletters and parents' evenings
Key person	A practitioner working with individual children to provide continuity for them and their parents and carers
Senior member of staff	Overseeing students in the setting during their training
Resources manager	Required to order stationery, resources and maintain resources already in use
Outings organiser	The member of staff who books venues, sends out letters for nursery outings, and so on

Think it over

How can staff be given extra responsibility without causing conflict within a team?

Commitment from team members and effective leadership

Team development requires both strong leadership and commitment from team members. A successful team is made up of individuals who are valued for their contributions and expertise, and they will probably have taken part in some of the decision-making about the sort of culture they are involved in. Managers need to analyse how they involve teams in this process and look at ways of motivating them.

Creating a non-dependent culture

The nursery had its first inspection (inspections were at the time carried out by social services). The report stated that the nursery was well run and the children appeared happy and their learning needs were being met. However, there was a concern that, should the nursery manager be out of the setting for more than a couple of hours, things would come to a standstill. Staff at the setting were too dependent on the initiative of the manager – they were unable to function without her. The manager of this setting then had to set about creating a non-dependent culture within the team. The next inspection report stated that this had been turned round and that the nursery could now run effectively without the manager's constant guidance and intervention.

- What strategies do you think the manager might have put in place in order for this change to take place?

In response to the case study 'Creating a non-dependent culture' you may have suggested letting the staff become more involved and take on responsibility. This team did in fact have a meeting, when the manager put 'the cards on the table' and explained the situation. Although anxious at first, the staff did gradually take on more responsibilities, as part of an action plan and with the guidance and support of the manager. The manager was open to ideas but also looked at the strengths of the individual team members to ascertain who would be best placed to take over certain activities and responsibilities. This process was measured and evaluated regularly.

Chapter 1 looked at the role of leadership and discussed the importance of particular attributes or skills a manager needs in order to lead an effective team. The manager is part of the team and key to ensuring its effectiveness. The manager must be a good role model for the staff and show respect for team members, while being supportive of their professional development. Effective managers can solve problems and balance the needs of all within the team. A good relationship with the staff will ensure that team members:

- relate positively to other groups – outside agencies, visitors, the wider community
- form good relationships with children and their parents and carers
- are enthusiastic about new challenges
- are willing to take on and train for new responsibilities
- have confidence to evaluate and look at making improvements to practice when needed.

The level of commitment is important, but can be one of the most difficult factors to guarantee. Staff are generally willing to work well as part of a team only if they:

- work for efficient managers
- are allowed to think for themselves
- are assigned interesting work
- are informed
- see the end result of their work
- are listened to

- are respected
- have their efforts recognised
- are professionally challenged
- have opportunities to increase their skills.

Consequently, managers must:

- be efficient and effective
- give authority to make meaningful decisions
- listen to employees' comments
- give positive feedback
- make group decisions
- ensure staff have variety in their work, to maintain interest
- communicate well with staff
- motivate staff
- offer guidance and support in times of change.

Managers need to know how to identify the strengths of their individual team members and use their distinctive contributions to the team in the most effective way. When looking for new staff, managers will be looking for professionals who will complement the team they already have in a positive way.

Good communication

Good communication is essential within a team in order for it to be effective. With this in mind, managers recruiting new staff will look for those who demonstrate this skill. Good communication encourages open dialogue which is non-threatening and useful in terms of evaluating and sharing good practice. Section 6.6 covers communication in more detail.

6.3 Recruitment, selection and retention of staff

The recruitment and selection of staff is a vital and often difficult aspect of a manager's job role. The success of the setting and the well-being of the children depend on the recruitment of reliable, appropriately qualified and experienced staff. In England since September 2008 managers have to meet the Welfare Requirements and Learning and Development Requirements of the Early Years Foundation Stage when they employ staff. This will involve selection and recruitment procedures that make sure all employees are safe to work with children and have current enhanced Criminal Records Bureau (CRB) checks. Providers must ensure that:

- adults looking after children, or having unsupervised access to them, are suitable to do so
- adults looking after children have appropriate qualifications, training, skills and knowledge
- staffing arrangements are organised to ensure safety and meet the needs of the children.

All adults involved in the setting must have a CRB check. A declaration of consent form (DC2) can be downloaded from the Ofsted website. The DC2 form asks for a self-declaration of criminal records and other matters that determine suitability to work with or be in contact with children. Enhanced disclosure includes additional information from local police forces. The CRB has published a code of practice and employers' guidance for recipients of disclosures to ensure they are handled fairly and used properly.

The following sources will be searched:

- the Police National Computer
- Protection of Children Act (POCA) list
- Protection of Vulnerable Adults (POVA) list
- information held under Section 142 of the Education Act 2002 (List 99).

Further information about responsibilities for carrying out CRB checks and about disqualification is provided in *Practice Guidance for the Early Years Foundation Stage*.

Find it out

Visit the Early Years Foundation Stage website and familiarise yourself with the welfare requirements regarding the selection of suitable staff.

The Children's Workforce Development Council (CWDC) is compiling an online database of recognised Early Years and Playwork qualifications so you can determine the appropriateness of candidates' qualifications.

Before a manager starts the recruitment process, thought must be given to the job that is available. It is necessary to analyse the job requirements, and to compile a job description, a person specification and to consider the legal requirement of placing advertisements that avoid discrimination. If time is spent on these aspects, problems such as high staff turnover, absenteeism and disciplinary problems can be avoided. Good recruitment and selection are important, as a more effective, better-motivated workforce can result.

The recruitment process must meet certain legal obligations – for example, individuals must not be discriminated against on the grounds of race, sex or disability, or refused employment on the grounds of membership or non-membership of a trade union. If an applicant feels they have been discriminated against, a claim may be made to an employment tribunal. If the tribunal finds in the claimant's favour, it may award compensation or recommend some other course of action to reduce or stop the effect of any discrimination. It is also an offence to employ a person with no immigration authorisation to work in the UK.

The number of people employed by a setting, and their qualifications, will depend on the current business plan and on the required staff:child ratios determined by current statutory legal requirements, for example the Statutory Framework for the Early Years Foundation Stage. It is interesting to note that managers themselves must have a minimum of two years' experience in an early years, or similar, setting.

The job description

The job description has three main purposes:

- to inform potential applicants about the job (prospective candidates can decide whether or not the job is for them)
- to ensure new recruits to the team understand the purpose, functions and accountabilities of the job from the outset
- to provide information to determine the selection criteria.

When analysing the position to be filled, consider the following points in order to ensure that the job description reflects the true nature of the position:

- the position's overall purpose and objectives
- whether it is temporary or permanent, full-time or part-time
- the level of seniority and qualifications required.

It is always good policy to research the requirements of the position by talking to colleagues within the same sector or to existing employees, and to draw on your own experience. If the position already exists, exit interviews can be a useful way to find out more about particular aspects of the job and provide useful insights for updating the role.

The job description can be used as the basis for the advertisement and application forms, as well as for the questions during the interview (see below). Although job descriptions will vary from setting to setting, a common format is as follows (see Figure 6.4):

- job title
- overall purpose
- principal elements of the job
- description of the establishment
- reporting arrangements
- salary
- location
- practical requirements.

Job title: Childcare worker

Responsible to: Nursery manager

Purpose: Work as part of the nursery team to ensure the children and families using the setting receive the highest standards of care and development in early years provision.

Location: Nascot Wood College, Harpenden Campus

Nascot Wood is a large college offering a wide range of courses on three separate sites in pleasant rural surroundings that incorporate a working farm (arable, sheep, cows and pigs). The nursery is now located in the old Manor House, which has been converted sympathetically to ensure an excellent working environment for staff and children. The children, aged from 6 months to 5 years, are divided into small working groups according to their age.

Main duties:

1 Act as key person to a group of children in your base room.

2 Alongside other staff, plan, develop and carry out a range of age-appropriate activities.

3 Keep up-to-date records of achievement that are shared with parents and used as a basis for planning.

4 Liaise with parents/carers and other staff to ensure all children have equal opportunities and experiences within the setting, while being aware of individual needs.

5 Work with and support children with special educational needs.

6 Undertake certain domestic jobs (e.g. preparation of some meals and snacks, cleaning of equipment) and ensure health and safety requirements are met.

7 Be conversant with developments in childcare practice and use appropriate materials to stimulate education in relation to curriculum requirements such as the Early Years Foundation Stage

8 Be willing to attend training and development courses.

9 Participate in the training of students on a range of childcare courses.

10 Assist the staff team in promoting the nursery's positive image and maintaining its reputation in the sector.

11 Assist and support fundraising activities.

12 Attend regular staff meetings.

13 Operate within college policies, including quality, equal opportunities and health and safety.

This job description is liable to variation to reflect or anticipate changes in the requirements in the post. While you will be allocated a room base associated with a specific age range of children, you may on occasion be asked to cover other base rooms and age ranges.

Figure 6.4. Example of a job description for a childcare worker (based on a job description supplied by Oaklands College Nursery, St Albans)

The person specification

A person specification should briefly describe the ideal person to fill the job. It is a profile of the skills, knowledge, experience and qualifications necessary to perform the role properly. This is useful during the recruitment phase, as it will help you find the ideal person to join your team. It can also be referred to when compiling the advertisement and drawing up a shortlist of candidates. At interview it can be useful as a checklist of points to be raised. It is normal practice to divide the elements of a person specification into desirable and essential and to include the elements shown in Figure 6.5.

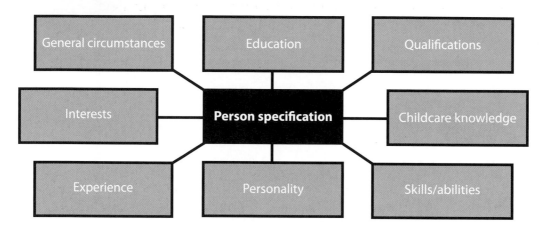

Figure 6.5 Example of the elements of a person specification for the job description in Figure 6.4

Essential:

- CACHE Award/Certificate/Diploma in Childcare and Education/ NVQ 3 Childcare or equivalent
- Recent and relevant experience of working with children between the ages of 6 months and 5 years
- Knowledge of the Early Years Foundation Stage
- Experience of implementing a wide range of activities for babies and young children
- Knowledge of child development, to ensure records and observations are up to date
- Knowledge of National Standards/Ofsted requirements
- Knowledge of health and safety requirements relevant to childcare settings
- Good written and verbal skills with adults and children
- Ability to work as a team
- Willingness to undertake further training and development
- Willingness to attend staff meetings outside normal hours

Desirable:

- Current first aid certificate
- Food hygiene certificate
- Experience of supervising students
- Full driving licence

Figure 6.6. Example of essential and desirable elements of a person specification

The job advertisement

It is necessary to target a range of potential applicants, but at the least expense. This can be done by recruiting from existing staff, by contacting local schools and colleges and by advertising in local newspapers and Jobcentres of the Employment Service. Online recruitment is also an option, as are commercial employment agencies and job fairs. Sector journals such as *Nursery World* and the *Early Years Educator* can also be used.

A job advertisement should be based on the job description and person specification so that readers of the advertisement know what is involved and precisely what is wanted. It needs to be eye-catching, brief, straightforward and non-discriminatory. Remember that the advertisement is a visual representation of your setting, so it is important to consider carefully the image projected. An example is shown in Figure 6.7.

The advertisement could include:

- the business logo
- the job title and location
- tasks and responsibilities
- salary and fringe benefits
- where and how to apply (e.g. an application form) or gain further information
- when to apply by.

The Jack and Jill Day Nursery

Nascot Wood College

Harpenden, Herts

We are a group of happy, professionally trained and qualified people working in a well-resourced, caring nursery. We are looking for a full-time, enthusiastic, trained person – CACHE Diploma in Child Care and Education (DCE) or equivalent – to join our team.

We offer:

> 39 hour week
> Salary £13,872–£16,710 p.a.
> 4 weeks' paid holiday
> Uniform

If you would like further information, to arrange a visit or an application form, please contact Pauline or Jamie on 01582 333 551.

> Closing date for applications March 4th.

Figure 6.7. Example of an advertisement for the job described in Figure 6.4

Diane's job advertisement

Diane has decided that she needs a person who has a Level 2 qualification, such as the CACHE Level 2 Award/Certificate/Diploma in Child Care and Education, to fill her post in the pre-school room. Diane's day nursery is in a pleasant area of Norfolk, near the coast, and has good relationships with the local school. At present the nursery cares for children aged 6 months to 5 years and has 30 children, although Diane is looking to expand the provision to accommodate an extra 8 or 9 places in the pre-school room. The salary is £6.50 an hour, and membership of the local hotel leisure centre is a fringe benefit. The position is temporary at present but may become permanent for the right candidate. Diane has designed an application form and requires two references.

- How would you present this information in an eye-catching advertisement?

- Where would you advertise?

- What personal qualities and skills would this role require?

Application form or curriculum vitae?

An application form can help you obtain the information you need to sift through applications. It can be used as a basis for the interview, but the form should ask only for information relevant to the job. Another method of screening candidates is to ask for a curriculum vitae (CV), in which candidates outline their previous experience and skills, employment and interests. The application form provides a standardised format for the presentation of information and enables candidates to be screened against criteria related to the specific needs of the setting. The curriculum vitae comes in several formats and pertinent questions may not be adequately addressed by the applicant. The lack of standardisation may hinder effective comparison of candidates.

The application form and the curriculum vitae should include details of at least two referees. To select the best candidate you will need to take up applicants' references. You may also wish to use a selection test.

Candidates should be short-listed for interview only if they meet the person specification. If no candidate is deemed wholly suitable it is possible to:

- re-advertise the position with changed specifications

- re-advertise at a later stage, and to use temporary staff in the interim.

Interviewing the candidates

An interview can be a stressful experience for the candidate, but it can also be daunting for the manager. There is a lot of pressure to get the choice right and managers are very aware that a wrong decision can affect the success of their business, in both the long and short term. Parents, for example, are quick to withdraw their custom if they find a member of staff abrasive or intolerant of the children. Most managers could tell you a horror story concerning the employment of someone who appeared on paper to be perfect but in reality was inefficient or damaging to the business.

Careful planning of the interview will help ensure a successful outcome. When the short-list for the interviews has been decided, prepare a letter to be sent to candidates that gives the date, time and venue. Include relevant information such as the setting's brochure, the timetable for the day (e.g. for observations and presentations – see below) and a map for the interview venue.

Prepare the questions beforehand and give thought to the structure, length, time and type of interview. Some employers like to observe the candidates working with the children or giving a presentation on some aspect of the work. A standard list of questions is fairer for the candidates and enables you to compare and contrast the answers. It is important to ask questions that give candidates the opportunity to show their knowledge and offer their opinions. Questions should be open-ended (those that cannot be answered by a 'yes' or 'no') and should not be discriminatory. It is a good idea to include some scenarios or 'what if…' questions, some examples of which are given below.

An informal interview; interview settings can be formal or informal.

- What would you do if a parent failed to collect their child at the allocated time?
- What would you do if you noticed cigarette burns on a child's arm?
- What would you do if a colleague repeatedly turned up late for work?
- What would you do if a parent commented about another child's behaviour?
- What would you do if a child was repeatedly biting others?

Possible areas to discuss are:

- the organisation
- the job
- the candidate's education, experience, skills, interests and general circumstances
- the candidate's aspirations.

Prepare the room to ensure comfort; candidates may not be at their best if sitting on an uncomfortable chair faced by a panel of interviewers across a large table. You may prefer a more informal approach, with comfortable chairs and a cup of coffee.

On the day of the interview ensure that visitors or telephone calls will not interrupt you. It may be necessary to have suitable cover arranged for that day to ensure you are free to concentrate, and that the applicants can be welcomed to the setting and put at ease.

At the end of the interview give candidates the opportunity to ask questions, and be clear about when you will contact them with the results.

Selection and job offer

When choosing new staff it is advisable to include existing staff in the process as it improves the chances of the team working well together. You can achieve this by including a staff member on the interview panel, or through discussions with staff at appropriate points in the process. However, the final decision belongs to the manager. It is important to remember that if there is any doubt about the suitability of a candidate it is better not to appoint at all. It can be a very costly and damaging experience if the wrong candidate is appointed.

An offer of a job can be made by letter or telephone. It is advisable to make any offer subject to satisfactory references, health and CRB checks and proof of relevant qualifications. You should also expect evidence of the right to work in the UK through a National Insurance number or a work permit. When the offer has been agreed and the conditions met, the unsuccessful candidates can be rejected. An unsuccessful candidate may request a debriefing session to help them understand why they were unsuccessful. It is therefore useful to write notes during the interview to help you recall your reasons for selection. Keep all notes you have made and interview forms so that you can give feedback to unsuccessful candidates.

Case Study

Staff involvement in selection

Nadira runs a Montessori pre-school and is in the process of employing a new member of staff. She discussed the job and person specifications with her present staff. She considered the strengths and weaknesses of the team and used this to assess the requirements of the person to be employed. After interviewing prospective candidates, she again consulted the team and took account of their comments in making her decision. The staff felt involved in the process and welcomed the new member of staff.

■ What would be the benefits of involving the team in the selection process?

■ Can you see any difficulties that could arise?

Staff induction

It is good practice to give each new member of staff an induction period. This will help new staff to settle in and will give you the opportunity to give them information about the setting and how it is organised. A successful induction period can lead to improved performance and better job satisfaction. It can also prevent high staff turnover and reduce absenteeism, resignations or dismissals. If there is more than one member of staff starting at about the same time their joint induction would reduce the demands made on you as manager.

Induction training can be part of wider, long-term staff development training with the aim of making employees more effective and motivated, and to extend their skills and adaptability in the workplace. A typical induction programme might include the elements shown in Figure 6.8.

The induction programme is a good opportunity to ascertain the training needs for your new (and existing) staff. It is also good practice to ask the new staff to complete an evaluation form of the induction programme to ascertain how effective it has been.

> **Key Term**
>
> **Induction –** introducing new staff to a setting or workplace to help them settle in, meet their colleagues and learn about the setting and how it is organised.

After induction you may wish to set a probationary period of 3–6 months, with a temporary contract and a review at the end. If progress has been successful a permanent contract could then be signed.

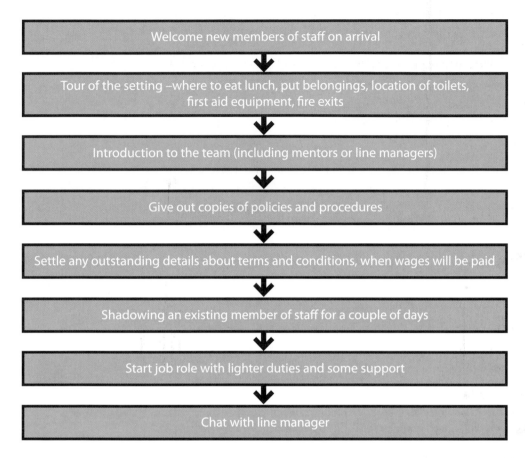

Figure 6.8. Elements of a typical induction programme

Think it over

A new member of staff is starting in the baby room. She has little experience of working in a day nursery, but has worked with babies over the past 10 years as a childminder. Consider how you would plan her induction.

Finding recruits

Many managers are finding there is something of a recruitment crisis in early years. It can be difficult to recruit and retain suitable staff, particularly as the average rate of pay is relatively low and differs across the country. The Pre-School Learning Alliance published figures from the Group Membership Questionnaire 2007 which show the average hourly rates of pay for each region (Table 6.4).

Table 6.4. Salary indicators in early years

	Leader	Deputy leader	Assistant
Eastern	£8.35	£7.28	£5.81
London	£8.98	£7.79	£6.05
Midlands	£7.82	£6.96	£5.64
North East	£7.46	£6.51	£5.57
North West	£7.99	£6.84	£5.62
South East	£8.50	£7.27	£5.88
South West	£7.96	£6.82	£5.99

In-house training

Some establishments are tackling this problem by recruiting unqualified staff and training them within the setting. The advantage of this is that the workforce meets their individual requirements, but there are also a number of disadvantages.

- It is still difficult to find appropriate candidates when there is a lot of competition from better-paid jobs.
- There is no guarantee that staff will stay when training has finished.
- It is also an expensive and time-consuming exercise, particularly as trainees are not included in the overall staff:child ratio.

There have been difficulties finding suitable training facilities; some training organisations, for example, do not receive funding for mature trainees, although childcare providers often prefer a range of ages among their staff and actively encourage older people to apply for work.

Work experience

Managers have found that they can spot potential employees from youngsters involved in work experience. If they show desirable qualities such as enthusiasm, reliability, flexibility, aptitude and a love of children, they are worth supporting and may be encouraged to follow a qualification route that suits them. Some colleges are working in close collaboration with employers to ensure that candidates are finding employment when they complete their courses, and some employers are even funding candidates through college.

There is also greater collaboration with employers and local schools, through the Centres of Vocational Excellence (CoVEs), launched in 2001. The CoVE programme, which is usually based in a college of further education, works with employers to provide appropriate training and encourage best practice. Through this work people are becoming more aware of the pressures and pleasures of working with children, and of the qualities and skills that childcare practitioners need. It is particularly important that careers advisers understand the true nature of a childcare career. In the past there has been too much emphasis on directing people with a low academic ability towards childcare. The childcare sector needs people who enter the career with their hearts, and employers who nurture and help people to develop their talents and fulfil their potential. There is also now a better career structure in place, which allows students to work their way up to management level – a prospect that is appealing to many in the workforce. The Children's Workforce Development Council (CWDC) is supporting the need for a better trained and qualified workforce through Level 3 qualifications and the Early Years Professional Status (EYPS). For more on this see Chapter 7.

Key Term

Early Years Professional Status (EYPS) – the new status for early years practitioners – a graduate leader in early years.

Retention of staff

Early years managers are naturally keen to maintain a steady workforce with a low turnover of staff. A stable team is able to plan together in the long term and feel secure that they have the mutual support of colleagues. There will be an air of confidence that encourages success. People will be aware of each other's strengths and weaknesses and know their own position in the team. Parents and children prefer a team to be stable and unchanging. A high staff turnover can give the impression that there is something wrong with the establishment and lead to clients losing confidence. The end result will be damaging to the setting's reputation in the local community. The manager nonetheless needs to ensure that a stable team remains motivated and embraces change or the setting can become stale and uninteresting.

It is natural and healthy for people to leave employment from time to time. There seems to be a high rate of pregnancy among early years workers, for example. This does give the opportunity for new members of staff to introduce ideas and freshen the team's approach. However, workers must be retained for a reasonable period; otherwise it is very difficult to establish a quality service that is competitive. If labour turnover is excessive it can indicate management problems.

Aids to staff retention

Managers are becoming very creative in the methods they employ to encourage retention of staff. The offer of fringe benefits is one from the wider commercial sector. These range from traditional pension schemes to membership of the local golf course or entrance tickets to race courses. Free car parking for employees is a perk that is particularly likely to appeal to staff in a densely populated area where parking charges are high.

Bonus schemes may be offered to reward staff for low absenteeism, and morale-boosting techniques include providing pleasant staff rooms, kitchen facilities and personal lockers. Subsidised childcare has proved to be an effective method of getting people back to work, as has flexible working. Some smaller establishments have introduced Christmas shopping days and bonuses as a reward for staff loyalty.

The wider aspects of retention of staff – for example that childcare workers must receive realistic wages for the job they do – need to be addressed at government level. However, there are some things that the manager can do, by participating in any forums on staffing problems and by raising the public awareness of the value of childcare.

The use of an appraisal scheme can also encourage retention of staff. This will give managers and staff the opportunity to review overall performance over a period of time and provide useful feedback. It will also facilitate mutual understanding of the objectives and requirements of the employee's job role and give the opportunity to set individual goals and meet aspirations, including future training needs. It is of paramount importance that staff feel that managers care about them and are prepared to invest in their future careers.

Key Term

Appraisal – the process by which members of staff are assessed on their performance, plan and monitor progress and discuss future aspirations; can be linked to performance pay.

Good practice checklist
Staff retention

- Pay particular attention to the interview and induction procedures. Ensure that the advertisements, job and person specifications are accurate and give a true picture of the job.
- Set appropriate standards so that you employ people who are satisfied by their job and not overstretched or bored.
- Help new recruits settle in and feel part of the team. Plan team-building activities and foster a team culture.
- Check that employees feel involved and that their contributions are valued. If an employee makes a suggestion make sure you give it proper consideration. If you decide not to act on the idea, thank the person for it and explain why it is impractical. Never make people feel silly for suggesting something or belittle their ideas.
- Communicate with all employees. Make sure they all know what is happening, not just a select few. This can be as simple as providing information about new equipment ordered.
- Implement pension and staff appraisal schemes.
- Employees should have the opportunity to discuss work and progress with the manager or line manager.
- Check that pay levels are still in line with those of similar local jobs, and that systems and methods of pay are fully understood and perceived to be fair by the staff.
- Ensure that working conditions are safe, healthy and clean and facilities such as toilets are up to standard.
- Offer regular opportunities for training and personal development on a fair basis. Ensure there is opportunity for advancement.
- Reflect on the management style and whether it is acceptable to staff. Implement training for all levels of management on human resources.
- Check that employees are not being discriminated against because of their race, sex, disability, sexual orientation, religion or belief.
- Find out why people leave and what workers like or dislike about the establishment.

Harassment and bullying

Employees sometimes leave employment as a result of harassment or bullying. This can be difficult to uncover, as many people prefer to keep silent about bullying and will just find employment elsewhere. It is often difficult to recognise that a person is being bullied; it may not be obvious and may be insidious. Those who suffer it may think it is normal behaviour in the organisation, or be worried that others will think they are weak or not up to the job if they complain. They may be accused of overreacting or think that they will not be believed if they report incidents. There is often fear of retribution too and people are unlikely to take action if they are afraid of the consequences for themselves. Colleagues may even collude with the bully to avoid being bullied themselves.

Harassment and bullying take many different forms. Bullying can be characterised as offensive or intimidating behaviour that may undermine or humiliate the individual. Generally harassment is seen as unwanted conduct that affects the individual's dignity and is unacceptable. Table 6.5 compares the two. Further, harassment can take place on any of the following grounds:

- ethnicity, colour or national origin
- gender, marital status and family circumstances
- disabilities and learning difficulties
- criminal record
- trade union membership and activity
- age
- socio-economic background
- religious or political beliefs
- sexual orientation.

Table 6.5. Characteristics of harassment and bullying

	Harassment	Bullying
Definition	Any behaviour that is unwanted, inappropriate, unsolicited and unacceptable to the recipient and that causes stress, distress and a loss of self-esteem	Closely allied to harassment but involves persecution and intimidating, unfair, sarcastic, malicious or angry behaviour that causes the person to feel upset, threatened and beleaguered
Examples/ nature	• Telling inappropriate jokes • An abuse of power • Making offensive and abusive remarks • Derogatory nicknaming and comments • Cold-shouldering • Making unwanted and deliberate physical contact	• An abuse of power • Deliberately withholding information • Shouting • Setting unrealistic targets • Ridiculing the recipient's work, ideas or opinions • A one-off incident or a series of incidents over a period of time • Committed by an individual or a group

It is good practice for employers to give examples of what is considered professional behaviour for staff (Figure 6.9).

It is morally offensive for bullying to continue in an establishment, and if unchecked it can lead to poor morale and poor employee relations. There may also be a lack of respect for managers, poor performance, absenteeism and resignations.

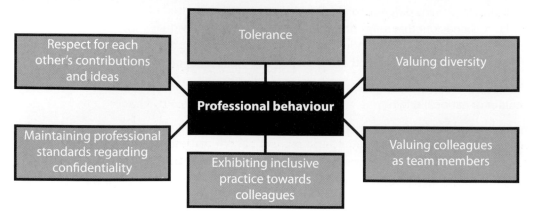

Figure 6.9. Professional behaviour

Managers therefore need to develop and implement policies to protect staff. In practical terms it is a good idea for early years settings to produce a simple policy on bullying and harassment. It should include a statement from management that bullying and harassment will not be tolerated and give examples of unacceptable behaviour. Staff should be involved in the writing of the policy to give it greater authority.

Setting a good example

Managers must set a good example and encourage a culture where employees are consulted and problems are discussed. For example, there should be a fair, prompt and objective method of dealing with complaints, and a strong commitment to confidentiality. In some cases it may be possible to resolve issues informally, or by using a counselling service. If informal resolution of the problem is not possible the manager may need to investigate disciplinary procedures. Advice on individual cases can be obtained from the Advisory, Conciliation and Arbitration Service (ACAS).

6.4 Legal obligations

Establishments have certain legal obligations. It is necessary to have systems in place, for example, for controlling finances. The business aspects of running a childcare setting are covered in Chapter 8. This section looks at the obligations and responsibilities managers have in relation to the care and administration of their team. These are many and varied, and include, for example:

- ensuring that prospective employees fit the legal requirements for working with children
- ensuring that staff are working in a safe environment
- providing contracts of employment for staff
- ensuring employees are paid
- keeping appropriate personnel records.

Contracts of employment

A contract is a legally binding agreement between employer and employee, formed when the employee agrees to work for pay. A contract is made up of oral as well as written agreements. It can include both express terms (those that are explicitly agreed) and implied terms (those that are too obvious to mention). Some terms in the contract will be determined by law, for example the right not to be discriminated against on the grounds of race, sex or disability.

Changes to a contract should be made only with the agreement of both parties. The employee or employer, after giving the required period of notice, can terminate a contract.

All employees are entitled to a written contract that sets out the conditions of employment. As this is a legally binding document it is advisable to employ a suitably qualified person to draw it up. However, contracts should include the following details:

- the registered legal name of the employer
- the legal name of the employee
- job title and brief description
- date of commencement of employment and end date if fixed term
- address of place of work
- salary details
- hours of work
- holiday entitlement
- notice period
- sickness and maternity rights associated with the job
- probationary period, if being used
- retirement age.

It may be necessary to produce a staff handbook which includes details of dismissal, disciplinary and grievance procedures. These can then be referred to in the contract.

The employee and employer should both sign and date the contract, and both parties should keep copies. The employer will also need to keep copies of references and right to work documents.

It is best to ensure that contractual obligations are clear, as any confusion can lead to friction and misunderstandings. In the worst scenario this can lead to claims in civil courts or appeals to employment tribunals for breach of contract. Employees who consider that their contracts have been terminated unfairly may apply to a tribunal claiming they have been unfairly dismissed. If employers fail to give the required notice, the employee can make a claim to the courts or to an employment tribunal for damages for wrongful dismissal. If an employee leaves without giving the required notice, the employer has a similar right to claim damages.

Entitlement to work

Employers are also responsible for checking that potential employees are entitled to work in the UK under the Asylum and Immigration Act 1996. Citizens from the UK and the European Union do not require a work permit, and this can be evidenced by a P45, National Insurance card or a passport. If a work permit is required it is the responsibility of the employer to arrange it, at least 8 weeks before the period of employment starts. It is possible for employees to compare their foreign qualifications with UK qualifications through UK NARIC (see Useful websites).

Paying employees

It is important to develop pay arrangements that are right for your establishment and that reward employees fairly for the work they do. It is a good idea to make sure that your rates of pay are competitive; this will need to be reviewed annually. If you decide to make any changes to pay, consult colleagues to gain their agreement first. Make the payment system as simple to understand as possible and explain to employees how their pay is calculated. The system should be reviewed as often as possible and accountants approached to ensure that everything is kept up to date with legal developments affecting pay.

You may decide to use performance- or skill-based pay systems, where individuals are rewarded for the skills they possess or acquire through training. One day nursery is known to pay employees a fixed sum of £100 bonus on completion of 3 months' work without absence. Other establishments reward staff with additional days off or even free air-miles. It is also becoming common practice to reward staff with lunch parties or pampering sessions following a successful Ofsted inspection (see Chapter 8). Performance can be assessed through an appraisal system where managers and staff monitor progress, formulate action plans and decide on training needs (see Chapter 7).

Many small businesses use a computerised database system to manage the payment of wages, including taxation and National Insurance contributions. HM Revenue and Custom (formerly the Inland Revenue) gives precise information on all aspects of taxation, National Insurance contributions and Pay As You Earn (PAYE) schemes. An advisory booklet entitled Pay Systems is available from ACAS, and the Department of Trade and Industry's Employment Relations Directorate has factsheets that outline the legal requirements for the payment of wages. For example, it is a legal requirement to produce an itemised pay statement that gives the:

- gross amount of the wages or salary, i.e. before tax and other deductions
- amounts of any fixed deductions and the purpose for which they are made (e.g. trade union subscriptions) or the total figure for fixed deductions, when a separate standing statement of the details has been provided
- amounts of any variable deductions and the purposes for which they are made
- net amount of any wages or salary payable (after tax and deductions)
- amount and method of each part-payment when different parts of the net amount are paid in different ways (e.g. the separate figures of a cash payment and a balance credited to a bank account).

The difficulty faced by managers is ensuring that staff are paid competitive wages while continuing to provide affordable childcare in a well-stocked and innovative environment. Managers have to balance pay and fees amid difficulties in recruiting appropriate staff. Increases to the national minimum wage and employers' contributions to National Insurance mean that fees have risen in order for settings to maintain a suitable profit margin. It may be necessary to justify the reasons for fee increases and to be able to argue the case for competitive wages within the sector. This can be particularly difficult if the setting is in an area of low average wages, where parents are likely to have difficulty paying the fees.

Personnel records

Under the Data Protection Act 1998 employees are entitled to have access to all the personal details on them that are held on computers or as manual records. Personnel records are needed to fulfil legal requirements, such as for statutory sick pay, tax and National Insurance contributions. Information kept should include:

- personal details – name, date of birth, address, qualifications, previous experience, tax code, National Insurance number, and emergency contact number
- employment details – date employment started, job title
- details of terms and conditions – rate of pay, hours of work, holiday entitlement
- absence details – sickness and lateness
- details of accidents at work
- details of disciplinary action
- training and development courses attended.

Personnel records do not need to be complicated – a card index system can be effective or a computerised system can be used. An effective personnel system will enable you to keep track of staff and monitor individual performance, and to have better control of staff turnover, problems of recruitment and discipline issues. It may also assist in the creation of fair and consistent promotion and help in the development of a successful equal opportunities policy.

Pensions

Any business that employs more than five members of staff must make a stakeholder pension scheme available to all employees. Information on pensions and entitlements is available from the Pension Service.

6.5 Management of team working

As a manager or leader in an early years setting you must ensure that there is good-quality provision which can be audited and inspected by outside bodies. To guarantee stability of care and provision of service, your team will need to be involved in the processes and procedures and share the same visions and goals. *Effective Leadership in the Early Years Sector: The ELEYS Study* (2007) identified good leadership practice as the ability to provide direction and:

- translate strategic vision into specific plans
- make use of the collaborative knowledge base
- build a shared value base – promote collective knowledge
- support others to talk knowledgeably about issues concerning their work
- recognise how to improve services to be responsive and flexible
- work for equality
- develop a culture of high levels of responsiveness
- Know the legislative frameworks.

(Siraj-Blatchford and Manni, 2007, p. 14)

The study suggested that this can be implemented through:

- effective communication
- encouraging reflection
- monitoring and assessing practice
- commitment to continuing professional development (CPD)
- distributed leadership
- building a learning community and team culture
- encouraging and facilitating parent and community partnerships
- leading and managing; striking a balance.

Key Term

Continuing professional development (CPD) – a process of self-improvement based on reflection, in which you set your own objectives, evaluate your progress, gain useful experience and assess any practical benefits.

6.6 The manager as a communicator

Communication is seen as 'multi-functional and multi-directional – consultation; reciprocity (dialogue rather than monologue) and reflection' (ibid. p. 15).

On a day-to-day basis in the setting communication can be challenging and will depend on the individual's stressors as well as the external influences on staff and their role within the setting.

Why does communication matter?

Communication is vital to all organisations and is often singled out as one of the greatest challenges for a manager. It is the key to getting things done. It can be intentional or unintentional. Effective communication promotes achievement and success. Employees want to be listened to and informed. Communication is the responsibility not only of the manager but also of each member of the staff team; however, as the manager is the leader of the team it will be their ultimate responsibility.

Most (if not all) of the manager's role is about communication. Not only do managers have to communicate information about policies and procedures to their staff, but day to day they also need to communicate more subliminal messages, such as recognition of professionalism, empathy, respect and authority, to name but a few. The staff need to be clear about the manager's expectations in terms of the standard of their work, and they need to know that the manager will support and lead them.

Characterising communication

Good communication

Good communication has the following characteristics:

- it aids decision-making
- it enhances the setting's reputation
- it ensures effective and smooth running of the systems, policies and procedures.

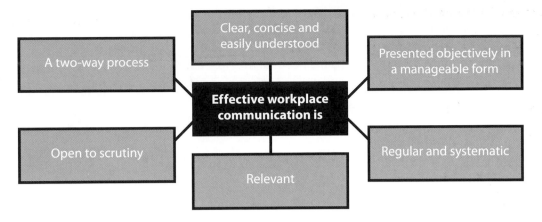

Figure 6.10. Elements of effective workplace communication

Poor communication

In contrast, poor communication results in:

- lack of information
- misinformation and misunderstandings
- unclear objectives
- people being inhibited
- poor relationships in the workplace
- values not being shared
- fear and rumour.

Clear communication can be hampered in early years settings by the physical environment – many settings are split into smaller groups or rooms. There can be challenges of:

- time – providing cover for people to attend meetings etc. when children's needs come first
- conflict between staff which cannot be resolved at the time it happens because the children need to be supervised – this can lead to bad feeling and unresolved issues
- dropping off and picking up times – an often hurried process when parents' motives can be misinterpreted
- few times when staff are together – sometimes causing 'sub-groups' to form within the setting
- shift work to meet the needs of parents and carers can mean that staff rarely all meet together.

Methods of communication

Communication can be spoken or written, direct or indirect. It does not need to be expensive or sophisticated. The mix of methods will depend on the size of the setting, the size of the team, working times and so on. Table 6.6 shows the advantages and disadvantages of a variety of methods.

Different methods of communication are useful on different occasions. For example, there is little point in holding a whole-team meeting to discuss a resource order when staff can be asked to put in orders for each room to the manager or deputy or the resources coordinator in person. Communication can work only if it meets the needs of the work environment. The ways in which a manager communicates will depend on:

- how many full-time and part-time staff there are
- opportunities and time for meetings
- technology within the setting (e.g. whether there is an internal telephone system)
- the budget available for staff training
- the size of the staffroom or meeting room.

Table 6.6. Methods of communication between manager and staff

Method of communication	Advantages	Disadvantages
Face to face (one to one)	Direct and swift, it gives the opportunity to listen to one member of staff informally, and feelings can be communicated.	It is an informal method and therefore difficult to record; also, it may cause difficulties with other members of the team if they feel 'they have not been told'.
Group meetings	Meetings can be valuable for discussion and feedback and can provide opportunities for team members to contribute ideas and identify challenges.	Meetings can drag on too long and often have rigid agendas, which can result in staff feeling that they are pointless.
Cascade networks	These are useful for passing on information quickly (especially in larger organisations).	If not clearly defined they are open to misinterpretation.
Written communication	Written communication can be especially useful when the need for information is permanent and the topic requires detailed explanation. It is particularly useful for holiday allocation, changes to opening hours and so on.	The wording needs to be checked as there may be room for gross misinterpretation and once written there is a tendency for it to remain 'written in stone'.
Employee handbooks/ induction bulletins	These are very useful as an 'official' way of informing employees of their job role, possible changes to it, work rotas and so on.	As with all written communication, it is very important that they are absolutely correct.

Method of communication	Advantages	Disadvantages
Notices on boards	Notices can be very useful for communicating with team members about items of interest such as staff outings or a social get-together.	Notices have a habit of 'falling off' boards! And if important but not very popular it is very easy for staff to say they did not see it.
Individual letters	People tend to take notice of things in writing.	Letters can be misinterpreted and it is sometimes possible for people to say they have not received them.
Staff training days	In-house days can be very useful in terms of professional development and as an opportunity to reflect on practice.	If not properly organised, staff training days can seem like a waste of time; also, not all members of the team may feel involved or feel the day is relevant to them.
Informal chats during work time	These can be held anywhere and at any time; they are often the way to get to know staff really well and keep up to date with what is happening.	Difficulties arise when there is a need for confidentiality, and if some staff have more opportunities for a 'chat' than others this can lead to discord within the team.
Electronically (email, fax, telephone)	Electronic means are useful to get information to a person quickly and have a good chance of a speedy reply.	They may be open to misinterpretation, are not always available in smaller organisations, and can be time consuming.

A simple but effective method of communication.

Styles of communication

Communication will be more effective if behaviour (i.e. what you do, as opposed to what you say) is taken into account. How you behave can help or hinder communication, as people are liable to judge you on the way you behave.

There are three general categories for style of communication:

- aggressive
- assertive
- passive (submissive, non-assertive).

Consider the following scenario. You are a busy manager trying to complete some notes you want to circulate to your team today, ahead of your meeting with them tomorrow. These notes are very important as they set out a draft policy for especially gifted and talented children and advice on how such children may be supported within the setting. You also have a stack of paperwork for children due to start next term which you need to complete, and the staff rotas need revising. A member of staff from the baby unit calls you on the internal telephone system and says he needs to discuss how the process of informing parents about their child's day can be improved. He has the time to come down now to talk to you, as they have the staff available at present. You would prefer to discuss the topic later, not now. Your response to this request, in terms of the above three styles, might be:

- Aggressive – 'You can't expect me to talk to you right now. I am in the middle of something really important. You'll just have to ring me back.'

- Assertive – 'Fine. I'll be happy to talk with you about these issues, but not just now. I'm in the middle of a report for the team for tomorrow. I suggest you ring me again after 2.00 p.m.'

- Passive (submissive, non-assertive) – 'Well, I'm really busy just now and a lot of people need to get the piece of work I am doing at the moment, but seeing as you have the time now…'

Aggressive   Assertive   Passive and submissive

Figure 6.11. Different styles of communication

Think it over

What type of response are you likely to make to a request that is difficult to grant – aggressive, assertive or passive?

As a manager it is often easier to be passive, as you may feel this is meeting the needs of the staff, but in the long run this can be destructive and your own work does not get done. If in the above scenario the manager had taken the time to talk to the member of staff, when would the notes be completed for the meeting? Would they be as effective if produced in a rush for the meeting? Would the other team members understand that the baby room member of staff took priority the day before?

Assertiveness

What assertiveness is

Assertiveness is based on a philosophy of personal responsibility and an awareness of the rights of other people. Being assertive means being honest with yourself and others. It means having the ability to say directly what it is you want, need or feel, but not at the expense of other people. It means having confidence in yourself and being positive, while at the same time understanding other people's points of view. Being assertive means being able to negotiate and reach workable compromises. Above all, being assertive requires you to have self-respect and respect for other people.

What assertiveness is not!

Being assertive is not:

- about getting your own way and winning every time
- a series of techniques to learn parrot fashion and then bring out in a difficult situation
- a way in which you can manipulate other people so that you can get your own way while looking as though you are considering others.

The benefits of being assertive

There are many benefits for both individuals and organisations when the people who work within them learn to be more assertive. For individuals they might include the following.

- People are happier in themselves and with the way they handle difficult or tricky situations.
- Individuals get the best from people at work, including themselves.
- People are much more likely to get results and outcomes that are satisfactory for everyone.
- Stress is reduced as people are more likely to manage conflict early and in a competent way.

For the organisation (i.e. the early years setting) they might include the following.

- Staff are more confident and competent.
- People work together better and are more flexible.
- There are fewer 'hidden agendas' and more direct talk.
- Issues are resolved at an early stage, before they become long-term problems.

Techniques for managers

There are various techniques you can use to communicate what you want to people without being rude or appearing self-centred. Figure 6.12 shows some of them.

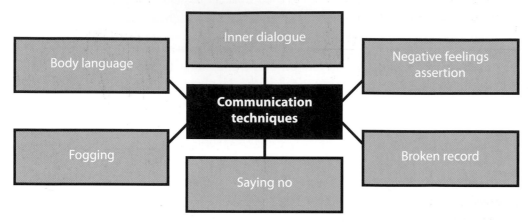

Figure 6.12. Techniques that do not make managers seem rude or self-centred

Inner dialogues

All of us talk to ourselves regularly, usually inwardly. If done negatively, it can guarantee a self-fulfilling prophecy of real disaster! For example, a negative inner dialogue before a meeting could go like this.

'It's Friday… the meeting is today… it's a difficult enough meeting at the best of times but when I tell them I have to cut back on resources they are not going to like it. They will tell me I haven't done enough forward planning. It's not my fault the cost of things has gone up so much. Especially Jill… she is always so on the ball… I ended up giving in to her the last time…'

All of this, of course, is very negative and causes a downward spiral, leaving little room for assertive behaviour.

The world of sports discovered a way to use this kind of inner thinking in a positive way quite a few years ago, and consequently there are many books about the 'inner game' of tennis, golf, squash and so on. The positive inner dialogue technique is very useful before a crisis to coach yourself into doing your best in the given circumstances. It is not a question of thinking rosy thoughts so that you can pretend it will be all right with a false sense of optimism. It is a way of stopping the downward spiral with positive but realistic options.

'It's Friday – the meeting is today… it is not going to be an easy meeting but I do have a good case and can present a valid argument. Not everyone will be helpful… but I do know how to be assertive should there be any comebacks… yes I believe my case is a good one. Now, what else is happening today?'

As you can see from the examples, with a positive inner dialogue it is so much easier to move onto the next thing and not remain trapped in a difficult situation.

Negative feelings assertion

In many cultures and situations it is much easier for people to tell others what they 'think' about something rather than what they 'feel'. Human beings are not robots, however, and feelings are important. It would be unrealistic to think that feelings were left at home in a box marked 'Personal'. At work it is often the case that feelings are shown reluctantly or as a last resort. While no one wants to be overcome all the time by feelings when at work, people have to find a way to say what they feel before they erupt, become angry and lose control. Negative feelings assertion is used to tell someone what is happening and how you feel in a constructive way. It is very useful for people who tend to be either aggressive or passive. Two examples of negative feelings assertion are given below.

'When you shout and lose your temper with me it becomes hard to listen to your message. I feel upset when you do it, so I'd like to take it more quietly.'

'Each time you arrive at the meeting unprepared it means we have to recap for your benefit only. I feel irritated about this. In future I would like you to prepare in advance.'

Broken record

Children are experts in the use of the broken record technique. Sometimes people pay very little attention to what you have to say as they are 'wrapped up' in their own concerns. This technique makes sure that your message gets through without nagging, whinging or whining. You simply keep on repeating the same message until it can no longer be ignored or dismissed. For example:

'I'm afraid we will not be able to take your child until the 15th. I realise this may cause you problems but we will not have a space before the 15th. However, I can promise that we will take your son from the 15th for as many sessions as you require.'

Saying no

Saying no can be tremendously difficult for some people, for many different reasons. Some people just like to please others and feel that 'No' would be an unwelcome response. Others are afraid of an aggressive reaction a 'No' might provoke. On the other hand, some people are just unthinking or unrealistic about what they are able to deliver. Conversely, some people's natural reaction is to say 'No'. It is interesting that one of the first words many children learn to say is 'No'. They may enjoy saying 'No' so much that sometimes they say it when they mean 'Yes'! If your first reaction is to say 'No', then it is important for you to think about why you do so.

If 'No' is the appropriate response to a request, then you should find a way to say it as directly as possible, without making excuses and beating about the bush, or giving long-winded explanations. The key to an assertive 'No' is to remember that you have the right to say it without guilt. Saying no firmly and reasonably is quite acceptable to most people, and much better that letting them down later. It can be helpful to think about the kinds of things you find it hard to say no to, and also what kind of people are hard to refuse. Is it doing favours for friends? Turning down staff who need overtime? Saying no becomes easier with practice and saves a lot of worry and lack of self-respect later. It is worth trying!

Fogging

When people behave aggressively they tend to expect disagreement and charge ahead, not listening. Fogging is used to slow them down by an unexpected response. It is a way of side-stepping their issue and still retain your point of view and integrity by agreeing with some part of what they say. It is called fogging because the effect is very like suddenly being faced with a bank of fog when the way appeared to be clear. Fog is not solid but is hard to get through – it is necessary to hold back a bit and pay attention to what is being encountered.

Saying 'Yes' is one way of fogging, as the word can take an aggressive person by surprise and help to calm matters. For example, if someone said 'Well, that was a pretty stupid way to behave in a meeting!' and you wanted to 'fog' you might say 'Yes. I can see that you think it was a pretty stupid way to behave.' You are not agreeing that you behaved stupidly – only that you can see that the person thinks it.

Fogging gives you time to get things on a more even keel and can calm a potentially explosive situation.

Body language

It has become quite fashionable in recent years to talk about body language as though it were a recently discovered way of communicating. A number of books have been written about this subject by experts who have studied and analysed what each gesture and action means, but children soon manage to learn to tell whether someone is angry or approachable, happy or sad.

Body language is an important aspect of assertiveness. It is no good if you have the right words and then contradict them with your posture and demeanour. Table 6.7 lists the differences between assertive, aggressive and passive body language, and these are illustrated in Figure 6.13.

Assertive   Aggressive   Passive and submissive

Figure 6.13. Types of body language

Table 6.7. Assertive, aggressive and passive body language

	Assertive	Aggressive	Passive
Posture	Upright/straight	Leaning forward	Shrinking
Head	Firm but not rigid	Chin jutting out	Head down
Eyes	Direct, not staring; good and regular eye contact	Strongly focused, staring; often piercing or glaring eye contact	Glancing away; little eye contact
Face	Expression fits the words	Set/firm	Smiling even when upset
Voice	Well modulated to fit content	Loud/emphatic	Hesitant/soft, trailing off at the ends of words/sentences
Arms/hands	Relaxed/moving easily	Controlled/extreme; sharp gestures, fingers pointing	Aimless/still
Movement/ walking	Measured pace suitable to action	Slow and heavy or fast, deliberate, hard	Slow and hesitant or fast and jerky

Dealing with conflict

There will be times when, as a manager, you have to deal with conflict. This can be:

- within the team
- between individuals
- between the manager and the team
- with someone outside the setting.

Conflict is an inevitable part of human interaction and cannot be avoided entirely. Conflict can also be healthy in open and honest relationships, and the outcome can be both creative and rejuvenating. It is possible to cope with conflict, but not all conflict is resolvable. If staff become too embroiled in inner conflict and hurtful gossip, it may be worth taking full charge of the situation, even at the risk of becoming unpopular.

There are different responses to conflict:

- avoidance – denial, working round the problem, not being explicit about issues
- diffusion – smoothing things over, dealing with minor aspects only
- facing it – admit conflict exists, raise it explicitly and address it as an issue.

Good practice checklist
Resolving differences

- Be open about what you want and need.
- Establish what the team members want and need.
- Negotiate – search for some kind of common ground. This may well be both parties wanting what is best for the setting.
- Mediate – listen to both cases to facilitate communication and encourage understanding.
- Produce ideas to address differences.
- Build on and develop suggestions.
- Turn conflict into cooperation by giving constructive objective feedback.
- Summarise to check that both sides understand and agree.

What do you do if it all goes wrong?

- Take time out – arrange a date when the matter can be discussed again.
- Reflect on what happened before, during and after. What were the triggers? Is there a history of conflict? What were the consequences of the conflict?
- Review the way the staff communicated – was it assertive, aggressive or passive/submissive?
- Decide how you will move forward – plan how to address the original and any further conflict.

There are also certain negotiation skills which can be utilised to open communication after conflict has become entrenched. These are shown in Figure 6.14.

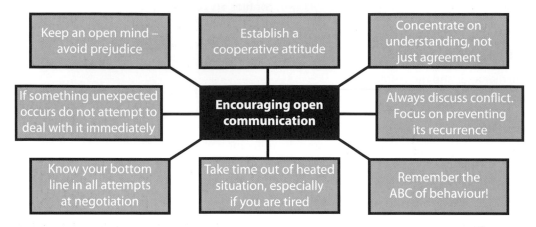

Figure 6.14. Negotiation skills can open communication to resolve conflict

6.7 The manager as a motivator

What can a manager do to meet the differing motivational needs of the staff? It would seem that managers who want to motivate their staff need to get to know them; they need to have an interest in each team member as a person. In order to do this the manager must find out what interests them and get to know their strengths and weaknesses. Good managers will ensure that all team members have the opportunity to utilise their strengths and play to them. They will also ensure that weaknesses are addressed through staff training and appraisal.

The team members will want to increase their skills, so they will need to be provided with training opportunities and challenges in their job. This will entail some delegation of responsibility on the part of the manager, which many find quite difficult, as there is an element of risk involved.

Moving boxes

Case Study

Jack is a very busy manager of a large nursery. A large delivery of resources arrives at the reception area and the maintenance person is off-site. The children are beginning to arrive for the afternoon session and the boxes are in the way and causing a health and safety risk. Jack is aware that the staff are not required to lift heavy items, but is also aware that some of the team have just finished a meeting along the corridor. He goes into the meeting room and finds four of his staff chatting. At this point he does find it a little difficult to cover his feelings (after all, they are standing chatting and there is bedlam ensuing in the reception area). He interrupts their chat and says quite loudly: 'There are loads of boxes cluttering up the reception area and the children are arriving. Please come and give me a hand to move them… Now.' The team members respond by muttering a variety of excuses and reasons for not going down to reception, keeping their backs to the manager: 'Oh, I need to get back' and 'I can't – I have a bad back.' Jack was cross but left the room and went along and piled the boxes as safely as possible until the maintenance person got back.

- How do you think Jack handled the situation?
- Would you say the team had respect for Jack?
- Could you hazard a guess as to some of the underlying problems within this team?
- What do you think Jack should have done?

Look at the case study 'Moving boxes'. You might have thought that this response was indicative of other problems within the team. The way a team is treated in these sorts of situations demonstrates the manager's ability to work as part of the team to make them feel included. If Jack had taken this opportunity to ask the staff to help him in this particular emergency and appeal to them as colleagues, he might have met with a more positive response. For example, Jack could have said:

'I apologise for interrupting. I know you are all just finishing your meeting… Joan, don't you come because I know you have a bad back, but would everyone else mind giving me a hand to move these boxes out of the children's way? I wouldn't ask ordinarily but the maintenance man is on his break.'

This manager's attitude to the staff could be seen as demotivating. He has given the staff cause to complain about his indecisive behaviour and has not used the opportunity to involve the staff enthusiastically. If the team are unwilling to take part in the smooth running of the setting they are less likely to be enthusiastic about larger challenges. The manager who is positive and responsive motivates and enthuses staff. The case study demonstrates an example of a small opportunity to motivate which was lost and instead the manager only demonstrated his intolerance.

Giving praise and encouragement is vital for motivating staff and does not need to wait until a team member is having an appraisal. This helps to boost self-esteem and show staff that you value their contribution. It is also motivating for staff to:

- involve them as much as possible in the decision-making
- seek their views
- consult them on potential changes.

Sharing information about how things are going guarantees staff involvement and encourages them to take ownership of their setting.

Figure 6.15 summarises the things that motivate staff teams. In contrast, what will reduce their motivation is a manager who allows them little or no control over their own jobs. Similarly, supervision that is too close can cause team members to feel stifled and patronised. Allowing team members to take some of the control is not only motivating for the staff, but also beneficial for the effective running of the setting.

Figure 6.15. Ways in which to motivate staff

6.8 The role of the manager in managing change

Change is essential in providing good-quality care and education, and is necessary to help the growth and development of a setting. It is important that we respond effectively to changing needs and apply new-found knowledge to our practice. Although we all experience change in our everyday lives, the process of change can make people feel uncomfortable and threatened. Many early years staff may feel that some changes are a threat to their professional practice, and will therefore resist change passionately. Change is often resisted by team members and so requires good planning and implementation.

Rodd describes leaders as 'orchestras of change' (2007, p. 182) and has found that leadership for change requires:

- vision and inspiration
- careful planning
- decision-making skills
- effective communication
- confident conflict management
- sensitive handling of people.

Change is inevitable and necessary. Change can be planned for, but because it is resisted by many people can cause stress and tension. Rodd also tells us that change is not to be made for change's sake, and that the most effective changes are so because they are essentially being made for good and valid reasons and to develop and evolve the team's vision. Rodd (2007, p. 185) places types of change into six categories (Table 6.8).

Table 6.8. Rodd's six categories of change

1 Incremental change	Small modifications introduced on a day to day basis – small changes to which little attention is given
2 Induced change	A continuous decision on an aspect of the provision to do with people, processes or structures – this can be done to meet a crisis or be an innovative idea to improve quality for example
3 Routine changes	Common, everyday changes on a daily basis in response to a problem situation to improve quality or meet the needs of children and their families
4 Crisis change	A direct response to any unexpected occurence in the setting – often an authoritarian decision made by the manager to precipitate a crisis
5 Innovative change	A result of creative problem solving. This is more likely to take place in a strong well motivated team where the team are seeking to find more effective ways to improve the service
6 Transformational change	Occurs at crisis point to radically alter the present provision – this could be actioned after a poor Ofsted inspection for example

Managers need to recognise that change can have quite serious effects on team members, and appreciate that a well-planned execution of change can be successful. Every team member's view of the change needs to be recognised by the manager and any conflict needs to be handled tactfully to manage stress levels among the team. Rodd (2007, p. 189) also tells us that the common sources of resistance are:

- fear about people's personal future
- ideological factors – values and belief systems
- individual personalities – negative or pessimistic people with low self-esteem
- lack of trust in the leader
- self-interest – what is in it for me?
- lack of understanding
- lack of ownership – imposed from outside
- excessive change – too much in a short period of time.

An effective manager will deal with this resistance in the following ways:

- encourage staff to express their concerns early on
- help staff to understand the rationale behind the change
- encourage staff to participate and be involved – this can act as a motivator and reduce fears and stress
- use listening skills and conflict management to strengthen the level of trust in the group – spend time doing this to support staff to adjust
- offer incentives and benefits to the team members who are resisting
- convey their confidence in the team's ability to manage the change process
- prepare well – support early to make change easier in the later stages
- stabilise the situation with ongoing support and evaluation

- provide regular feedback on success
- keep staff informed
- encourage team members to support each other
- encourage staff to feel in control and take ownership of the change.

The resistant team

I have been a manager for many years. I have always considered myself to be a fairly good manager who listened and responded to my team. I do not have a problem with leading the team and usually find they are open to working with me to implement necessary changes.

Just recently after an Ofsted inspection we were actioned to make changes to the curriculum. These changes had to be made quickly, so I held a meeting and discussed the actions and set about changing the curriculum planning, which meant changing individual work plans for the team members. For the first time in my career as a manager I encountered real resistance. Staff seemed to be deliberately difficult, and at times they were almost hysterical when I told them about the changes to their working practices.

- Reading 'between the lines', what do you think the manager could have done differently in managing the change?
- Where were there opportunities to consult and negotiate?
- What were the obstacles for the manager?

Having met with such resistance last year I learned from the situation and asked the team to meet early this year to plan ahead. This meeting went well – the team were pleased to have an input and I gave each team leader responsibility for their own area. I also invited another supervisor from another setting, who shared his experiences of a similar change. Within the week the team all came to me with new plans ready to go; they also shared ideas they wanted to implement to make the changes smoother.

- What had the manager learned from this process?
- Why did the staff react differently this time round?
- Why did the team come up with ideas to make the changes more effective when they had resisted it the year before?

Conclusion

Managers will need to work tirelessly to offer ongoing support to the team to facilitate change. They will need to diagnose early on skills and preparation needed, and support staff to adapt by using appropriate communication skills. To make a change is to learn something new. Managers need to note that not all changes are successful, but commitment to the change is essential if they are to be effective managers.

Check your understanding

1   Outline the main factors that influence the culture of an organisation.

2   How to team building exercises foster the development of a cohesive team?

3   What are the main advantages of working in a team in an early years setting?

4   Identify a list of possible leadership roles within settings.

5   What can a manager do to ensure commitment from team members?

6   What are the three main purposes of a job description?

7   What is meant by a 'person specification'?

8   Outline the most effective way to conduct and organise an interview.

9   What is considered good practice in retaining staff?

10 Outline the legal obligations of employing staff.

11 Describe the facets of good communication and team working.

12 What is the role of the manager in managing change?

References and further reading

Bunch, M. (1999) *Creating Confidence. How to Develop Your Personal Power and Presence*. London: Kogan Page.

Cava, R. (1991) *Dealing with Difficult People*. London: Judy Piatkus.

Department for Education and Skills (2003) *Every Child Matters*. London: DfES. Available at www.dfes.gov.uk.

Dickson, A. (1982) *A Woman in Your Own Right. Assertiveness and You*. London: Quartet Books.

Fullan, M. (2001) *Leading in a Culture of Change*. San Francisco, CA: Jossey-Bass.

Handy, C. and Aitken, R. (1986) *Understanding Schools as Organisations*. London: Penguin.

Honey, P. (1997) *Improve Your People Skills* (2nd edn). London: Institute of Personnel and Development.

Lyrus, V (1998) *Management in the Early Years*. London: Hodder and Stoughton.

Makins, V. (1997) *Not Just a Nursery. Multi-agency Early Years Centres in Action*. London: National Children's Bureau.

Moyles, J. (2007) *Effective Leadership and Management in the Early Years*. Maidenhead: Open University Press.

Nicolson, P. and Bayne, R. (1990) *Applied Psychology for Social Workers* (2nd edn). London: Macmillan.

Penn, H. (ed.) (2000) *Early Childhood Services. Theory, Policy and Practice*. Buckingham: Open University Press.

Petrie, P. (1989) *Communicating with Children and Adults. Interpersonal Skills for Those Working with Babies and Children*. London: Edward Arnold.

Pre-School Learning Alliance (2005) *Report on the Early Years Workforce*

Recruitment and Retention of Disabled People – A Good Practice Guide. www.surestart.gov.uk

Rodd, J. (1998) *Leadership in Early Childhood* (2nd edn). Buckingham: Open University Press.

Rodd, J. (2007) *Leadership in Early Childhood* (3rd edn). Maidenhead: Open University Press.

Siraj-Blatchford, I. and Manni, L. (2007) *Effective Leadership in the Early Years Sector: The ELEYS Study*. London: Institute of Education.

Smith, A. and Langston, A. (1999) *Managing Staff in Early Years Settings*. London: Routledge.

Tuckman, B.W. and Jensen, M.A.C. (1977) '*Stages of small group development revisited*'. Group and Organization Studies, 2: 419–27.

Useful websites

Ofsted: www.ofsted.gov.uk

ACAS: www.acas.org.uk

Belbin – work of Dr R. Meredith Belbin: www.belbin.com

Council for Awards in Children's Care and Education: www.cache.org.uk

CWDC (Children's Workforce Development Council): www.cwdcouncil.org.uk

Department of Trade and Industry: www.dti.gov.uk

Early Years Educator (EYE) magazine: www.earlyyearseducator.co.uk

Early Years Foundation Stage: www.standards.dcsf.gov.uk

Early Years National Training Organisation: www.early-years-nto.org.uk

HM Revenue and Customs: www.hmrc.gov.uk

National Day Nurseries Association: www.ndna.org.uk

Nationwide Payroll Company – provides payroll services for pre-school establishments, etc.: www.nationwidepayroll.co.uk

Nursery World magazine: www.nurseryworld.com

Pensions Service: www.thepensionservice.gov.uk

Pre-School Learning Alliance: www.pre-school.org.uk

Sure Start Business Success for Childcare: www.surestart.gov.uk/ support4business

UK NARIC – national agency providing information and expert opinion on vocational, academic and professional skills and qualifications: www.naric.org.uk

Sure Start: www.surestart.gov.uk

7 Management and Development of Self

In the current climate of change, professionals working with children, young people and their families are required to be evaluative and reflective thinkers with the ability to review their performance, research practice and make appropriate changes in order to improve and broaden their skills. Working towards good-quality practice involves developing excellent practitioners and teams. An effective manager will need to ensure that each member of the team is given opportunity to access the necessary tools to become more effective and reflective in their practice. In this chapter we will explore the importance of self-development and reflection for the individual practitioner, and consider ways in which the manager can support staff with the correct tools to manage continuous improvement and quality through staff training. This is a gradual process which may be unfamiliar to practitioners, particularly if they undertook their training some time ago.

We will look closely at the appraisal system as a means for practitioners to improve their individual performance. The use of appraisals is a key aspect of continuing professional development and improvement of the quality of the provision for children. The chapter will provide information for managers on how to encourage employees to build on their successes by considering their strengths and weaknesses and recognising their training needs. The advantages of appraisals to individuals and to settings are also discussed.

This chapter covers the following areas

7.1 The importance of self-development

The world of childcare and education does not stand still. It is continuously developing and evolving with the prime purpose of improving the quality of the provision for all children. As we have seen, within the past few years alone the Children's Workforce has seen the implementation of the *Every Child Matters* programme, the Early Years Foundation Stage, the introduction of the Welsh Foundation Phase, the Children and Young People's Plan and the Children's Workforce Development Council, to name just a few. For the manager and staff of an early years setting it can be challenging to keep up with all the changes.

However, it is imperative to do so for a number of reasons. Firstly, the workforce must continually assess and reflect on these changes and the effect they will have on their work practice. This is particularly important if the changes are likely to impact on the registration and inspection of services. Staff and managers must also allocate time to update their knowledge in order to improve the quality of the provision they offer children and build a cycle of continuous reflection and improvement.

The National Standards for Leaders of Sure Start children's centres stress the relationship between continuous professional development and the sustained improvement of services for children. Managers need to be aware of this and foster a working environment that encourages staff to question, reflect and develop their practice. They can achieve this by establishing a common goal within the team to improve provision for the children. The manager must understand the importance of continuous training and staff development and promote training programmes that meet the learning needs of all those involved. The staff will need to be encouraged to take personal responsibility for their own learning and development.

Self-development also enables staff to update their skills and remain marketable in the workplace, and may determine their future career direction. One of the key reasons for childcare practitioners to undertake self-development is to ensure that they are able to stimulate and enthuse the children they work with. Children will love to learn if they are surrounded by adults who also love to learn and who work in a context that stimulates and encourages learning. Children should be supported by adults who are curious to understand their own practice better and who are determined to continually improve.

Points for reflective practice

Research one of the current initiatives in childcare and education. It may be a government initiative or an influential piece of research.

- Consider the main features of this initiative.

- What are the implications for your practice?

- What are the implications for your setting?

- How will you ensure that all staff members have the opportunity to learn about and reflect upon this new initiative?

A new team member working with the manager.

7.2 Review of personal strengths and celebration of practice

When a new team member begins employment the manager will have ensured that they are appropriately qualified and taken up references to ensure suitability. The new team member will also have had an enhanced Criminal Records Bureau (CRB) check before being employed. This initial investigation is just the beginning of the manager getting to know the practitioner and the beginning of their developmental journey.

It is also essential for managers to have their own opportunity to develop in this way. We need then to consider the ways in which we can review the personal strengths of all team members. Recognition of personal strengths is a good starting point when looking at the overall characteristics and attributes of a practitioner and at ways to help them develop their practice. This recognition will:

- build the self-esteem of the practitioner
- define ways in which their strengths can be applied to the working environment
- support the practitioner's ability to contribute to wider team working
- help to identify areas for improvement.

Key Term

Criminal Records Bureau (CRB) – the agency that checks police records and identifies people who may be unsuitable to work with children or other vulnerable members of society.

Think it over

Make a list of your strengths in terms of:

- organisational skills
- creativity
- communication
- particular skills (for example IT skills).

When you have made your list, reflect on ways in which your particular strengths could be used in the following settings:

- sessional day care
- nursery classroom
- as an assistant manager in a private day care setting
- women's refuge.

We will look later at a personal development plan which asks the practitioner to review their personal strengths and successes in order to improve and develop their practice. Practitioners need to be aware of their successes in order to move forward and become reflective practitioners as part of teams working towards the same goals. The manager can support the practitioner to decide:

- what sort of practitioner they want to be
- how they can develop themselves as practitioners to achieve their aspirations.

When a practitioner is new to the setting this can be difficult to know right away and the manager will need to give them time to settle in, bond with team members and find their place as part of the team. As part of ongoing supervision or mentoring the manager can then support the practitioner to identify their strengths and any areas for development.

The ELEYS Study (Siraj-Blatchford and Manni, 2007) looked at the methodology of effective leadership and stated that effective practices needed to be identified in the setting for 'ensuring shared understandings, meanings and goals' (p. 14). The study found that staff members of effective settings were encouraged to attend staff development sessions and were provided direction by their leader or manager to share the same vision of what they wanted their service to look like. The DfES (2005) draft paper 'Championing Children: A shared set of skills, knowledge and behaviours of those leading and managing integrated children's services' highlighted the provision of direction as a key aspect of leadership. The manager therefore needs to ensure that they identify the strengths of the team members and give them clear and purposeful direction to work towards a common vision. The DfES document (cited in Siraj-Blatchford, 2007) states that the shared vision should be translated into specific plans and that managers should:

- make use of a collective knowledge base and common purpose
- support others to talk knowledgeably about issues concerning their work and area of expertise
- work for equality
- develop systems to support a high level of responsiveness for the team.

Effective managers must understand the learning needs of their staff and recognise that new and inexperienced staff will need more support to identify their strengths, needs and direction.

Celebrating individual and team success

An effective and forward-thinking team will find that success is celebrated. The manager should provide opportunities for the team as a whole and for individual members to do this. This can be achieved in a variety of ways.

- In everyday situations: meeting in the corridor; congratulating a team member for a particular thing (e.g. a member of the team received an order of books and unpacked them, catalogued and displayed them).

- At a team meeting: congratulate the team for a particular piece of work and discuss the strengths of the work.

- Displays: a display is a good way of celebrating a success so that everyone can be involved and informed.

- Newsletters and information: given to parents, carers or other stakeholders; information about an event which has been particularly successful for the setting.

If practitioners work in settings where they feel valued because their strengths and skills have been put to good use, and because success is celebrated, they will be more likely to be committed and loyal to the setting's vision. Curran (1989) discusses the stages of team development and in 'collaborating as an effective team' states that 'the team rewards its performance by articulating a sense of pride concerning its achievements' (cited in Rodd, 2007, p. 158).

Points for reflective practice

Consider the ways in which your team:

- celebrates team success

- congratulates members for individual success.

Reflect on how you are involved in the above – are there ways in which your setting could improve?

7.3 Tools for self-development

Between 2007 and 2010 it is planned that £117 million will be invested in the early years workforce. Some of this money will be used to provide cover so that early years workers can take part in continuing professional development (CPD). The Graduate Leader Fund will also be boosted so that every full-day care setting will be led by a graduate by 2015, with two graduates per setting in disadvantaged areas.

For early years workers and managers it can be seen as an exciting time to be working in the children's workforce, as career progression and upskilling is pushed firmly to the forefront. One means of improving career opportunities is to undertake self-development and work towards improving personal skills and knowledge.

Personal Development Plans

In order to be successful when undertaking self-development it helps to be aware of personal strengths and areas for improvement and to understand the tools which are available to help you. You can start by assessing your current skills and interests and your areas of knowledge and experience. This will help you ascertain any gaps in your knowledge, and can be done by discussions with:

- current and previous work colleagues
- the parents of the children you work with
- your current line manager
- the people you currently manage.

The information you gain from these discussions can be logged and formed into a personal development plan (PDP) that identifies your learning needs and goals.

Key Term

Continuing professional development (CPD) – a process of self-improvement based on reflection, in which you set your own objectives, evaluate your progress, gain useful experience and assess any practical benefits.

Table 7.1. Example of a personal development plan

Date:			
Summary of performance over past 12 months.			
Strengths			
Areas that require development			
Objectives	Measurement	Delivery date	Performance summary

When you have identified the areas you wish to develop you will need to decide the action you are going to take. Self-development can take place through:

- training courses
- developing reflective practice (see section 7.4)
- maintaining a professional learning log or diary to help you analyse what you are learning from everyday work experiences

- working with a mentor to provide support and direction
- reading professional journals and magazines
- involvement in professional organisations.

Self-development may involve formal structured learning.

Effective learning

Whichever method of self-development you choose you will be involved in a learning experience that will move you to a deeper level of understanding. In order for learning to be effective you should:

- expose yourself to new ideas, experiences and challenges
- build on your previous experiences
- practise the new skills you learn
- process and assimilate new information
- make time for professional discussion with colleagues.

Peter Honey and Alan Mumford (2000) conclude that we learn either through formal structured activities such as lectures and books, or informally through our experiences. In their view learning from experience is the most important of all life skills and gives the opportunity to acquire knowledge and skills, to improve practice and adapt to change. However, this so-called experiential learning must be a structured and conscious process in order to be most effective. Honey and Mumford maintain that a conscious learner from experience will be:

- clear about what they have learned
- able to communicate their learning to other people
- able to help others improve
- comfortable with change
- able to learn from successes and mistakes

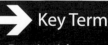

Key Term

Experiential learning – an individual learns through direct, first-hand experiences and reflects and acts on those experiences for improvement and self-development.

- able to transfer learning from one situation to another
- more purposeful in extracting learning from all experiences, even mundane routines.

Learning styles and preferences

People learn in different ways, and Honey and Mumford have identified four different learning styles: activist, reflector, theorist and pragmatist. They suggest learning activities to support each style. For a small cost you can complete a questionnaire on their website to discover your individual learning style preferences (see Useful websites).

Think it over

Consider how you learn.

- Do you learn best when you are sitting in a classroom listening to a tutor, or do you prefer to learn from practical experience?
- Think about an occasion when you had to learn a new skill, e.g. driving a car or using a computer. What did you find easy? What did you find challenging?
- Observe other people involved in learning a new skill. This could be on a television programme. What strategies do they use? What difficulties do they face?
- Consider barriers to self-development and how you will overcome these.

Honey and Mumford also identify four key stages in the learning cycle (Figure 7.1).

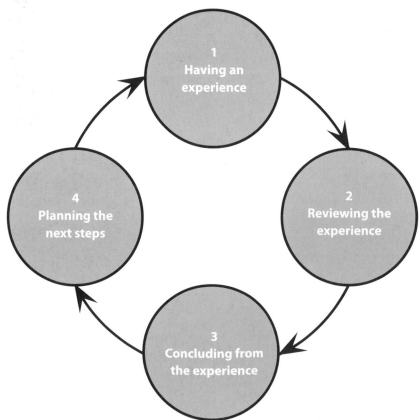

Figure 7.1. Honey and Mumford Learning Cycle

If you follow this idea it seems logical to use a learning log or diary as a tool in your self-development journey. The log could take the form of a simple record of experiences and reflections generated by the experience. A reflective log should not be onerous for the writer, but to be meaningful you must be disciplined in your approach, focused on improvement. You will also need to develop the skills of reflection. Writing down your thoughts will help you to clarify your thinking and focus on your development and progress. You may see a pattern emerging that will help you to concentrate on how you can improve your practice. A learning log can also provide a basis for discussion with colleagues and staff members.

7.4 The reflective practitioner

Reflective practice

Reflective practice can be seen as the process of making practice more effective through deeper thinking, consideration, action research and further learning. The way in which you do this can be individual. You will need to evidence your reflective practice, however, so that it is part of your review of practice and your CPD. To do this you can use a variety of recording methods:

- minutes of meetings – informal and formal
- reflective logs or diaries
- photographic evidence of action research
- findings from research
- note taking from observation and thoughts or ideas
- record of ongoing review and evaluation of activities
- records of reflective conversations.

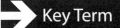 **Key Term**

Reflective practice – thinking about your role and practice with the aim of evaluating it and making any changes to improve its quality.

What is a reflective practitioner?

Reflection is the way in which we become better at something. A reflective practitioner will:

- ask reflective questions
- be able to identify effective practice and evolve that practice
- research new ways of working
- understand themselves
- take part in reflective conversations
- refine and modify current practice
- learn about new ways of working
- focus on concerns and consider various alternatives
- access a greater range of knowledge and skills

- connect research to practice

- reflect on the past

- examine attitudes and preconceptions

- become involved in active research

- look back at what happened

- reconstruct what happened.

Moyles (2007, p. 14) says that 'a great deal of reflection is involved in the process of self evaluation'. Moyles also cites (Ghaye and Ghaye, 1998; Gold and Evans, 1998; Yorke-barr, 2001): 'Reflecting on one's role and on policy and practice is the same as reflecting on anything else in our lives: it is about thinking deeply and contemplating how things "are". In reflecting in depth, people also analyse whether everything is as it should be or whether changes are needed' (ibid.). They also go on to say that active reflection has the 'potential to empower individuals'. A reflective practitioner will become more effective, knowledgeable and experienced through the process of reflection.

We need to acknowledge that reflective thinking is not an easy process and has to be worked at, involving colleagues in discussion to support the process. So, what do we need to do to become reflective? (See Table 7.2.)

Table 7.2. Opportunities for the reflective process

Have time to reflect and analyse	It is important that the practitioner is given time and space for reflection – this will not be easy in a busy setting, but nonetheless needs to be valued as essential.
Access to CPD (continuing professional development)	All practitioners will have good opportunity to reflect when taking part in CPD – it will give them new ideas and also offer them time to examine their own practice and ask questions.
Identify own understanding	Practitioners will need time to focus on areas of strength and areas that need improvement. They can then look at ways in which they can extend and enhance their skills and build on their professional competence.
Observe the practice of others	Even if this is within their own setting the opportunity to observe others is invaluable. It will open up many questions for the practitioner and heighten awareness in the setting.
Have opportunities to find out about things	If a practitioner wants to know more about something or explore an idea as part of their reflective thinking, time needs to be given to this part of the process.
Have support of manager or supervisor	Without the support of the manager or supervisor reflective practice can easily become stifled and practice become stale.
Observe children	Observing children is an essential learning tool for the reflective practitioner – so much is to be learned if this is well documented, and every opportunity to observe a child can be used in researching and analysing practice.
Take part in action research in setting	As part of the reflective process all practitioners should use action research to pilot new ideas and look for more effective ways of working.

Within the StEPS project (Moyles and Adams, 2001) it was shown that the benefit of reflection for managers and leaders was 'an enhanced sense of self-efficacy in which practitioners began to think differently about themselves'.

Think it over

Are you a reflective practitioner? If you think you are, can you list ways in which you are reflective and how you evidence that?

Experiential learning

Experiential learning is seen by some as integral to reflective practice. A spiral of 'steps' can be used to demonstrate the way in which to examine ideas simply (Figure 7.2).

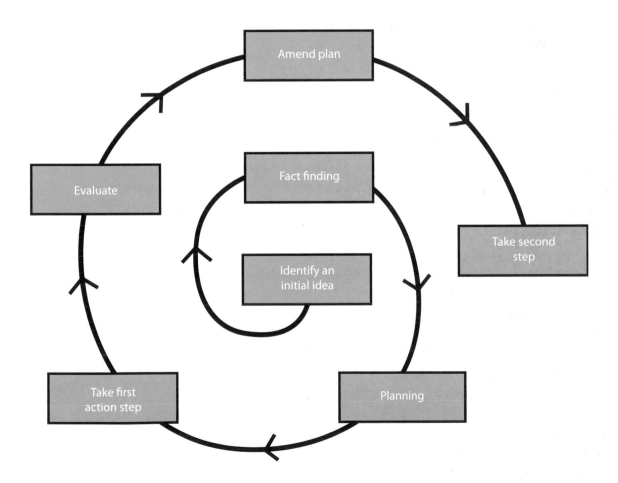

Figure 7.2. The spiral of steps in experiential learning

As this process is spiral, there will be opportunites to reflect more than once in order to really improve practice. Kolb and Fry (1975), also well known for contributions to thinking around organisational behaviour, created a model of four elements of experiential learning (Figure 7.3).

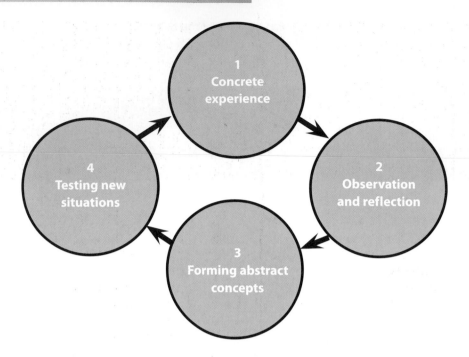

Figure 7.3. The four elements of experiential learning

The concrete experience (1) is where the practitioner will carry out an action and see the effect of the action. At stage 2 the practitioner will formulate an understanding of the action and decide if it would have different outcomes, for example with a different group of children. At stage 3 the practitioner makes a decision on the general principle – does this action always have this effect? Kolb then suggests that stage 4 will be the point at which the practitioner will use this knowledge to test new situations and return to carrying out the action – stage 1. Jarvis (1995), building on the work of Kolb and Fry, suggested that this model did not give room for the reflective process and said that the process could be more complex, giving opportunity for experimentation and reasoning and reflection. He said that reflective learning consisted of:

- contemplation: the person considers and then makes an intellectual decision
- reflective practice: reflects on the action having taken part in it
- experiential learning: the way in which pragmatic knowledge may be learned.

Find it out

Look at the list at the beginning of this section under 'What is a reflective practitioner?'. How does this list link to the theories of Lewin, Kolb, Fry and Jarvis (Figures 7.2 and 7.3)? Do these models work in practice or is reflective practice more complex than these models? You might also want to link this to the Honey and Mumford model looked at on page 214.

7.5 Managing the continuous improvement and quality of the provision through staff development and training

Provision for professional development is a key factor in providing quality in early years settings. However, the training itself needs to be of a high standard and delivered by knowledgeable and suitably qualified people. The Children's Workforce Development Council (CWDC) is the Sector Skills Council responsible for the development of qualifications designed to raise the skills levels of the childcare workforce. Any awarding body that develops a qualification for the children's workforce must first gain the support of CWDC before the qualification can be accredited. Early years managers can now access the CWDC's database of suitable qualifications for preparing a knowledgeable and skilled workforce in order to check the validity of qualifications held by prospective employees and to see progression routes for established staff.

The Common Core of Skills and Knowledge for the Children's Workforce

All qualifications currently being developed are expected to contain a Common Core of Skills and Knowledge for the Children's Workforce. These skills and knowledge are described under the headings:

- Effective communication and engagement with children, young people and families
- Child and young person development
- Safeguarding and promoting the welfare of the child
- Supporting transitions
- Multi-agency working
- Sharing information.

Over time it is expected that everyone working with children, young people and families will be able to demonstrate a basic level of competence in these six areas of the Common Core, which it is hoped will contribute to a rise in the quality of provision offered to young children.

Every local authority has a training and development department as part of its children's services team. Funding is available to assist staff members with professional development. This is generally channelled through the local authority, which will arrange courses, conferences and networking meetings either free of charge or at a subsidised fee for practitioners. Information about courses can be accessed through the local authority website.

As part of the Children's Workforce Strategy the government launched the Transformation Fund in 2006 to support the national development of the children's workforce. The aim was to support the development of the workforce without compromising the affordability of childcare, and from 2006 to 2008 £250 million has been available to provide training routes towards a new graduate-level status for early years professionals. It is the intention to ensure that all full-day childcare settings employ a graduate with Early Years Professional (EYP) status by 2015. The intention of the fund was also to invest in promoting the skills and qualifications of staff employed in private, voluntary and independent (PVI) childcare settings, in particular by increasing the numbers achieving a Level 3 qualification.

Early Years Professionals (EYPs) will work in a range of settings, lead practice and be central to delivering a high-quality service to children and their parents. The Children's Workforce Development Council states that EYPS has been developed in response to research that identifies staff qualifications as one of the key indicators of the quality of childcare in a setting. EYPs will therefore support the well-being, learning and development of all children. There are four different pathways to achieving the Early Years Professional Status to meet a variety of needs and these can be researched through the CWDC website. Regardless of which pathway is used all candidates will go through the same assessment process. This process includes:

- a one-day review of skills to provide feedback to the candidates;

- five written assessment tasks based on experiences of early years practice;

- a one-day assessment visit in an early years setting, including a tour of the setting, a review of the written tasks, an interview with the candidate and interview with others who know the candidate's work.

Since 2008 the Graduate Leader Fund (GLF) has replaced some aspects of the Transformation Fund, and represents the main investment in improving the quality of the early years workforce. The GLF demonstrates a commitment to the introduction of graduate leadership of early years settings in the PVI sectors. Other funding will be available from the Outcomes, Quality and Inclusion block of the Sure Start, Early Years and Childcare Grant.

The Children's Plan

Published in December 2007 by the Department for Children, Schools and Families, the Children's Plan expects local authorities and Children's Trusts to champion improvements in the lives of children across the five outcomes of the *Every Child Matters* agenda (see also Chapter 8). As part of this the Centre for Excellence and Outcomes (CfEO) in Children and Young People's Services was established and became operational in July 2008. This will focus on coordinating local authorities and providers in the provision of best practice for children and families, one based on dedicated graduate practitioners offering high-quality service to children and their families. The CWDC vision for the early years workforce is clearly laid out on their website.

Qualifications and courses available

The CWDC Early Years and Playwork Qualifications Database will provide up-to-date information on all available courses. This information will also allow:

- Ofsted Child Care Inspectors (CCIs) to judge whether early years and playwork providers meet the national standards relating to staff qualifications

- employers and practitioners to identify which qualifications are suitable for specific job roles within early years and playwork settings

- childcarers who wish to be approved under the Childcare Approval Scheme to determine whether the qualifications and/or training held by the carer meets the requirements.

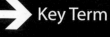

Key Term

Early Years Professional Status (EYPS) – the new status for early years practitioners – a graduate leader in early years.

Key Term

Children's Plan – a government initiative, launched in 2007, that aims to achieve world-class standards in the provision for children in England by 2020.

The awarding bodies that develop qualifications at present include CACHE, City & Guilds and Edexcel. Each awarding body submits qualifications to Ofqual, the Office of the Qualifications and Exams Regulator (formerly the Qualifications Curriculum Authority) for accreditation. The process of accreditation is vigorous to ensure quality, and the submission of a qualification does not guarantee accreditation.

In addition to the awarding bodies mentioned, numerous other training organisations and national charities provide training within the early years sector. These often appear in *Nursery World* magazine. These courses cover all aspects of childcare and education, from first aid to dealing with difficult behaviour. They are an excellent way to increase and update knowledge and re-energise staff members.

Good practice

A team can become a dynamic learning environment with the right sort of encouragement from a manager. As part of good practice all staff, even those who are more recently qualified, should be encouraged to further and update their skills.

As a manager you will need to ensure that valuable staff time is not wasted taking part in training which is not effective. All training, whether internal or external, must be appropriate for the individual learner. Much time is wasted by many establishments sending staff on training courses that they feel are neither relevant nor suited to their individual learning styles. This leads to staff being demotivated, and they may begin to perceive training as a 'chore' rather than something that will help and support them as individuals. If staff have a 'voice' in the selection of their training and are given opportunities to research possible courses, for example, they are more likely to make a commitment to the training and become actively involved. The manager should also understand the nature of the training that is available in order to match courses to appropriate members of staff and ensure training is most effective.

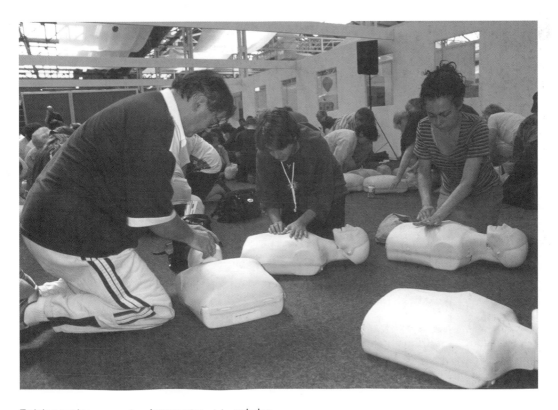

Training can increase and update your team's knowledge.

Much of the training and development of staff in early years settings can take place through work done on-site. For example, more experienced staff can coach or mentor the junior members of the team by sharing their expertise (mentoring is discussed in more detail below; see also Chapter 2). The more experienced members of staff have a wealth of expertise to share, and will find that sharing this knowledge also gives them the opportunity to consolidate what they already know.

In-house training can involve an exchange of skills within the team. For example, having identified their individual strengths, members of staff can be encouraged to form teams based around their interests. Each team then puts together a learning programme to develop skills and exchange ideas.

Key Term

Mentor – trusted and experienced professional person who can provide training, advice and support in an organisation or institution.

Think it over

Look at ways in which you could develop practice with your team by in-house training. How would you evaluate the training and share good practice with other settings?

A team learning plan

It can be useful to develop a team learning plan, which gives members of the team the opportunity to work on things such as:

- a staff newsletter
- a bulletin for parents and carers
- a yearly outing for parents, staff and children.

This can be a way of developing staff skills. It is important that the staff are aware at the outset of both the learning and organisational objectives.

Delegating duties to team members not only builds their self-esteem but can also increase their knowledge and experience. For instance, they may be given the opportunity to register and introduce a new child to the setting, coordinate with the parents and carers and get feedback from the staff on the child's progress. Other opportunities for staff to train and develop their knowledge and skills include the following.

- *External development teams or networks*. This involves networking with other professionals.
- *Project-based work*. There may be an area within the nursery, such as use of information technology, which needs improvement; a team can set about researching the present provision and investigating needs.
- *Specialist training for special needs coordinators*. This may be necessary for them to keep abreast of the latest information and knowledge on the support of children with special needs. This information can then be disseminated to the rest of the team within a staff development session.

Such opportunities will lead to multi-skilling and integrated team working. They also empower staff to make decisions and become involved. The manager will be moving away from the authoritarian image to one of leader, facilitator and coach.

Training and development plan

It is crucial, however, that there is a development plan in place rather than an informal approach, for the following reasons.

- Team members need to know in advance when they will be going on training sessions.

- You will need to arrange cover (allowing for travel and evaluation and dissemination time).

- If there is no set plan for training, some less motivated team members may feel that it is not worth asking to take part in courses – especially if the same (more motivated) people get the opportunities to do training every time.

- If the development plan is in place it can be holistically designed with the staff team to meet the needs of the setting and reinforce good practice.

- A well-organised, well thought-out training plan will challenge staff, offer encouragement and build the expertise of the staff team.

The first step is to identify the needs for training and development. This can be done in a variety of ways:

- through a SWOT analysis of present skills

- by directives from outside agencies, for example Ofsted or curriculum guidance

- from staff themselves (perhaps in appraisal or collectively at team meetings)

- as a result of statutory training requirements such as first aid and food hygiene.

It will then be possible to produce an appropriate plan for the professional development of the staff. This will need to take account of the following factors:

- the budget for training and development

- staff commitment to further training (such commitment can be initiated at interview and induction of new staff)

- staff time (good-quality staff cover will need to be provided, which also has cost implications)

- the availability of suitable facilities for on-site training.

The professional development plan should be linked to the needs of the setting and not to the needs and wants of individual staff, with the proviso noted above that staff should not be sent on courses that they feel are irrelevant.

> ## Key Term
>
> **SWOT/SWOC –** analysis of strengths, weaknesses, opportunities, threats or challenges; a way to organise a thorough analysis of your current position in order to plan for greater effectiveness.

Points for reflective practice

Formulate your own SWOT or SWOC (strengths, weaknesses, opportunities, challenges) analysis of your practice. Discuss it with a colleague, then reflect on ways in which you can plan to make effective changes to your practice.

Table 7.3. Three broad categories of training for the early years setting

Purpose of training	Type of training and possible venue	Benefits to the setting
To meet statutory Ofsted and curriculum requirements	Training to meet statutory requirements such as first aid, food hygiene, NVQ training to train staff to correct level. Also specialist training for the special educational needs coordinator. These types of training could take place on- or off-site and will require training provider input (e.g. St John's Ambulance/Red Cross, local further education college, NVQ assessment centre).	To ensure all staff are trained to required standard. This will benefit the profile of the setting and education of the children.
To develop good practice	This part of the training could cover a plethora of subjects such as anti-discriminatory practice, curriculum development, working with parents, team-building. This could be in-house training or on short courses offered by independent trainers or Early Years Development and Childcare Partnerships.	This will improve overall working practice if disseminated to the team. New strategies for working with children and policy development will be promoted.
Personal and professional development of individual team members	Individual members of the team could identify specific areas of professional development, such as further courses of a higher level, which could take place off-site in the voluntary sector or in higher education.	It will reflect in the performance of individual team members if they feel valued by being allowed time to do further training.

The three areas of development shown in Table 7.3 can make up the essential components of an effective plan for training and development. You will need to analyse needs through appraisal and team meetings, and link these to statutory requirements. If the plan is well thought through it will benefit the setting in terms of its smooth running and improved practice, and will ensure that team members feel valued. It is good practice to give staff the opportunity to share knowledge gained through training by disseminating it to other team members, as this is cost-effective and allows staff to take on another role in mentoring and tutoring.

Barriers to further training

The biggest barrier to taking part in training is time, especially for workers with family responsibilities. Many people participate in courses in their own time, so that settings do not have to pay for cover. Some courses are becoming available through online distance learning, which will help people to study outside working hours.

The cost of courses can also be a barrier, particularly in settings that make little or no profit. Early Years Development and Childcare Partnerships offer a solution by providing free or subsidised courses. There are also concessions available on selected courses and for people on a low income; it is worth checking with the provider of the course or training. The Partnerships also offer their own courses for settings and individuals within their area, and these are generally free.

Figure 7.4. Common barriers to participating in further training

Another significant barrier for early years workers can be a lack of confidence. Many people have not been involved in education for themselves since leaving school and are daunted by the prospect of sitting in a classroom again. Others found school an unsatisfactory experience and have deep-seated feelings of low self-esteem. A manager will need to identify these barriers and work with the member of staff to overcome them. Simply acknowledging their existence can be sufficient, as can emotional support and encouragement and providing a mentor.

It is often a good idea to encourage staff to attempt a short course initially so that they can build their confidence with a sympathetic trainer. Many people find that once they start doing courses they enjoy them so much that they continue attending until they have accumulated an impressive number of qualifications. This success will be transferred into their approach to work, and the setting will reap the benefits.

Mentoring

Mentoring is a largely untapped resource for professional development in the early years sector. Every student who takes one of the new Sector Endorsed Foundation Degrees for Early Childhood Practitioners should have a personal mentor. Mentors are not responsible for the teaching of students, but support their learning through regular meetings with them, looking at the assessment work they need to do for their course and verifying their practical skills in the workplace. This role benefits the mentor and the person being mentored, as both can learn from the experience: the mentor has skills and experience to pass on but can also learn from the student's course material (if he or she is doing a qualification) and discuss new ideas. If the mentoring does not work with one pairing, the student should switch to a different mentor, rather than deciding that mentoring itself is unsuccessful.

Evaluation of training and development

After the training or staff development has taken place it is really important that:

- it is evaluated
- information is disseminated (particularly after 'development of good practice' training).

The two may be combined on a single form, such as that shown in Figure 7.5. This type of evaluation provides the team member with the opportunity to feed back first to the manager. If the information would be useful to disseminate to the team, the manager will need to provide time in either a team meeting or an internal staff development session to do this. Alternatively, the manager may feel that it would be useful to copy handouts for other staff to use as a reference. Such forms could also be used in appraisal (see section 7.6) to consider how the individual team member is able to make use of training. As part of a team-building exercise, the results pooled from evaluation forms can be discussed in order to put together future training plans. The evaluation form is only one suggestion for a way in which training can be made to benefit the whole team. Teams themselves are likely to suggest a variety of ways to evaluate training and disseminate information.

	Information for manager to disseminate
Name:... Title of training:... Provider:...	
Please list briefly the key points of the training.	
How do you think the training will be of benefit to you in your role?	
List some aspects which you feel would be useful to disseminate to the rest of the team.	
Were you given any handouts or resources on your training? If so, please list them.	

Figure 7.5. A sample form to evaluate training and record what information the manager needs to disseminate

7.6 Managing the development of staff through appraisal

Appraisal

All contracted staff should receive some sort of appraisal with their line manager. This will vary from setting to setting in terms of time allowed and its exact nature.

When new members of staff start work they are usually given a probation period, during which their employment is still of a temporary nature. They should go through an induction at the setting and possibly be allocated a mentor to guide them through their probationary period (see Chapter 6). When the probation time is up, the line manager will meet with them to discuss their progress and at that point confirm their full employment status. It is at this point that the new employee becomes one of the team, and this will be recorded in a staff file at the setting. After that initial meeting there should then be regular appraisal meetings between the member of staff and line manager.

How often appraisal meetings take place will vary from setting to setting, but there should be at least two a year. These meetings are special because they are:

Key Term

Appraisal – the process by which members of staff are assessed on their performance, plan and monitor progress and discuss future aspirations; can be linked to performance pay.

- confidential
- one to one
- for the purpose of discussing that person's progress only.

The appraisal meeting is not an opportunity to discuss other members of staff, children or resources, unless it has a direct effect on that member of staff's development. Together the member of staff and the line manager will discuss a number of topics (Figure 7.6).

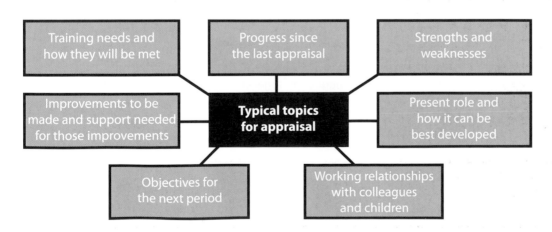

Figure 7.6. Common topics for appraisal

People being appraised should go to the meeting well prepared: this means having objectives and ideas for training in mind. The appraisal meeting is a time set aside for them exclusively and should be an opportunity for them to discuss any personal or professional issues that might have affected their performance. The line manager will note these details on a confidential appraisal form. If something is written on the appraisal form it will need to be actioned by the manager as agreed at the meeting in support of the member of staff. Both people will sign the appraisal form. At the next appraisal meeting the objectives will be reviewed once more. If the member of staff has not met the objectives the latter can be revised, or the line manager may express concerns at this point. It is important that the appraisal scheme is taken seriously, and neither the member of staff nor the line manager should make false promises at this meeting. It is far better that the manager encourages the member of staff to set realistic objectives, and is realistic about the amount of support that can be offered to the member of staff to meet those objectives.

Advantages of appraisal to the setting

- Staff who are listened to feel valued and their performance will consequently improve.
- Procedures such as appraisal demonstrate a professional approach to other practitioners and service users.
- In appraisal there are opportunities for the manager and the team member to discuss any issues and resolve any conflicts.
- Targets can be set for the team member which will have a direct, positive effect on the practice in the setting.

Advantages of appraisal to the individual team member

- Staff who have an opportunity to discuss their personal and professional progress confidentially are less likely to harbour grievances.
- During this allotted time the team member will have the line manager's full attention; this should make them feel valued and listened to, which in turn will make them a stronger member of the team.
- Appraisal is an opportunity for the manager to praise the team member 'officially' and put it in writing.
- If there are any concerns an appraisal session is a good time for these to be addressed. The manager and member of staff can then negotiate targets for improvement; without appraisal there is a risk that poor performance will be discussed in front of other members of the team.

Management skills – ELEYS Study

The ELEYS Study (Siraj-Blatchford and Manni, 2007) listed management skills as part of an assessment tool for managers and leaders in the sector. Stem 2.1 states that an early years manager should: 'Ensure effective human resource management and administration'; 2.1 c is to 'Be an effective appraiser of staff, be encouraging, supportive, firm and constructively critical where necessary (this involves setting achievable individual goals for staff and having professional development targets)' (p. 70).

As part of this stem the manager is required to assess:

- what your strengths are
- which areas need improvement
- what you can do to build on your strengths
- what you need to do to improve your skills and capabilities.

The Care Management Standards LMC A1.2 also declares that managers can manage and develop staff by:

- developing and implementing written agreements for supervision and performance reviews
- supporting workers to reflect on issues and processes raised in supervision and performance reviews
- acting on supervision and review outcomes
- identifying areas of learning.

Unspoken ambition

Case Study

You are a manager of a children's centre. You have worked with your team of outreach workers for one year and supervised and appraised all members of the team. One of your team, James, comes to you and says that he would like a 'change of direction' and, although never having discussed this with you at appraisal, now wants to become involved in researching an aspect of children's development. This will cost extra money you have not identified as being needed for training before because this is the first time you have heard about it. When you ask James why he has not mentioned this before he says it is because he feels you 'lead' him in appraisal and he has actually always wanted to pursue this but felt he could not. When you examine his appraisal documents there is no record of this.

- What would you do?
- What steps might have been taken to ensure this could not happen?
- How would you deal with the accusation that you 'lead' the appraisal?
- What would you do to ensure this did not happen again?

Vocational training

Claire left school at 16 with four GCSEs at grades C and B. She was encouraged to stay on at school to take an A-level course but had never really enjoyed school and was keen to leave. She worked for a while in a supermarket and as a receptionist at a health centre, but neither of these positions gave her fulfilment. Claire had always enjoyed babysitting her younger cousins and helping out at the local Brownies on Monday nights, so she decided to apply for a childcare course at a college of further education. Claire was put on the CACHE Diploma in Childcare and Education and within two years had successfully completed the course and gained employment at a day nursery. Over the next five years Claire worked her way up the career ladder and, encouraged by her manager, attended several short courses and eventually became deputy manager of the day nursery. She recently completed the Foundation Degree in Early Childhood Studies course at her old college and now has her sights set on a manager's position within the chain of day nurseries. Claire cannot believe how successful she has been and friends and family notice how she is much more confident and self-assured.

■ Consider the challenges Claire now faces and how you would support her.

■ Reflect on the next step for Claire and the progression route she can take.

Conclusion

This chapter has outlined the focus for the children's workforce to be highly trained and well qualified by 2020, and as part of this plan practitioners will find that they need to complete training and gain qualifications. By 2020 the expectation is that the majority of practitioners will hold a full Level 3 qualification, with many working at Level 6. A current key initiative is the drive towards equipping practitioners to have Early Years Professional Status (EYPS). This move towards a graduate-led profession represents a huge transformation of the early years workforce.

In this chapter we have looked at the importance of self-development, as well as the development of others and ways in which reflective practitioners can celebrate success and work for continuous improvement and quality of provision.

Check your understanding

Give a brief summary of the following.

1 Why is self-development important for the reflective practitioner?

2 How can we recognise personal strengths and celebrate good practice?

3 Name some of the tools that are useful for self-development.

4 How does the manager ensure the continuous improvement and quality of the provision through staff development and training?

5 How can staff be developed through appraisal?

References and further reading

Bartholomew, L. (1996) 'Working in a team', in S. Robson and S. Smedley (eds) Education and Early Childhood. Abingdon: David Fulton.

Cottrell, S. (2003) The Study Skills Handbook. Basingstoke: Palgrave Macmillan.

Department for Education and Skills (2005) Championing Children: A shared set of skills, knowledge and behaviours of those leading and managing integrated children's services.

Honey, P. and Mumford, A. (2000) The Learning Styles Helper's Guide. Berkshire: Peter Honey Publications.

Honey, P. and Mumford, A. (2000) The Learning Styles Questionnaire: 80 Item Version. Berkshire: Peter Honey Publications.

Jarvis, P. (1995) Adult and Continuing Education. Theory and Practice 2e, London: Routledge.

Kolb, D.A. and Fry, R. (1975) 'Toward an applied theory of experimental learning; in C. Cooper (ed.) Theories of Group Process, London: John Wiley.

Lewin, K. (1948) Resolving social conflicts; selected papers on group dynamics. Gertrude W. Lewin (ed.). New York: Harper & Row, 1948.

Lewin, K. and Lippitt, R. (1938) 'An experiential approach to the study of autocracy and democracy. A preliminary note'. Sociometry 1: 292–300.

Maynard, T. and Thomas, N. (2004) An Introduction to Early Childhood Studies. London: Sage Publications.

Miller, L. and Devereux, J. (eds) (2004) Supporting Children's Learning in the Early Years. London: David Fulton.

Moyles, J. and Adams, S. (2001) Statement of Entitlement to Play: A Framework of Playful Teaching. Buckingham: Open University Press.

Moyles, J. (2007) Effective Leadership and Management in the Early Years. Maidenhead: Open University Press.

Rodd, J. (2007) Leadership in Early Childhood. Maidenhead: Open University Press.

Siraj-Blatchford, I. and Manni, L. (2007) Effective Leadership in the Early Years Sector: The ELEYS Study. London: Institute of Education.

Useful websites

CACHE: www.cache.org.uk

Children's Workforce Development Council (CWDC): www.cwdcouncil.org.uk

City & Guilds: www.cityandguilds.com

Edexcel: www.edexcel.com

Every Child Matters: www.everychildmatters.gov.uk

Honey and Mumford Learning Styles Questionnaire (LSQ): www.peterhoney.com

National Standards for Leaders of Children's Centres: www.surestart.gov.uk

Nursery World: www.nurseryworld.co.uk

Ofqual: www.ofqual.gov.uk

Skills for Care: www.skillsforcare.com

skills4study.com – a free online study skills resource: www.palgrave.com/skills4study/index.asp

Teachernet – online publications for schools: www.teachernet.gov.uk/publications

8 Administration of the Early Years Setting

The administration of early years settings has become increasingly complicated over recent years as managers are required to understand how to run their establishments as businesses and compete in a competitive market. The need for good-quality childcare is paramount and is supported by unprecedented government financial commitment and involvement. Parents and carers are increasingly aware of the elements of good-quality provision and are seeking well-run settings that are able to meet their diverse needs and those of their children.

Managers will need to keep themselves up to date in order to ensure that their early years settings are run as efficiently and effectively as possible. In the current market small businesses are competing with well-run chains of nurseries and therefore must reflect a similarly professional approach. This will involve understanding appropriate legislation and how to meet current requirements of registration and inspection. Managers must understand how to lead and support their teams when writing and following the necessary policies and procedures that reflect the regulatory requirements and legislation.

The number of women in full-time paid work has risen, and with smaller and wider-spread families the increased workforce must rely on childcare that is flexible, affordable and reliable. Since 1997 there has been steady growth in the amount of childcare provision, with 644,000 new childcare places created by September 2006 (www.labour.org.uk/early_years). If this trend continues in the next decade, settings may consider expanding their businesses to meet the demand. This chapter outlines the important aspects of the administration of childcare settings.

The chapter covers the following areas:

8.1   The National Childcare Strategy and current developments

8.2   The business aspects of managing an early years setting

8.3   Legislation, registration and inspection

8.4   Policies and procedures

8.1 The National Childcare Strategy and current developments

In May 1998, the government launched its National Childcare Strategy in the Green Paper *Meeting the Childcare Challenge* (Department for Education and Employment, 1998). This strategy was relevant across the whole of the UK, but dealt specifically with England. The Secretaries of State for Wales, Scotland and Northern Ireland issued their own documentation in relation to childcare.

The aim of the strategy was to support families and to ensure they had access to the childcare that met their needs. The background to the strategy lay in the recognition that:

- there were not enough childcare places
- the cost of childcare put it beyond the reach of many families
- it was difficult for parents to access information about childcare in their area.

The general feeling was that childcare provision had failed to keep pace with the needs of families, employers and society as a whole. It was also noted that the quality of provision was variable.

The National Childcare Strategy was an important document as its principal aim was to ensure that good-quality childcare for children was available in every neighbourhood. This included formal childcare, such as playgroups, out-of-school clubs and childminders, as well as informal childcare, for example relatives or friends looking after children. Figure 8.1 shows its more specific objectives.

Figure 8.1. Specific objectives of the National Childcare Strategy

The National Childcare Strategy was government led; however, the role of parents in making choices for their children was recognised and reiterated. The vision was for the government to provide for the standardisation of services to enable all parents to make informed choices about the type of childcare that suited their needs and those of their children. The day-to-day administration of the strategy was down to the local authority through the Early Years Development and Childcare Partnership in each area.

In December 2004, the Ten Year Childcare Strategy: Choice for Parents, the Best Start for Children, was published (www.surestart.gov.uk). This supported the work already started under the National Childcare Strategy by incorporating four key themes:

- choice and flexibility
- availability
- quality
- affordability.

The emphasis is, at the time of writing, on parents having greater choice in being able to balance their work commitments and family life through enhanced parental leave and easy access to Sure Start children's centres.

The government has pledged to have a Sure Start centre in every community, with a total of 3,500 by 2010. Future funding of £351 million will pay for the development, extension and modification of existing centres in less disadvantaged areas and represents an unprecedented investment in early years provision. The Sure Start centres build on existing successful initiatives such as Neighbourhood Nurseries and Early Excellence Centres and ensure that high-quality provision is available for all communities. The vision is for this provision to be staffed by a skilled, well-qualified early years workforce with full day care settings being led by professionals and having a strengthened qualification and career structure. The provision will be made affordable to parents through increased tax support.

In December 2007 the Children's Plan set out ambitious goals to improve the lives of families, children and young people by 2020 and local authorities play a key role in delivering these reforms, alongside Children's Trusts and in accordance with the five *Every Child Matters* outcomes. The Children's Trusts will work with local authorities to ensure local services are meeting the local needs of children and their families (see Chapter 7).

▶ Key Term

Sure Start – Sure Start brings together service providers from health, social services, early education and voluntary, private and community organisations to provide integrated services for young children and their families that meet local needs. Sure Start is a key part of the government's campaign to tackle childhood poverty and social exclusion.

▶ Key Terms

Children's Plan – a government initiative, launched in 2007, that aims to achieve world-class standards in the provision for children in England by 2020.

Children's Trusts – bring together all services for children and young people in an area. The trusts are underpinned by the Children Act 2004 duty to cooperate, which focuses on improving the lives of children across the five *Every Child Matters* outcomes (see Chapter 9) and social exclusion.

Think it over

Research the role of the local authorities and Children's Trusts in determining local need. Useful websites for information are www.everychildmatters, www.surestart.gov.uk and www.dscf.gov.uk/localauthorities.

The main role of the local authorities is to focus on the long-term delivery of reliable childcare services within their area and to ensure that the private, statutory and voluntary sectors are meeting local demand efficiently and cost-effectively. They must ensure that they:

- are not duplicating services
- are making maximum use of local providers
- are providing training, advice and information for those providers and for parents and carers.

Quality

Managers of early years provision must ensure that their setting offers a good-quality experience for the children attending and provides the care and education of children that meets the needs of the parents in accordance with the Children's Plan.

There are numerous ways of doing this, including:

- through highly trained staff
- sharing of good practice
- leading by example
- by performing successfully when examined against nationally agreed standards
- through meeting quality assurance schemes.

Ofsted monitors the quality of the childcare and education provided in any early years setting through the regulation and inspection process, and by grading individual provisions it recognises the importance of high-quality service. The use of a quality assurance (QA) scheme can enable settings to develop and maintain a high-quality service.

According to Brunton and Thornton (2007) a quality assurance scheme helps the management of a setting to set and maintain high standards for the service they provide. As part of the quality assurance, clear policies and procedures will contribute to the day-to-day running. Settings will also be able to identify the aspects that require attention if improvement of service is to take place.

When a setting has achieved a quality accreditation staff will feel motivated and be more aware of the important part they play. It will also have a beneficial effect by reassuring parents that the setting offers a high-quality service and contribute to the long-term stability and financial viability of the business.

Find it out

Research your nearest Early Excellence or Sure Start centre, perhaps by visiting it and recording examples of good practice that are taking place. Similarly, research the work of your local Early Years Development and Childcare Partnership.

Quality assurance schemes

Quality assurance schemes may be developed by a local authority, but there are also nationally recognised schemes, such as:

- 'Aiming for Quality' – the Pre-School Learning Alliance
- Quality Counts – the National Day Nurseries Association
- Aiming Higher – the 4 Children organisation.

Local authority schemes generally provide a portfolio of criteria to be met by the setting in order to achieve accreditation. The portfolio will include agreed standards by which each setting is judged. This forms a guide to good practice for all those providing care, early years education and out-of-school care and will be applicable to all providers:

- childminders
- day nurseries
- pre-schools
- 'wraparound care' (i.e. breakfast and lunch clubs)
- after-school clubs or
- holiday play schemes.

The standards will have been agreed after extensive consultation with providers of services, including private and voluntary settings as well as independent and maintained schools, and will represent a broad consensus of views. Local authorities are committed to encouraging and supporting higher standards for the benefit of all children and their families.

A mentoring system may be provided to assist in the achievement of accreditation, with one-to-one assistance or group workshops. Settings are encouraged to build bonds with other providers in similar circumstances in order to create a feeling of camaraderie and an ethos of quality. Cluster groups are established to form a support system. It is generally believed that staff can learn from sharing good practice.

When a setting feels that it is ready for accreditation, and that all the criteria have been met, a verifier will visit to assess the quality of its work. If all is satisfactory the verifier will recommend accreditation. A report is then sent to the local authority, which has the power to grant accreditation if it is satisfied with the evidence. Verifiers are chosen for their early years experience and other relevant skills.

- They must have sound knowledge of what makes an appropriate environment and of child development.
- They must be committed to parental involvement, equality of opportunity and anti-racism.
- They will also have the ability to communicate effectively, both verbally and in writing.

The verifier will want to meet the manager and to talk to representatives of the staff and parents, as well as some children, if appropriate. Verifiers will also want to see evidence of where the setting considers it has met the criteria.

Quality Improvement Principles

Until 2007 the government provided an accreditation for quality assurance schemes, the Investors in Children award, but this has now been superseded by the National Quality Improvement Network (NQIN) which is managed by the National Children's Bureau (NCB).

These NQIN principles have been developed by key organisations with interests and involvement in promoting high standards in early years provision. They are used in the development of quality assurance schemes that:

- guide and support settings to improve outcomes
- encourage settings to be inclusive and reduce inequalities
- strengthen values and principles in settings

- promote effective practice and its delivery in settings

- increase the capacity of settings to improve quality

- promote integrated working within and among settings

- challenge and support key people in settings to lead quality improvement

- build on settings' proven workforce development strategies

- support settings through the self-evaluation and improvement processes

- local authorities and national organisations use to monitor quality improvements and communicate achievements

- local authorities and national organisations use to ensure quality improvement is achievable, continuous and sustainable

- operate fair, inclusive and transparent accreditation processes.

Leading to Excellence (Ofsted, 2008), a report based on the evidence of 90,000 inspections between 2005 and 2008, analyses how childcare and early years settings are led, managed and organised to promote positive outcomes for children. This review ascertained that 5 per cent of childminders and 16 per cent of day care provision were part of a quality assurance scheme. The report found that high-quality day care settings that were using a quality assurance scheme shared some key features:

- excellent teamwork

- staff with a clear understanding of their own responsibilities and how their roles fit alongside others

- staff who are fully involved in planning and evaluating activities and who contribute to children's individual records

- managers and teams working together to promote children's learning

- staff who are highly committed and continually strive to improve their practice

- adults with thorough understanding of child development

- leaders who are fully aware of strengths and areas for improvement

- good links with homes to support children's progress

- children who are effectively involved in planning.

Points for reflective practice

Practice Guidance for the Early Years Foundation Stage refers to quality improvement. Read the following statement (Point 1.21, p. 8) and reflect on how you can meet this expectation.

'It is important that all providers consider how best to create, maintain and improve a setting so that it meets the highest standards and offers the best experience for young children. All providers should continuously think about how to improve what they are offering to children and families. This might include using self-evaluation tools, or becoming involved in local authority or national quality improvement initiatives, making sure that parents' views are understood and considered.'

Training

The National Childcare Strategy recognised that it can be hard for workers within the sector to add to their qualifications and progress in their careers. It was noted that there were a large number of disparate qualifications that did not relate clearly to each other and were not always recognised by employers on a national basis. For this reason it was decided to instigate a framework of training and qualifications that would be recognised by employers and that would enable workers to progress in their careers, moving freely around the country and from employer to employer.

As a result, the training of childcare workers has been scrutinised and attempts made to ensure that courses meet the criteria outlined by the appropriate sector skills councils, for example the Children's Workforce Development Council (CWDC) and the regulatory body OfQual (Office of the Qualifications and Exams Regulator), which has replaced the Qualifications Curriculum Authority (QCA). All courses are rigorously compiled and assessed to ensure continuity in the standard of the qualification as the CWDC works towards the vision of a graduate-led profession (see Chapter 7).

As a manager you need a good understanding of the qualifications available, and the level of training they provide, in order to ensure that you are employing appropriately qualified staff. As a general rule it is useful to remember that workers need a Level 3 qualification to be in charge of a setting. The CWDC's Early Years and Playwork Qualifications database will enable parents, employers and Ofsted to check the validity of individual qualifications.

Regulation and inspection

Parents need to feel comfortable with the childcare that they choose, and much of this confidence is based on the registration procedures. The Childcare Act 2006 introduced two new registers for people caring for children:

- the Childcare Register
- the Early Years Register.

The Childcare Register lists providers who are registered to care for children from birth to 17 years. The register has two parts:

- the voluntary part, which providers who are not eligible for compulsory registration may choose to join (mainly people looking after children aged 8 and over, or providing care in the child's home)
- the compulsory part, which providers must join if they care for one or more children from 1 September following their fifth birthday until they reach their eighth birthday.

Details of inspections are available for providers on the Childcare Register and the Early Years Register in the document *Are you ready for your inspection?* (Ofsted, 2008).

Provision will be inspected under the new requirements and links to the statutory Early Years Foundation Stage (EYFS). *Are you ready for your inspection?* clearly lays out the requirements, and guides managers in preparing their staff for an Ofsted inspection.

Table 8.1 summarises what inspectors consider when making judgements about the provision in settings on the Early Years Register and shows how they link to the general requirements of the EYFS. You can find more details about these and other judgements that inspectors make in inspection guidance documents such as *Using the early years evaluation schedule* and *Conducting early years inspections*, which are available on the Ofsted website.

Table 8.1. Information from *Are you ready for your inspection?* (Ofsted, 2008, pp. 13–14)

Judgement	What inspectors consider	Links to the general requirements of the EYFS
How effective is the provision in meeting the needs of the children?	Overall how well the early years provision: ■ meets the needs of all children who attend ■ supports every child so that no group or individual is disadvantaged ■ helps children make the best possible progress in their learning and development, and promotes their welfare ■ works in partnerships with others to ensure good-quality early education and care ■ plans for improvement and has effective processes of self evaluation.	All learning and development, and welfare requirements. Note specific welfare requirements: All providers must have and implement an effective policy about ensuring equality of opportunities and for supporting children with learning difficulties and disabilities. Providers must promote equality of opportunity and anti-discriminatory practice and must ensure that every child is included and not disadvantaged because of their or their parents' ethnicity, culture or religion, home language, family background, learning difficulties, sexuality, gender or ability.
How effectively is provision led and managed or, in the case of childminders, organised?	How well you (and/or the leaders and managers of the provision): ■ strive for improvement to provide high-quality care and early education ■ monitor provision and outcomes for children; and identify and make the necessary improvement ■ safeguard all children, including making sure that adults looking after children or having unsupervised access to them are suitable to do so ■ promote inclusive practice so that the learning and development, and welfare needs of all children are met ■ work with parents, carers, other providers, services and employers to promote children's care and early education ■ maintain records, policies and procedures required by the EYFS to ensure that the needs of all children are met.	All learning and development, and welfare requirements, specifically: Providers must take necessary steps to safeguard and promote the welfare of children. Providers must ensure that adults looking after children, or having unsupervised access to them, must be suitable to do so. Adults looking after children must have appropriate qualifications, training, skills and knowledge. Staffing arrangements must be organised to ensure the safety and to meet the needs of the children Outdoor and indoor spaces, furniture equipment and toys must be safe and suitable for their purpose Providers must maintain records, policies and procedures required for the safe and efficient management of the settings and to meet the needs of the children.

Judgement	What inspectors consider	Links to the general requirements of the EYFS
How effectively are children helped to learn and develop?	How well you and any assistants or staff: ■ use information from observation and assessment to ensure that all children achieve as much as they can ■ support their learning ■ plan the learning environment, and for children's play and exploration ■ plan for individual children ■ identify and provide for additional learning and development needs ■ involve parents and carers as partners and other agencies and providers in children's learning and development.	Learning and development requirements relating to the: ■ early learning goals – the knowledge, skills and understanding which young children should have acquired by the end of the academic year in which they reach age five ■ educational programmes – the matters, skills and processes which are required to be taught to young children ■ assessment arrangements – the arrangements for assessing young children to ascertain their achievements. Welfare requirement: ■ Providers must plan and organise their systems to ensure that every child receives an enjoyable and challenging learning and development experience that is tailored to meet their individual needs.
How effectively is the welfare of the children promoted?	How well you and any assistants or staff ensure that: ■ steps are taken by key people to safeguard and promote the welfare of the children ■ children's good health and well-being are promoted, the necessary steps are taken to prevent the spread of infection, and appropriate action is taken when children are ill ■ adults teach children about keeping safe ■ children are encouraged to develop the habits and behaviour appropriate to good learners, their own needs, and those of others ■ the outdoor and indoor spaces, furniture, equipment and toys are suitable and safe	Welfare requirements: The provider must take necessary steps to safeguard and promote the welfare of children. The provider must promote the good health of the children, take necessary steps to prevent the spread of infection, and take appropriate action when they are ill. Children's behaviour must be managed effectively and in a manner appropriate for their stage of development and particular individual needs. Outdoor and indoor spaces, furniture, equipment and toys, must be safe and suitable for their purpose.

Tax credits

Parents who work may be able to claim for childcare costs through tax credits up to 80 per cent of the costs to a maximum of:

- £175 per week for one child
- £300 per week for two or more children.

The amount depends on income, with lower-income families receiving more tax credits. The childcare must be registered and approved, for example from a childminder, nursery, play scheme or out-of-school care in a school setting. Generally each parent must be working 16 hours or more a week to claim assistance. Further information is available from HM Revenue and Customs (HMRC).

Other financial assistance

Further money has been made available to develop new out-of-school childcare, especially for families from ethnic minorities and those whose children have special needs.

Employers are also being encouraged to play an important part, for example through childcare partnerships. In addition they are being encouraged to adopt 'family-friendly' policies. There is an emphasis on helping employees balance work and family life.

Effects of the drive to increase the number of places

Partly as a result of the above arrangements for financial assistance there has been an increase in demand for childcare places. This has put some pressure on current providers to expand their businesses and has encouraged new providers to establish settings. There are difficulties in finding appropriate staff to fill vacancies and some providers fear a flooding of the market. Avenues of funding available for expansion and setting up a new business are discussed below. Local authorities have improved the availability of information for existing settings and also have staff available to advise on business and financial matters.

8.2 The business aspects of managing an early years setting

Running a childcare setting, whether it is a day nursery or an after-school club, can be a costly business. There are a number of start-up costs that need to be accounted for and continuous running costs that need to be considered for sustainability. Initially you will require funding for:

- premises
- conversion
- equipment
- recruitment

- marketing
- working capital to cover early trading losses.

In the longer term, funds will be needed for:

- administration costs
- telephone and postage
- rent and service charges
- insurance
- staffing.

In addition you will regularly need to replace play equipment and supplies such as paper and pens.

This section looks at starting up an early years setting, sources of funding and the expansion of a setting. The matter of planning permission will arise in connection with both setting up and expanding. Finding a market for your provision and marketing the setting are crucial aspects of management, and these are also covered.

The business plan

To analyse the cost of starting up a business, and to define your aims, you should draw up a business plan. It is also a helpful way of raising financial backing and demonstrating the viability of your ideas.

The business plan should be easy to read and understand. It should be based on accurate research and assessment of the market. It could include the following elements.

- *Executive summary*, with the key objectives and level of funding needed. This will include the timescale for development and the amount of finance required.
- *Sector analysis*, with a brief explanation of the marketplace and developments that may affect demand.
- *Market analysis*, to include your market research on potential customers, the competition and its strengths and weaknesses. You could also include a SWOT analysis of your business.
- *Operational plan*, with business objectives and means of achieving them. This should include the legal structure of your business – whether you are a sole trader, partnership or limited company. It should also state the features of the childcare provision, such as the curriculum, the hours of opening and the nature of the care. You will also need to include details of the premises and your support systems, such as Information Technology.
- *Management team*, giving clear details of everyone involved in the business, including their relevant experience and qualifications. This should also outline details of the staff to be recruited.
- *Implementation plan*, to explain how your targets will be met.
- *Financial information*, with predictions about how your business will develop and indications of the cash flow forecast, profit and loss and balance sheet.
- *Appendices*, including your financial data, the curriculum vitae for each of the management staff, proof of registration and copies of policies and procedures.

Key Term

SWOT/SWOC – analysis of strengths, weaknesses, opportunities, threats or challenges; a way to organise a thorough analysis of your current position in order to plan for greater effectiveness.

Find it out

Contact your local bank or building society and ask for information regarding starting up a business.

Funding

Both existing early years settings and proposed ventures may wish to apply for funding. For the latter, family and friends are the easiest and quickest source of funding, and banks might consider funding if you have capital or assets of your own. Banks will supply information on setting up and sustaining small businesses. They will also provide information and advice on the help available for those starting a business, such as the government loan guarantee scheme.

Funding is available from a variety of sources and it is advisable to research all possible avenues. Many applications are turned down for funding because the applicant has not carried out enough research. It is important to ensure that the interests of potential funders match the aims of your setting. Figure 8.2 shows some possible sources of funding or information on funding, with useful websites listed at the end of the chapter.

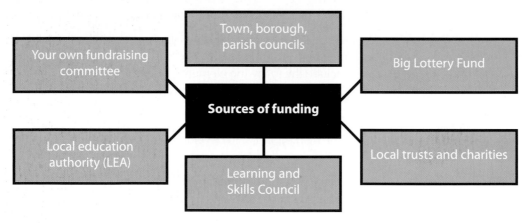

Figure 8.2. Sources of funding or information on funding

Potential sources of funds will depend on the type and status of the organisation, as well as the nature of the proposed spending.

The Pre-school Learning Alliance has fundraising ideas for members who are pre-school settings. A new free electronic costing tool has been developed by the National Day Nurseries Association, working with the Department for Children, Schools and Families, to help nurseries manage their finances. This joint project aims to provide information to aid the financial planning decisions that nurseries need to make and to offer advice on business strategies and marketing.

Expanding an early years setting

Many settings have found that expansion is a good way to achieve sustainability. By offering more services they increase income and become a vital resource in the community. They are also responding to the changing needs of families and children. Some of the many ways of expanding an existing service include after-school clubs, breakfast clubs and holiday schemes.

Advice is available from local authorities or from the Pre-school Learning Alliance, which has experienced local development workers.

To be in a position to expand:

- your existing provision must be in a strong financial position
- the provision must be well managed and well resourced
- demand must be assessed (as with starting a new business)
- a business plan must be drawn up for the expansion
- good management procedures must be in place to keep everything running smoothly.

It is all too easy to spread yourself too thinly. It is also necessary to consider the drawbacks to expansion as well as the benefits. It may not, for example, be as easy to be hands-on in the everyday management of two or more settings, or even of one larger one.

Good practice checklist
Expanding the setting

- Ensure your current setting is well financed and managed, and has a good structure.
- Recognise that you may need managerial assistance, particularly if you are considering opening another setting.
- Seek advice from professional organisations and high street banks.
- If you are building on a new site do not compromise on position. Location is important.
- Make sure your property is big enough for the financial viability of expansion.
- Be realistic about availability of staff and training costs.
- Research government funding to see if you are eligible, but remember it will run out eventually.
- Be realistic about competition and threats to your future business, and plan accordingly.
- Do not overestimate profits.

Planning permission

Planning permission is usually required for the expansion of existing premises or to convert a property for the purpose of establishing an early years setting. It is essential that you check with planning departments before purchasing or leasing premises. Planning permission will be required if you intend to:

- erect a new building
- change the use of a building
- undertake external work, including extending existing buildings
- carry out works around the building, such as installing a children's playground.

Car parking is often an issue that leads to planning permission being refused, so it is worth spending time researching the area and assessing the views of local residents. The nearest neighbours to your proposal will be informed of your plans and invited to comment or object. They may also object to an increase in the level of noise generated by children at play. Access to the area will also be considered, as will the number of similar businesses in the locality. The conversion of a residential property into a business such as a day nursery may also be disallowed if the local authority wishes to keep the area for residential use.

Conditions are invariably applied to any planning application, and these might limit the number of children catered for or the hours of opening. You will need to take these into account when considering the financial viability of your project.

Finding your market

Whether you are considering starting up a setting for the care and education of children or expanding an existing provision, you must first consider the needs of the local community and the nature and extent of the competition; for example, you should establish whether the local nurseries are full and what childcare services they offer. You will need to establish these in a systematic way. Good sources of information about your area include:

- the recent local authority childcare audit and plan
- the local Children's Information Service
- the library
- directories of childcare services
- major employers (there may be a need to provide childcare for their employees)
- local parents.

You can conduct desktop research and establish an overview of the current situation within which you are aiming to develop your service. Statistical information which has been gathered for a range of different purposes may enable you to identify gaps in the market that your business can fill. Possible sources of information would be reports from the Daycare Trust and Ofsted.

You may find it useful to conduct a survey to determine the exact nature of childcare needs in your area. Figure 8.3 shows some methods for gathering information.

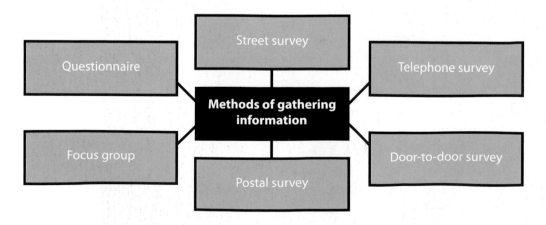

Figure 8.3. Some methods of gathering information

Whichever method you choose you should try to contact as wide a selection of relevant people as possible. For any of these methods, you are likely to want to use questionnaires of some sort, and these are considered below.

Street survey

This can be done in an informal way by simply asking people questions and recording their responses. You could use a questionnaire as a basis for your questions, notes or a checklist. This method enables you to obtain information quickly and to clear up any misunderstandings immediately. The response rate is high and you can ask supplementary questions, although it is a time-consuming method of gaining information. You may also need permission from the local council.

Street surveys can be useful, but may not always be convenient.

Telephone survey

This is a quick way to access information and reaches more people than postal surveys; but it may be considered intrusive by respondents. Inaccurate responses could be given if respondents feel pressured by time.

Door-to-door survey

It is important to get the timing right for this method – for example, avoid mealtimes and peak television viewing times.

Postal survey

In this method respondents have time to think and may express their true feelings. The response rate is low and you should bear this in mind when choosing this – an average response rate is 10 per cent, even when stamped addressed envelopes are provided for the return of questionnaires.

Focus groups

These can be made up of existing or potential users of your service, and are a good opportunity to raise awareness about your plans and establish local needs at the same time. You may need to employ an experienced market researcher to facilitate the group.

Questionnaires

Questionnaires are a good way to collect information in the types of survey outlined above. However, it is harder to write a questionnaire than many people think. An example is given in Figure 8.4. Much thought needs to be given to its layout and the precise nature of the information sought. It is important to stick rigidly to the task in hand and not to include any superfluous questions. You will also need to consider the piloting, distribution and return of questionnaires.

It is important to ensure that the questionnaire is typed and that instructions are clear. Spaces between the questions will help the reader, and later make it easier for you to analyse the results. Take care over the order of the questions and think carefully about the impression you are giving to potential clients. Ask a friend or colleague to check the questionnaire, and to pay particular attention to the wording of the questions.

- Do they fit your purpose?
- Is there any ambiguity or assumption?
- Are you asking for knowledge respondents may not have?
- Are the questions misleading or offensive?

It is a good idea to pilot a questionnaire by sending copies to a similar group of people to your target group. It will then be possible to see if the questionnaire has been worded correctly to give you the information you are seeking.

Make sure you add a date for the questionnaires to be returned by and consider how you will distribute them and get them returned. You can also use local organisations to translate your questionnaire into different languages. It may be possible to ask the local school to distribute your questionnaire to all their parents, or to place copies in the doctor's surgery and health clinics. Community groups may also help with distribution. In such circumstances it is a good idea to place a box somewhere accessible for the return of the completed questionnaires, to increase the response rate.

Dear parent,

The Wise Old Owl Pre-school in Bury Lane is considering expanding the service it offers. We are currently open on Tuesday and Thursday mornings from 9.30 a.m. to 12.00 noon. We would welcome your views on expansion and would like to establish what you would find most useful. Please complete the form below and return it to us in the envelope provided by June 21st. We will be using your comments to guide our plans but all answers will be strictly confidential.

Thank you for your help.

1. Please give the postcode for your area……………………………………..

2. Please give the ages of all your children…………………………………...

3. Please identify whether you are currently using our provision by circling the appropriate answer.

        Yes   No

4. How likely would you be to use new provision at this pre-school?

        Very likely   Quite likely   Not likely

5. If you have circled 'Not likely' please explain briefly why and return the form to us.

6. If you circled 'Very likely' or 'Quite likely' please tick the box(es) for the provision you would use:

	Extra morning session on Monday/Tuesday/Wednesday
	Afternoon sessions 12–4 p.m. (with lunch)
	After-school sessions 4–7 p.m. (with tea)
	A lunch club 12–2 p.m.
	A breakfast club (with breakfast) 8–9 a.m.
	A holiday club

7. Would you be interested in attending a 'focus group' to discuss the findings of this questionnaire?

        Yes   No

If you would like to be advised if/when these services start, please complete your name and address.

NAME:

ADDRESS:

Figure 8.4. Sample questionnaire (based on information supplied by the Pre-School Learning Alliance)

Market research

Linda is a pre-school worker in the south-east of England. She has worked for various employers since leaving the local college in 1990 with an NNEB qualification. Her experience of different settings is wide and she has knowledge and understanding of the needs of pre-school children and their families. Recently she participated in the successful award of accreditation at her workplace and completed the CACHE Advanced Diploma in Childcare and Education in 2001.

Linda has always dreamed of owning her own nursery, and with a colleague as her partner this is a dream that should soon be realised. They have found suitable premises in the centre of their town, near a church and local playing field. Having lived in the town for 11 years, Linda has a good understanding of the provision in the area and now needs to identify gaps in the market on which to base a successful business.

- What research will Linda and her partner need to conduct?

- Suggest sources of support for their plans.

Marketing

It is essential continually to research your market and satisfy the needs of your customers. This is a component of staying in business. As a manager you will need to continue to offer a service to your customers that is set at a marketable yet profitable price. You will also need to define and market your unique selling point (USP), which differentiates your setting from others in the area and encourages parents to use your service above all others. In order to market your early years setting you will need to establish a package that identifies clearly what you are able to offer prospective clients and the individual qualities that your setting has. Think carefully about product, place, price and promotion.

Product

- What are the benefits to the children and parents?

- What quality is offered?

- What training and qualifications do the staff have?

Place

- Is your establishment in a convenient setting?

- Do young families populate the location?

- Is it welcoming?

- Do you have good facilities?

- Are you near local bus services?

- Is parking available?

Price

- Set your fees carefully – too cheap and clients will not value you; too expensive and they will go elsewhere.

- Bear in mind the going rate for your type of setting and find out what the local competition is charging.

- Consider your costs.

Promotion

- How are you going to tell potential clients about your provision?

- In what areas can you sell your setting?

- Regularly review your marketing methods.

You will need to think carefully about the image of your setting and the key aspects you wish to market to the public. This is known as 'branding' in the advertising world and is the way you can effectively disseminate the vision and values of your service to prospective clients. The brand should be synonymous with the service you provide and ensure people remember what your setting is all about. You will need to ensure that the image you are projecting to prospective customers is the one you want, which might entail asking customers about their perception of your setting.

The marketing plan

It may be possible to formulate the above points as a marketing plan. This should involve the whole staff team. It can be decided who does what, how and by when; it will give you an overview of your marketing strategy. The plan could include a timetable, marketing objectives and budget.

Think it over

Consider the different tactics you could use in marketing an early years setting. These could include:

- brochures
- open days
- leaflets
- networking
- the Internet
- local press.

What are the benefits and practical implications of each strategy?

A brochure is a good way of marketing your establishment and could set out the philosophy of your setting. This is a chance to establish your views on education and how these will be applied. The organisation, opening times and management of the setting can be included, as can staff experience and policies and procedures. Prospective clients will also be interested in your approach to behaviour and discipline. Many people now use the Internet when researching childcare provision so it is worth considering creating a website and an e-brochure, which is an electronic version of the paper-based brochure. Websites and e-brochures are constantly available for parents to peruse and can reach a wider audience. You must ensure that the website is easy to access and navigate, and portrays the image you wish to project. It is also important to keep all the information up to date.

Many settings are marketed mainly by 'word of mouth'. The location of new settings and their quality soon get around, via the playground communication system. Clients are very knowledgeable and discerning. By organising an open day and producing leaflets to accompany this you will be able to kick-start the process. It is always a good idea to get parents involved from the beginning, and to show the achievements of the children by organising events. This will also give you the opportunity to understand the needs of the local community better, as well as to market your setting.

The local press can be a good means of advertising your service, so cultivate positive relationships there. They will appreciate any new activity you are doing, particularly if it is of interest to the general public.

The local authorities across the country have their own Childcare Information Service (CIS) which includes directories of all registered childcare provision in the area and your provision will need to be on this list (see section 8.1).

However you choose to market your setting, the key to a successful business is to listen to the parents and prospective clients and respond to their needs in the service you provide.

8.3 Legislation, registration and inspection

Managers of childcare settings must keep up to date on legislation to ensure that they are meeting requirements for registration and inspection. Legislation takes the form of primary legislation (Acts of Parliament) and secondary legislation (such as regulations and standards). Current legislation of particular importance for managers is the Childcare Act 2006 and the Early Years Foundation Stage (EYFS) which is given legal force through an Order and Regulations made under the Act.

It is essential to keep abreast of current practice, and most managers do this by attending training, reading literature and through discussion with colleagues. Training, advice and support are available through national associations such as the Pre-school Learning Alliance, the National Childminding Association and the National Day Nurseries Association.

Find it out

Research other Acts an early years manager needs to have some knowledge of. This could be through national associations such as the Pre-school Learning Alliance and the National Day Nurseries Association. The legislation could relate to sex or race discrimination, health and safety, fire safety, food safety or employment rights.

The Early Years Foundation Stage encompasses the *National Standards for Under-8s Day Care and Childminding, Curriculum Guidance for the Foundation Stage* and the *Birth to Three Matters* framework (see Chapter 1). These are enforced by Ofsted's Early Years Directorate. The statutory framework for the EYFS stipulates a set of requirements relating to, for example, space per child and staff ratios, and these must be met in order for a setting to be registered.

Registration

The registration process assesses the suitability of the personnel and premises to provide care and education for children under 8 years of age. This is to ensure that all providers:

- meet the EYFS standards for their area of provision;

- protect children;

- ensure that all children are safe, well cared for and participate in activities that contribute to their development and learning;

- promote high-quality in the provision of care and learning;

- can reassure parents that the setting is providing suitable care and education for their children, and that all staff are suitably qualified and CRB checked.

There are different processes of application for registration and the documents *Guidance to Registration on the Early Years Register* and *Guidance for Registration on the Childcare Register* outline these. The documents are available from the Ofsted website. Briefing sessions for childminders are also provided by local authorities.

Key Term

Criminal Records Bureau (CRB) – the agency that checks police records and identifies people who may be unsuitable to work with children or other vulnerable members of society.

Inspection

Ofsted inspectors are trained to inspect childcare and early years provision and must adhere to a specified Code of Conduct to ensure inspections are of a high professional standard. This Code of Conduct is available on the Ofsted website. Inspections are carried out randomly for settings which are only on the Childcare Register, and therefore may be at any time. During this visit the inspector's role is to ensure you are meeting the requirements of your registration. During the inspection the inspector will:

- talk to you, any parents, the children (if present) and any staff members and observe the provision to make sure policies are being put into practice

- check registration details and assess your compliance with, and understanding of, the requirements and any conditions of registration

- assess the safety of the premises and the risk assessment you carry out

- assess understanding of policies and procedures

- look at your recruitment policies, where applicable

- look at your arrangements for making sure unvetted (not CRB cleared) people do not have unsupervised access to children.

After the inspection you will receive a letter confirming either that you have met the requirements for registration or that further action is needed. Letters and other inspection reports are published on the Ofsted website.

Settings registered on the Early Years Register will be evaluated on the quality and standards of their provision in line with the principles and general and specific requirements of the EYFS. Inspections will be at least once within the first three or four years of the implementation of the EYFS. Newly registered early years providers will normally be inspected within a short period of their registration, if they have children on roll.

Inspections will always be prioritised for settings where:

- the last inspection concluded that the quality of childcare and/or early education was inadequate

- there have been significant changes since the last inspection, such as the appointment of a new manager; a high turnover of staff or, in the case of childminders, a change of premises.

Settings are encouraged to complete a self-evaluation form prior to the inspection, which can be downloaded from the Ofsted website.

Inspectors will provide feedback and a short report to settings after each inspection and grade the provision from Category 4 (Outstanding) to Category 1 or 2 (Inadequate) in their report, with further action identified. The report will include a summary of the effectiveness and quality of the provision. Inspection reports are published and a copy sent to the local authority.

You will need to continue to demonstrate your suitability to be a provider throughout the time that you remain registered. Ofsted will monitor this through regular inspections and other visits, and by following up any complaints received about the service you provide. If there are any changes to the conditions of registration, Ofsted will normally work with a setting in order to minimise disruption to the service being offered. However, in some circumstances Ofsted has the power to shut down a setting with immediate effect.

Written records required for an Ofsted inspection

All providers are required to keep the following written records of:

- complaints received from parents and their outcomes
- all medicines administered to children
- accidents and first aid treatment
- Criminal Record Bureau checks
- the following information for each child in your care
  - full name
  - date of birth
  - the name and address of every parent and carer who is known to the provider
  - which of these parents or carers the child normally lives with
  - emergency contact details of the parents and carers
- the name, home address and telephone number of the provider and any other person living or employed on the premises
- the name, home address and telephone number of anyone who will regularly be in unsupervised contact with the children attending the early years provision
- the names of the children looked after on the premises, their hours of attendance and the names of the children's key workers
- a risk assessment, clearly stating when it was carried out, by whom, date of review and any action taken following a review or incident. A risk assessment must be carried out for each specific outing with the children.

Providers must also record and submit certain information to their local authority about individual children receiving the free entitlement to early years provision.

8.4 Policies and procedures

In order to conform to the EYFS, and the inspection and registration process, each establishment must ensure that certain mechanisms are in place. These include policies and procedures and the organisation of the setting.

As a team it is important to work together to create workable policies and procedures that cover all areas of the statutory requirements of the EYFS. Policies refer to a course of action agreed by the setting and procedures dictate the way in which the task is to be performed.

A policy is a written document that sets out the rules by which a setting operates. All the members of staff should agree to it so that they feel part of the process. A policy will need to be reviewed regularly and should be considered a living document that is adapted in pace with changes in your setting. All staff must be given a copy of policies, perhaps in the form of a booklet or portfolio, which must be kept up to date. This must also be accessible for everyone involved in the setting, including students on placement as part of their course

9.1 Government initiatives

Children are high on the government's agenda. A Minister of State for Children has been appointed. The first-ever governmental National Childcare Strategy was launched in 1998 (see Chapter 8). The strategy was part of a package of policies designed to tackle child poverty and social exclusion, the aim being to end child poverty by 2020. This section covers a few other important initiatives. Sources of further information on these appear in the list of useful websites at the end of the chapter.

Figure 9.1. There have been great changes in the care and education of young people; gone are the days of 'chalk and talk'

Every Child Matters – Change for Children

In September 2003 the Department for Education and Skills published the long-awaited Green Paper *Every Child Matters*. This new way of working looks at the welfare of children and young people from birth to age 19 years. Whatever the child's background or experience, the aim is to support five key outcomes for all children and young people.

All agencies have to work together to provide services and these five outcomes for children. These agencies are able to share information to protect children and young people from harm and support them to achieve what they want in life.

The government continues to set up new projects within this agenda, encompassing areas such as:

- Invest in a Children's Fund
- Support schools in working with mental health practitioners

The following behaviour is considered unacceptable in the nursery, whether towards an adult or another child:

- Biting
- Hitting
- Pinching
- Inappropriate language
- Throwing/breaking toys/equipment/furniture.

Nursery staff will encourage and support children to develop a sense of right and wrong by helping children to cooperate in the nursery.

Staff will always try to explain, reason with and calm the child.

If the antisocial behaviour continues, the staff will direct the child to more positive activities.

If a child has hurt/upset another child they will be encouraged to apologise to the injured party.

As a last resort the child will be removed from the situation and asked to sit with a member of staff for a few moments to calm down.

Any incident of discipline will be brought to the parents' attention and discussed with them.

Staff will be aware of the age and stage of development of the child and of any cultural, linguistic or particular needs.

Shouting or physical punishment will not be used. Physical intervention, i.e. holding, will be used only to prevent injury to the child, other children or an adult, or serious damage to property.

Figure 8.6. Example of a discipline policy

New staff should be given copies of policies and procedures as part of the induction process and given the opportunity to discuss them with their line manager. As a manager you may wish to compile a staff handbook or pack and ask new staff to sign documentation to say they have read and understood the policies and procedures of the setting. Many establishments do this in the induction period to ensure new members of staff are conversant with the policies and procedures of the setting from the start of their employment (see Chapter 6).

A framework for writing a policy could be to include:

- the aims of the policy
- methods of implementing the policy
- procedures for monitoring and reviewing.

Good practice checklist
Writing a policy or procedure

- Ensure you have a clear aim in mind and that you understand the focus of the policy.
- Base the aim of your policy on the shared values and vision of the whole team.
- Make sure legislative requirements are met (e.g. Ofsted standards) and regularly reviewed.
- Make sure the policy is written down and regularly reviewed.
- Staff should be part of the process of writing policies.
- The resulting documents should be readily available for all to see, including staff and parents.

Points for reflective practice

As a manager it is worth regularly reflecting on the nature of the policies that you have in place.

- How could you ensure that all policies are up to date?
- How could you ensure that they cover every area of the care and education of children and meet National Standards?
- How could you ensure that staff and management read, understand and agree to the policies and procedures?
- What kind of consultation process might you implement to review documentation?

Conclusion

This chapter has looked at the administration of the childcare setting and has considered the role of the manager in running a successful establishment that offers quality provision. The emphasis has been on business responsibilities and legal obligations, and ways in which to meet these, for example through the creation of policies and procedures.

Check your understanding

1. In the area where you live or work, what childcare is available? Is there room for expansion? How would you find out this information?

2. Consider how you would market a new nursery in your area.

3. How would you ensure you were providing a quality service?

4. How would you make the childcare you provide accessible and affordable?

References and further reading

Brunton, P. and Thornton, L. (2007) *The Early Years Handbook*. London: Optimus Publishing.

Department for Education and Employment (1998) *Meeting the Childcare Challenge* (Green Paper). www.surestart.gov.uk.

Department for Education and Skills (2000) *Curriculum Guidance for the Foundation Stage*. www.standards.dfes.gov.uk.

Department for Education and Skills (2002) *Birth to Three Matters*. www.standards.dfes.gov.uk; www.surestart.gov.uk.

Department for Education and Skills (2003) *Every Child Matters*. www.everychildmatters.gov.uk.

Department for Education and Skills (2003) *National Standards for Under 8s Day Care and Childminding*. www.surestart.gov.uk.

Department for Education and Skills (2007) *Early Years Foundation Stage: Setting the Standards for Learning, Development and Care for Children from Birth to Five*. www.teachernet.gov.uk/publications.

Department for Education and Skills (2007) *Research Report Childcare and Early Years Survey: a Study of Parents' Use, Views and Experiences*. www.dcsf.gov.uk/research (published May 2008).

Ofsted (2008a) *Are you ready for your inspection?* A guide to inspections of provision on Ofsted's Childcare and Early Years Registers.

Ofsted (2008b) *Guidance for Registration on the Childcare Register*.

Ofsted (2008c) *Guidance to Registration on the Early Years Register*.

Ofsted (2008d) *Leading to Excellence*. Practice Guidance for the Early Years Foundation Stage

Proctor, T. (2000) *Essentials of Marketing Research*. Oxford: Pearson.

Useful websites

Big Lottery Fund – allocates money for good causes from the National Lottery: www.biglotteryfund.org.uk

Charities Aid Foundation: www.cafonline.org

Childcare links – provides links to Children's Information Services: www.childcarelink.gov.uk

Criminal Records Bureau (CRB): www.crb.gov.uk

Daycare Trust – promotes affordable childcare for all, and offers advice and information: www.daycaretrust.org.uk

Every Child Matters: www.everychildmatters.gov.uk

FunderFinder – resources for those seeking grants: www.funderfinder.org.uk

Health and Safety Executive (HSE) – gives information on health and safety at work: www.hse.gov.uk

HM Revenue and Customs (HMRC). www.hmrc.gov.uk

Information Commissioner's Office: www.dataprotection.gov.uk

Laing & Buisson – independent company providing statistical information on availability of childcare (may require payment): www.laingbuisson.co.uk

Leading to Excellence: www.cwdcouncil.org.uk; www.ofsted.gov.uk

Learning and Skills Council – funding for training: www.lsc.gov.uk

National Childminding Association: www.ncma.org.uk

National Children's Bureau (NCB): www.ncb.org.uk

National Day Nurseries Association: www.ndna.org.uk

Nursery & Childcare Market News – newsletter for childcare workers: www.nurseryandchildcaremarketnews.co.uk

OfQual (Office of the Qualifications and Exams Regulator): www.ofqual.gov.uk

Ofsted (Office for Standards in Education): www.ofsted.gov.uk

Pre-school Learning Alliance: www.pre-school.org.uk

Sure Start: www.surestart.gov.uk

Teachernet – online publications for schools: www.teachernet.gov.uk/publications

9 Political and Social Issues

At the beginning of the twentieth century, children in the UK were treated very differently from the children of today. We have seen vast changes in the way children and their parents and carers are perceived and treated. In more recent years, children have become the subject of political debate and they are now at the top of the government's agenda. Parents and carers have, through legislation, been given clarity about their responsibilities and a voice in how their children are treated by professionals. Consequently, early years professionals have seen many changes in the care and education of young people.

Managers in early years settings – in children's centres, day nurseries, nursery schools and pre-school settings, some of which will be in the private and some in the voluntary sector – are at the front line of the implementation of government strategies and guidelines. This has meant that today's nursery manager has had to keep abreast of all that is happening in the early years world. It is essential that managers keep themselves up to date with current thinking, practice and policy. It is beneficial for them to be involved in networking with other professionals and local authorities, to help keep the channels between the implementers and the policy-makers open. They are the most experienced in dealing with children, parents and carers on a day-to-day basis.

This chapter looks at the wider issues surrounding early years services. Some of these issues may not directly affect what happens in the everyday management of an early years setting, but it is vital for the manager to be aware of what is taking place across the sector. Managers who have a wide knowledge base are far more likely to be respected by their teams and will feel more confident in dealing with outside agencies. Managers will have to implement changes. These changes can be externally enforced, or they may need to take place for a variety of reasons internal to the setting. This chapter also helps the manager to understand the making of policy and the resulting legislation.

The chapter covers the following areas:

9.1 Government initiatives

9.2 Children's rights and legislation

9.3 Safeguarding children and young people

9.4 Working with children, young people and their families

9.5 Supporting good health

9.6 Policy affecting practice

9.1 Government initiatives

Children are high on the government's agenda. A Minister of State for Children has been appointed. The first-ever governmental National Childcare Strategy was launched in 1998 (see Chapter 8). The strategy was part of a package of policies designed to tackle child poverty and social exclusion, the aim being to end child poverty by 2020. This section covers a few other important initiatives. Sources of further information on these appear in the list of useful websites at the end of the chapter.

Figure 9.1. There have been great changes in the care and education of young people; gone are the days of 'chalk and talk'

Every Child Matters – Change for Children

In September 2003 the Department for Education and Skills published the long-awaited Green Paper *Every Child Matters*. This new way of working looks at the welfare of children and young people from birth to age 19 years. Whatever the child's background or experience, the aim is to support five key outcomes for all children and young people.

All agencies have to work together to provide services and these five outcomes for children. These agencies are able to share information to protect children and young people from harm and support them to achieve what they want in life.

The government continues to set up new projects within this agenda, encompassing areas such as:

- Invest in a Children's Fund
- Support schools in working with mental health practitioners

- Staying safe consultations – balancing protection of children with allowing them to take risks

- Developing fun, safe and effective children's play with the Department of Culture, Media and Sport

- A Children's Plan to examine prevention of problems, tailored support services, positive childhood and the role of families.

As part of the Change for Children agenda there are areas that, as a practitioner you should know about, even if you are not directly involved.

Find it out

Research what the *Every Child Matters* agenda is doing to support youth – Targeted youth support – as part of the Youth Matters Green Paper (July 2005) and Next steps (March 2006).

The Ten Year Childcare Strategy

The government's Ten Year Childcare Strategy was published in December 2004. This set out the government's long-term vision to ensure that every child gets the best start in life. It aims to offer:

- Choice and flexibility – parents to have greater choice about balancing work and family life

- Availability – for all families with children up to 14, and childcare places to suit their circumstances

- Quality – high-quality provision with a highly skilled workforce

- Affordability – families able to access high-quality childcare that they can afford (www.treasury.gov.uk).

The strategy recognised that early childhood is a vital time in a child's development and acknowledged the need for awareness of the considerable challenges faced by families in balancing their family life with work commitments. It also recognised that the country's economic prosperity relied to some extent on an offer of high-quality childcare and support of parents to ensure that there was a response to this need. There has been an investment in setting up a strong foundation of services and support for parents. The Ten Year Strategy set out to create a sustainable framework for childcare provision and support to build upon the government's *Every Child Matters* agenda.

Think it over

Research 'Choice for Parents, the best start for children: a ten year strategy for childcare'.

Can you see the main aims of this strategy in the local provision in your area? Consider the changes you have seen take place in the last five years.

The Work and Families Act 2006 also responds to the need to offer more choice and flexibility for parents by extending maternity and adoption pay and creating new rights for employed fathers.

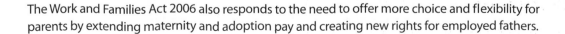

The new initiatives should ensure that children and families are supported in their choice of childcare.

The Children's Plan – Building brighter futures (December 2007)

Building on a decade of reform, the Children's Plan aims to respond directly to strengthen support for all families during the formative years of children's lives. Five principles underpin the Children's Plan and are shown in Figure 9.2 (see also Chapter 7).

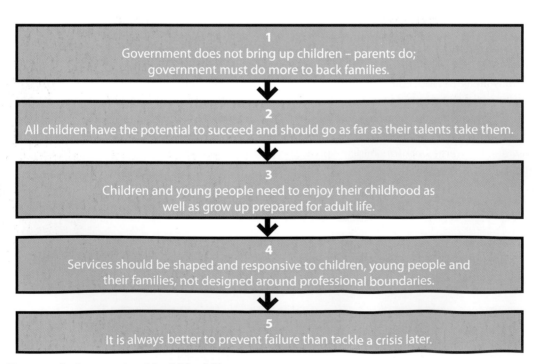

1
Government does not bring up children – parents do;
government must do more to back families.

2
All children have the potential to succeed and should go as far as their talents take them.

3
Children and young people need to enjoy their childhood as
well as grow up prepared for adult life.

4
Services should be shaped and responsive to children, young people and
their families, not designed around professional boundaries.

5
It is always better to prevent failure than tackle a crisis later.

Figure 9.2. The five principles of the Children's Plan

National Service Framework for Children, Young People and Maternity Services

The National Service Framework (NSF) was announced in February 2001. The aim is to develop standards across the National Health Service (NHS) and local authority social services for children. The programme intends to stimulate long-term and sustained improvement in children's health.

Children's Trusts

Children's Trusts bring together all services for children and young people in their area. They focus on improving outcomes for children and young people and they have a duty to cooperate in this (see also Chapter 7). Their core features are:

- clear short- and long-term objectives covering the five *Every Child Matters* outcomes
- a children's services director
- single planning and community functions, supported by pooled budgets, to facilitate the development of an overall picture of children's needs.

Sure Start

Sure Start is a government-funded programme which began in 1998 and is an integral part of the Children, Young People and Families Directorate (see also Chapter 8). The programme aims to achieve better outcomes for children, parents and families and communities by:

- increasing the availability of childcare
- improving the health and emotional development of children
- supporting parents as parents and their aspirations towards employment.

The programme is a comprehensive service to deliver the best start in life for every child in England, bringing together education, health and family support. It works through integrated early years services in:

- Sure Start children's centres – 2,907 established in June 2008, offering services to 2.2 million young children and their families. These centres bring high-quality services to communities.

- Early education – all three- and four-year-olds offered a free part-time place (12.5 hours, 38 weeks a year) in an early education setting. There is a code of practice on the provision of free nursery education places which can be viewed on the DfES website. The free places can be provided by maintained, private, voluntary and independent sector providers. There are currently 37,000 settings delivering these government funded places.

- Childcare provision – some 1.29 million registered childcare places – some of these will be extended schools; some will be with childminders. There is a free booklet available for parents and carers called 'Looking for childcare'.

Key Term

Children's centres – a variety of provision and services under one roof within the community, providing high-quality care to children and their families.

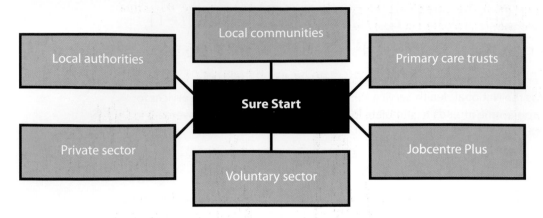

Figure 9.3. Sure Start model for integrating services

Sure Start principles

Families are supported from pregnancy right through until children are 14 years old, extended to 16 years old if children have special educational needs. The principles are:

- work with parents and children – meeting the needs of children and supporting parents to fulfil career aspirations

- services for everyone – responding to the varying needs of children and their families at different times in their lives

- flexible at the point of delivery; services provided to encourage access; accessible opening hours and location all under one roof; a single point of contact

- starting very early – beginning with the first antenatal visit giving advice on all aspects of life, from pregnancy and health to decisions about returning to work

- respectful and transparent – customer-focused and led by the customer

- community driven and professionally coordinated – expertise is shared in consultation with local people towards understanding their service priorities

- outcome driven – the core purpose is better outcomes for children. This includes a reduction in bureaucracy and simplified funding.

Points for reflective practice

Visit the Sure Start website (www.surestart.gov.uk) and investigate:

- Sure Start children's centre guidance
- the National Quality Improvement Network.

Ofsted and the inspection process

As we have seen from Chapter 8, since 2001 Ofsted has inspected all childcare provision in the UK against the Department for Education and Skills *National Standards for Under 8s Day Care and Childminding* (2003). There are different types of inspections, depending on the setting being visited, and they follow different legal frameworks:

- maintained schools (under section 10 of the Schools Inspection Act 1996);
- funded nursery education (under section 122 of the School Standards and Frameworks Act 1998);
- childcare (under Part XA of the Children Act 1989 and as inserted in the Care Standards Act 2000).

These standards will determine the expectations of the Ofsted inspectors when they inspect any setting under these headings.

In August 2003, Ofsted produced *Early Years: The First National Picture* (a very useful report, which you should obtain as it contains information about the outcomes of inspections, as well as complaints, investigation and enforcement – see references). This gave an overall summary of the make-up of childcare in England. It stated that:

> On 31 March 2003, Ofsted had 99,300 registered childcare providers in England on its database. Of these 68,200 were childminders, 9,600 full-day care providers, 11,600 sessional day care providers, 8,000 out of school care and 1,900 crèches. Around 1,700 providers were offering more than one type of care.

The Early Years Directorate of Ofsted has a statutory responsibility to ensure that providers of day care for children are suitable and that they comply with the National Standards. Ofsted has the power to:

- grant, refuse or cancel registration;
- impose, remove or vary conditions of registration, and grant or refuse requests for variations to the conditions of registration;
- prosecute providers for specific offences.

All day care providers must register with Ofsted and will require a named 'registered person' for inspection and registration purposes (see Chapter 8). Ofsted guidelines describe a 'suitable person' to be registered to run a setting by their qualification level – Level 3 with two years' experience of working with children. The setting will need to pay a fee for registration and there is an annual fee once it is registered.

A full programme of combined inspections by Ofsted began in April 2003. These combined inspections meant that all settings providing nursery education and receiving government funding for 3–4-year-olds would be inspected and scored on a three-point scale for the quality of nursery education – good, satisfactory and unsatisfactory. In these inspections judgements were made about the quality of leadership and management and its effect on the progress of children who receive funded nursery education. This was, of course, very important as the manager needed to demonstrate:

- leadership of the setting
- the ability of the setting to assess its weaknesses and strengths
- how effective the setting is at monitoring and evaluating the education it provides
- commitment to improving care and education for children.

From September 2008 this changed and settings are now inspected according to the Early Years Foundation Stage (EYFS) framework – which sets the standards for care, learning and development for children from birth to the 31 August following their fifth birthday. Childcare providers for this age group must join the Early Years Register and the Ofsted Childcare Register (OCR) – see Chapter 8. This is compulsory, although some services do not have to register:

- some crèches
- activity-based settings
- nannies caring for children in their own homes.

9.2 Children's rights and legislation

The majority of professionals working with children will probably state that most of their work underpins protecting the rights of children. The League of Nations drafted the first Declaration of the Rights of the Child in 1924. In the UK there has long been a concern about how to address the 'needs' of children, and there was little emphasis on ensuring their rights. Children are, of course, vulnerable members of society and are dependent, particularly in the early years, on adults advocating for them. In early years settings it is important that children's rights are considered when making decisions about their future or their developmental progress. Some children are faced with situations where, for reasons beyond their control (family breakdown, abuse, domestic violence or poverty), their rights are being taken away from them. It is important for early years practitioners to ensure that they know the legislation that supports children.

The United Nations Convention on the Rights of the Child

The 1989 United Nations Convention on the Rights of the Child (CRC) is one of the primary resources for anyone looking to develop services for children. It was ratified by the UK in 1991. The articles within it cover every aspect of a child's life (children are those under 18 years of age). The CRC highlights the need for countries to work together, and most countries have now ratified it (the USA and Somalia have not). All countries that ratify the CRC must produce a report after the first two years and subsequently every five years. The CRC says that the best interests of the child must always be considered and that their views must be taken into account at all times. The convention contains 54 articles, which address the rights shown in Figure 9.4.

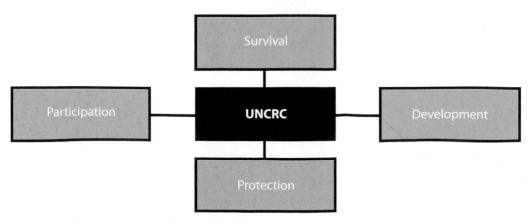

Figure 9.4. Children's rights addressed by the United Nations

The UN Committee on the Rights of the Child is responsible for monitoring the implementation of the CRC, and in October 2002 it issued a report on the UK. Some of this report praised what was going on in the UK and acknowledged positive moves in areas such as race relations legislation and promotion of children's rights in the UK's international aid policies. The Committee made a recommendation that the UK establish children's commissioners to ensure that the rights of children and young people are being upheld. Wales was the first nation in the UK to implement this and the first children's commissioner began work in March 2001. *Every Child Matters – Agenda for Change* stated that this will come into force in England as well. The commissioners' role is an independent one and therefore they have the power to:

- review proposed legislation
- listen to the views of children and young people
- ensure that children's best interests are being met.

This will include investigating the effectiveness of the law, practice and services. The UN Committee also had concerns about the lack of coordination across government departments, and the 'piecemeal' approach to putting some aspects of the CRC into law. The government now has strategies in place to address these concerns.

Law reform and the Implementation of the Convention of the Rights of the Child

This report (2008) covers 18 of the general principles and rights contained in the CRC, three of which have been identified as requiring further investigation:

- the process of law reform
- its place as part of a broad child rights strategy
- the actual impact of legislation of this kind on children.

This report will investigate these three subjects and report findings so that recommendations can be made.

UNICEF

UNICEF, the United Nations Children's Fund, works to support set goals for children internationally. In 1990 there was a World Summit for Children – the Millennium Declaration was a General Assembly resolution in September 2000. The declaration has eight chapters and key objectives adopted by world leaders during the summit:

1 Values and principles
2 Peace, security and Disarmament
3 Development and Poverty eradication
4 Protecting our Common Environment
5 Human Rights, democracy and Good Governance
6 Protecting the vulnerable
7 Meeting the special needs of Africa
8 Strengthening the United Nations

The Millennium Declaration

The declaration had 180 nations committed to 'A World Fit for Children'. This included 21 targets in ten years, focusing on four key priorities:

- promoting healthy lives
- providing quality education for all
- protecting children against abuse, exploitation and violence
- combating HIV and AIDS.

As you can see, these international goals are similar to the focus of the *Every Child Matters* agenda in the UK.

Between April 2001 and May 2002 some 95 million people in over 190 countries pledged their support for the 'Say Yes for Children' campaign which also supported the above goals. This campaign, promoted by the Global Movement for Children, was the largest petition ever according to the *Guinness Book of World Records*.

Find it out

Investigate the United Nations Charter and the Universal Declaration of Human Rights.

- How do they link to policy in Britain today?

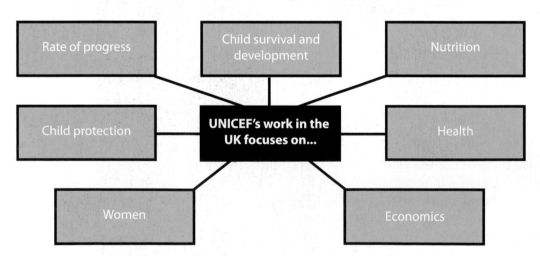

Figure 9.5. The focus of UNICEF's work in the UK

The UK National Committee for UNICEF was established in 1956. The committee works in the UK to champion and promote children's rights, and raise money for the work of UNICEF across the world.

Innocenti Research Centre

With the guidance of UNICEF principles and the Innocenti Research Centre in Florence aims to raise the national and international profile of children's issues. It undertakes research to promote the creation and distribution of information so different parts of the organisation can benefit from each other's experience.

- Child poverty and social and economic policy responses – this will look at the impact and context of socio-economic policies at national and international level on children's rights and to ensure that these are being realised.

- Implementation of international standards on children's rights – this area of work promotes awareness and understanding of standards internationally. It is also looking at how these standards are translated into national policy.

- Protection of children from exploitation and abuse – this looks at human rights violations committed against children during armed conflict.

Find it out

Use the Internet to investigate Innocenti's work on:

- global research on Ombuds for children
- cross-national surveys on children
- The Florence Report (2008) – Sexual Exploitation of Children and Adolescents.

Children's needs are paramount throughout the world.

Points for reflective practice

In the last century childhood has changed irreversibly. Andrew Bell (1808) was one of the founder members of the monitorial system of elementary education and he wrote in his book, *The Madras School* (1808, p. 292) that:

> It is not proposed that the children of the poor be educated in an expensive manner or to be taught to write or cipher. Utopian schemes for the universal diffusion of general knowledge would soon realize the fable of the belly and the other members of the body and confound that distinction of ranks and classes of society on which the general welfare hinges… there is a risk of elevating by an indiscriminate education, the minds of those doomed to the drudgery of daily labour above their conditions and thereby rendering them discontented and unhappy in their lot.

Look at ways in which we may have moved on from this perception of education of children. Where are there inadequacies in our present systems?

Figure 9.6. It is everyone's duty to promote racial equality and harmony.

Promoting racial equality

Equality is about making sure people are treated fairly and are given equal chances and access to services. Equality is not about treating everyone the same, but about recognising and celebrating people's individual differences. We have a public duty to promote equality and remove discrimination.

Legislation and the Commission for Racial Equality (CRE)

There is also a statutory duty to promote racial equality, and specific responsibilities have been laid down for schools. All managers of early years settings need to have read the guidance on the Race Relations Act 1976 and the Race Relations (Amendment) Act 2000, which are designed to eliminate racial discrimination and promote race equality and relations. Local authorities produce guidance for childcare settings, and the Commission for Racial Equality (2002) has published its own guidance for schools, which supports settings in implementing the requirements of the Race Relations (Amendment) Act 2000.

By May 2002 all settings were advised to have a written statement of policy for promoting racial equality. They were also expected to develop an assessment or action plan to look at the impact of this policy on:

- staff
- children
- parents and carers of different racial groups.

Early years settings must evaluate the effects on the above groups of the following aspects of their practice:

- care, learning and play
- admissions
- behaviour policies and management
- the curriculum
- staff recruitment
- guidance and support.

If the assessment or action plan is not carried out the CRE is empowered to issue a notice of compliance.

Ofsted's role

The ways in which a setting addresses inclusion and valuing cultural diversity will also be closely monitored by Ofsted. The registered person in the setting will need to show the strategies that are in place to 'overcome potential barriers to learning'. The staff team will be expected to monitor the children's behaviour to ensure that the setting does not have an adverse effect on the children's learning. Settings must be proactive and take steps to involve parents and carers from ethnic minorities. The setting will also need to collect and keep information on the ethnicity of all children and staff, for the purpose of monitoring equality of opportunity.

Key Term

Inclusion – the process of ensuring equality of learning opportunities for all children irrespective of their diversity.

Good practice checklist
Ensuring inclusion

The 2001 census showed that nearly one in eight pupils comes from a minority background. By 2010, the proportion is expected to be around one in five.

The Department for Education and Skills (2003b) has published the findings of a consultation. Data were gathered from 500 schools. The document identified certain characteristics of successful schools and found that there was a need to spread their good practice in the following areas:

- strong leadership – in implementing an effective strategy

- high expectations – all pupils encouraged to fulfil their full potential

- monitoring achievement and identifying areas of under-achievement

- effective teaching and learning – support for bilingual pupils, cultural identities reflected in the lessons

- ethos of respect and a clear approach to racism – a focus on prevention of racism, bad behaviour and bullying

- parental involvement – parents and carers and the wider community involved in the life of the school.

Although the study related to schools, the points of good practice also apply, to a great extent, to early years settings. It is interesting that leadership and reflective management rate so highly as factors in success! Managers of early years settings can use the school experience as a model for the provision of opportunities for all.

Points for reflective practice

As a manager, what practical things might you do to ensure the setting operates in a non-discriminatory manner?

What might you have to do to meet the requirements of the Race Relations Act?

Child poverty

Some people may find it hard to accept that many children are still living in poverty in the UK, but for some childcare workers and managers this will be readily evident in their setting. Childcare professionals are required to see the child holistically. Some projects and centres of excellence are working to address these needs.

According to Daycare Trust estimates (August 2008) some 3.49 million children in Britain live in poverty, a shocking 30 per cent of all children. In 1999 the government pledged to end child poverty and since then has lifted 500,000 children out of poverty by increasing benefits and supporting parents into work by the introduction of Tax Credits (see Chapter 8). However, some children, in particular asylum-seeking children, have suffered as a result of political decisions. Moreover, many anti-poverty proposals are long-term, and for parents living in deprived areas there will be no imminent change in their situation. Figure 9.7 shows factors other than low income associated with poverty within a region.

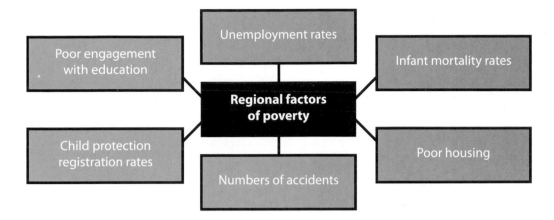

Figure 9.7 Poverty is not caused solely by low income

The emphasis of present government strategy is to:

- help parents into paid employment
- continue investing in good-quality, affordable childcare
- work to promote high-quality affordable childcare.

According to Daycare Trust, the typical cost of a childcare place for a child under 2 years old in 2008 is £159 per week. For some parents living on state benefits or a low wage this is unaffordable.

Think it over

Look at the Save the Children website (www.savethechildren.org.uk) and investigate the following reports on child poverty in the UK:

- Children in Severe Poverty in Wales
- Halfway House
- Persistent Child Poverty in Northern Ireland: key findings
- Hard Times.

Inclusion

In 2008 the Council for Disabled Children (CDC) undertook a project to identify best practice in including children with disabilities and young people in children's centres and extended schools. Sure Start and the Department for Children, Schools and Families commissioned the *Extending Inclusion* programme. This consisted of two projects – the first to review access to and inclusion in children's centres and the second to review access to and inclusion in extended schools. The projects were asked to:

- identify good practice in promoting access to services for disabled children and their families
- identify good practice in promoting participation of disabled children and their families
- share this good practice with others
- listen to the views of children with disabilities and their families
- develop partnerships with local authorities, services and volunteer agencies.

The government's current vision for children's centres is broadly inclusive and aims to target inequalities between disadvantaged children and the rest. The focus is on children fulfilling their potential. The government stated that 'Children with disabilities and/or special needs must be able to access all extended services' (DfES, 2005).

Working with the Disability Discrimination Acts (DDA) 1995 and 2005

The DDA sets out two main duties:

1 not to treat disabled children 'less favourably'
2 to make 'reasonable adjustments' for disabled children.

The Disability Discrimination Act requires all settings to make reasonable adjustments towards the inclusion of disabled children.

Failure to comply with these duties amounts to unlawful discrimination. These duties apply to the provision made by schools and local authorities, but can also apply to other agencies such as extended schools or provision in a children's centre which could be run by a voluntary agency or private company.

The Council for Disabled Children states that all providers need to have a shared understanding of responsibilities under the DDA, and need to discuss a definition of their duties, looking specifically at:

- shared understanding of any developments needed – what are the practical implications?
- areas to improve access and participation – how does the DDA apply in practice?
- a focus on children and young people with disabilities – an action plan to support and include them
- who counts as disabled
- what the barriers are and potential solutions
- commitment and capacity of the staff working with the children.

Points for reflective practice

What is the potential discussion needed for your setting in providing access and inclusion?

How has your setting ensured it complies with the DDA?

What it means in practice

Access to all types of provision for children and young people with disabilities is often hampered by a lack of information and clarity. Many of their parents do not know what services are available and are very often dependent on their individual point of contact, that is health visitor, social worker or GP. 'Knowledge of the Children's Information Service (CIS) is low and they are perceived as being largely irrelevant for disabled children' according to Daycare Trust (2007).

Although some settings are welcoming they may give parents the impression that they have not thought about how best to provide the correct service to the child or young person. The Council for Disabled Children (CDC) found that very often all the parents need is for someone to say; 'How can we support your child?' Practitioners need to have information and training to help them provide the best service for children to meet their support needs.

Think it over

Investigate one of these published studies which look at barriers for children with disabilities and their families:

Joseph Rowntree Foundation (2006) report – Inclusion of children in primary school playgrounds.

Daycare Trust (2007), Listening to parents of disabled children – a report for the London Development Agency.

9.3 Safeguarding children and young people

One of the most important responsibilities of anyone working with children is to protect them. The protection of children in their care is an integral part of childcare and education workers' duties and moral code.

The death of Victoria Climbié in February 2000 at the hands of her guardian brought child protection into the limelight once again and highlighted a need for further structural changes to local authorities. The subsequent report by Lord Laming (2003) was (at the time of writing) the latest of 67 inquiries into severe child abuse that have been held in England since 1945. Many of the proposals made in the report into Victoria's death have had a profound effect on policy and have led to early intervention to prevent something similar happening again. The fact that there were 12 opportunities to save Victoria highlighted the need for seamless provision of services for children, and the need to ensure that everyone who comes into contact with children is accountable.

Even though early years practitioners may never come face to face with a child in the same situation as Victoria Climbié, this does not give cause for complacency. Vigilance is required and procedures must be followed. The registered person is responsible for the safety of the children. The manager of the setting (usually the registered person) may be the person the staff or parent or carer will approach with a concern about a child's well-being.

All early years settings are required to have a 'designated child protection person' and managers will need to allocate this role to an experienced team member or take on the role themselves. The designated person needs to remain objective and professional. The priority is to pass on all concerns to the relevant agencies. An early call to a fellow professional could save a child's life, or at the very least assure the manager that all is well. If there should be any concerns raised, all staff should follow the correct procedures. The manager will need to support staff and let them talk through their anxieties and fears. Staff should be encouraged at appraisal to attend courses in child protection (these are especially useful for non-qualified staff). The manager will need constantly to keep up to date with any changes to the law or local policy.

Michelle's concerns

Case Study

Michelle is head of room in a busy day nursery. There is a child whose behaviour has been concerning her for some time. She discusses this with the new manager, Claire, and relates some incidents which have worried her; Michelle also discusses a conversation she has overheard between parents. Claire asks Michelle to make notes so that they have a written record of her concerns. Michelle carefully records observations of the child, with times and dates when the child was less communicative. Michelle speaks to Claire a second time and gives her the written record. The manager says that she will handle it, but offers Michelle no further information or advice. Michelle is very upset by this response and leaves the office feeling indecisive about what to do next.

- What mistake did Claire make?
- How could she have handled this situation differently?
- Would you say Claire works well with her staff team, based on this incident?

The case study 'Michelle's concerns' illustrates a difficult situation for any member of staff, one that can cause a great deal of worry. Childcare professionals need to work together for the good of the child, and to ensure that everything observed is documented in line with local child protection procedures. In the main, the case study relates to a lack of communication within the staff team and reluctance on the part of the manager to share information with the staff member, which causes the latter to feel isolated.

It is important that staff teams are aware of the setting's procedures and are aware of whom to contact if there is cause for concern. Each area will have a child protection procedure, which will include contact information for all the professionals working within the child protection team. Area child protection teams are maintained by the Department of Health and it is their role to develop agreed local policies and procedures for multi-agency working to protect children and promote their welfare. Managers should ensure they have a good relationship with local health visitors and other professionals, as they are a useful source of advice and guidance, and may also know the children within the setting.

> ### Key Term
>
> **Multi-agency working** – involves different services, agencies and teams of professionals working together to provide support that meets the needs of children and their families.

Find it out

To further explore safeguarding children you might want to look at the Common Assessment Framework (CAF).

Consider your possible involvement in this process.

Generally, managers will be dealing with comparatively minor incidents within their settings. Staff may be concerned about a parent or carer who seems unusually stressed and impatient with a child; or a situation when a child and family are experiencing temporary difficulties caused by:

- loss of a parent or guardian
- redundancy
- financial pressures
- illness in the family
- the family moving house
- a parent's new hours of working, or promotion
- a new baby
- difficulties in dealing with the child in a particular stage of development, such as tantrums, toilet-training or challenging behaviour.

In such cases the manager will need to allow the family (both the child and the parents or carers) individual time. Parents may need to have time to have a friendly chat with the

> ### Key Term
>
> **Common Assessment Framework** – a holistic assessment tool used by early years practitioners to identify at an early stage the additional needs of children and young people who are achieving poorly on the *Every Child Matters* outcomes.

manager, and during this time the manager will be able to offer advice or discuss the possibility (if needed) of involving other support, for example a health visitor. It is important that managers have information and contact details on the types of support available.

In terms of safeguarding children the manager will be responsible for making sure there is good practice that meets the needs of children and their families and fulfils legislative requirements. They will also need to support and advise parents, carers and members of staff about any issues that may come up.

Good practice checklist
Safeguarding children

- Ensure all staff are recruited effectively by obtaining references and CRB disclosures (see Chapters 7 and 8).
- Ensure there is a clear child protection policy.
- Ensure that all staff can demonstrate a confident understanding of the policy for safeguarding children.
- Use documentation from the local safeguarding children's board.
- Appoint a lead person whose job it is to ensure that every member of staff receives continuous training so that they know what to do if they are worried that a child is being abused.
- Ensure that parents are aware that staff have a duty to share child protection issues with other professionals and agencies.
- Ensure that if a child protection incident were to occur good support is in place for children, their families and staff.

9.4 Working with children, young people and their families

Historically, parents and carers developed their own integrated service by drawing on the support of grandparents, relations, pre-schools and schools, and neighbours. This would have been achieved within a strong community network. In the present day, however, this can be difficult, as families are often dispersed and not part of a familiar, close-knit community. Parents and carers are often faced with trying to find suitable childcare if they are working and not able to depend on close family or neighbours (as they might have done formerly). In doing so, they will need to take certain factors into consideration.

- Who is to provide the childcare – childminder, nursery, friend, after-school club?
- Are they reliable and dependable?
- Are they trustworthy and suitably qualified?
- Where is childcare to be provided – at work, near work, near home?

- What will it cost?

- Is it worth doing? (Will we be better off?)

Integrated services should be able to provide for a variety of diverse needs (see Figure 9.8). The most effective service for families is one which provides for all. One example is a 'wraparound' service – day care, sessional care, nursery, school and extended schools. Similarly, health services for families dealing with long-term illness or medical conditions should also offer practical, emotional and financial help.

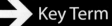

Key Term

Integrated working – professionals working together to deliver frontline services to children and their families. This means that provision will be under one roof and accessible for all.

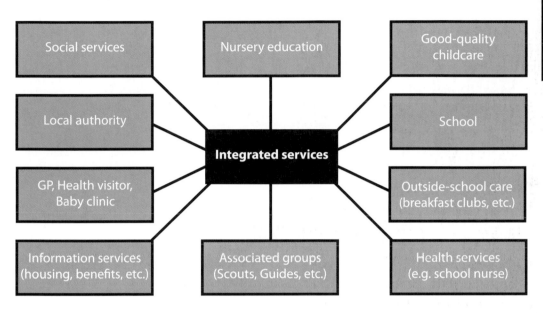

Figure 9.8. An integrated service provides good-quality services for all the family.

Improving life chances

Children's centres are currently the way forward in ensuring that the government's agenda for multi-agency working can be established and be successful. The changing context of children's centres relies on good local authority leadership, close partnership working and effective multi-agency teams. They need to offer services that are attractive to parents and support the local community to improve life chances for children.

As part of the drive to provide children's centres with good-quality care, there is also a drive to ensure that all staff are highly trained and qualified. Volunteers have an important role in the effective running of a children's centre and will require training and good supervision.

Centres are expected to monitor the progress of each child and use records which help keep parents up to date with their progress, encouraging them to be actively involved in their child's learning. The centres work with statutory, voluntary, private and independent sector partners to provide:

- early years provision

- a childminders' network

- parenting education

- family support services

- health services

- education, training and employment services.

In areas where there is less need and fewer deprived families, the job of the children's centre is to signpost parents to local services rather than duplicating what is already available locally.

In order to establish effective multi-agency working the professionals will need time to get together, and this can mean that professionals such as health visitors, family support workers and midwives may work in the same location, helping them to identify common ground. It is important that everyone in a multi-agency team is aware of the line management structure and that they all have regular opportunities to meet and have joint training to discuss and make joint decisions.

Points for reflective practice

In your current role, look at ways in which you can improve or take part in a multi-agency team approach.

Parents and families need support at particular times in their lives when facing new challenges such as:

- the birth of a new baby or sibling
- a child starting school
- health issues or feeding problems
- if the child has an identified particular need
- problems in the parents' relationship.

The care that young children receive from their parents or carers is pivotal for their development and emotional security. Authoritative parenting that combines consistent boundaries with warmth and love improves a child's self-esteem and confidence. If parents and carers feel supported, it can make a significant difference to the life chances of the child. Parents may, in some cases, feel that they are unable to ask for support. Figure 9.9 shows some of the reasons why people may find it difficult to ask for help.

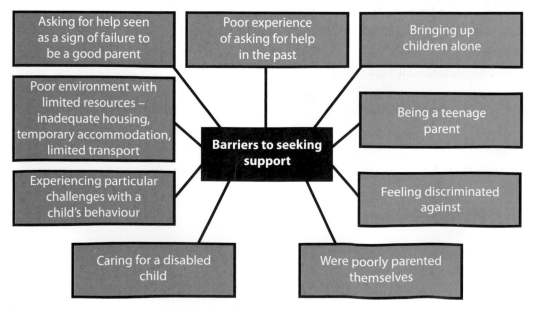

Figure 9.9. Some reasons why people may find it difficult to ask for help and support

All settings need to overcome any barriers the parents and carers may have to discussing their difficulties with the staff or asking for information about support they could access. If a parent or carer has a particular need it is also important that staff have knowledge of support services on offer.

Find it out

Investigate some of the following agencies to gather information to support parents and carers for particular issues:

- Mellow Parenting
- Triple P (Positive Parenting Program)
- PEEP – Learning Together
- Race Equality Foundation – Strengthening Families, Strengthening Communities
- Parents as First Teachers
- PIPPIN (Parents in Partnership Parent Infant) Programme.

9.5 Supporting good health

The government's public health White Paper *Choosing Health: Making healthier choices easier* (2004) highlighted the importance of children's health needs from pre-conception and throughout life. The paper looks at ways in which we can reduce health inequalities in the UK through improvements in education, housing and financial stability. The *Every Child Matters* outcomes also note that health and well-being are essential for development and long-term prospects. If a child is not healthy it can hold them back in every facet of their lives, preventing them from enjoying their lives and reaching their full potential.

Health professionals are, of course, the first point of contact in a child's life, and they have contact with the parents before the child is even born. This gives them the ideal opportunity to:

- establish a good relationship with the parents
- influence parenting practices right from the start
- promote a healthy lifestyle
- empower parents to care for themselves and look after their own health
- make sure parents have all the information they need to give their child a healthy start in life.

We are more aware than ever of the importance of healthy diet and exercise.

Most parents are at this time susceptible to encouragement and advice to ensure their child has a good start in life. The role of the health services is to prevent possible negative effects of deprivation at this point. They can do this by:

- promoting and supporting breastfeeding
- reducing smoking in pregnancy
- improving mental health of children and their parents
- encouraging an immunisation programme
- encouraging good dental health
- informing parents of ways to prevent accidents with young children
- informing parents about childhood screening
- intervening early to address any particular needs.

Think it over

How do you ensure that information is readily available to parents in your setting regarding health?

How do you integrate health promotion into the daily routine in your setting?

Find it out

Look at the following websites for information to support health promotion within your setting:

- www.dh.gov.uk
- www.communityhealthprofiles.info
- NHS immunisation: www.immunisation.nhs.uk
- the Child Accident Prevention Trust (CAPT): www.capt.gov.uk
- Department of Health Brushing for Life Initiative: www.dh.gov.uk
- The healthy schools programme: www.healthyschools.gov.uk

As with all development of services, the Department of Health (DH) has arrived at the current state of play through investigation, exploration and research. There has been a long-term effort in producing the current thinking on ways in which we can combat health inequalities and improve life chances through good health care and support. Table 9.1 outlines how we have arrived at this current level of service.

Table 9.1. Development of new health agenda and legislation

The Health of Children and Young People (2001)	A report which shows analysis of health and health-related behaviour among those aged under 20 years in the UK between 1990 and 2001. It looks at how health during childhood can impact upon well-being in later life. Health inequalities in health and health-related behaviours are summarised using geography, social groups and ethnicity so that we might have a better understanding of ways to combat such inequalities.
The National Service Framework for Children, Young People and Maternity Services	One of the events which prompted this was the death of Victoria Climbié in February 2000. The 8-year-old girl came in contact with a range of service providers (health, police, social care, etc.) who failed to recognise and prevent the abuse that led to her death. Lord Laming undertook an enquiry, publishing a report on 28 January 2003 that outlined 108 recommendations to avoid as far as possible another event like this one occurring in the future. This case increased the government's commitment to vulnerable children and raised the profile for a coordinated approach to child protection services. In February 2001, the government announced that it would develop a new National Service Framework (NSF) for children, to set in place clear standards whereby service providers would be inspected.
The 2002 Spending Review	An announcement of a comprehensive Child and Adolescent Mental Health Service by December 2006; by May 2003 a comprehensive CAMHS service was defined (in the Emerging Findings of the NSF document).

2003, the first Minister of State for Children	The first Minister of State for Children in the Department for Education and Skills, Margaret Hodge, was appointed, taking responsibility for children's services, childcare and provision for under-5s, family policy (including parenting support and family law), and for the reform agenda to be set out in the Green Paper on children 'at risk'. Responsibility for children's social services was also transferred from the DH to the DfES.
Every Child Matters, Green Paper (Sept 2003)	This proposed a range of measures to reform and improve children's care and protect children from neglect and harm.
Every Child Matters: Next Steps (March 2004)	Published on the same day as the Children Bill was introduced to Parliament, this document set out the purpose of the Children Bill and the next steps for bringing about change of children's services.
The NHS Improvement Plan (June 2004)	This set out the next stage of the government's plans for modernising the health service. It signalled three big shifts: putting patients and service users first through more personalised care; a focus on the whole of health and well-being, not only illness; and further devolution of decision-making to local organisations. It required greater joint working and partnership between primary care trusts (PCTs), local authorities, NHS Foundation Trusts, NHS Trusts, independent sector and voluntary organisations.
The Treasury Child Poverty Review (August 2004)	This examined the welfare reform and public service changes necessary to advance towards the long-term goal of halving child poverty by 2010 and eradicating it by 2020. The review set out the key measures to reduce child poverty in the medium- to long-term, in particular through improving poor children's life chances, where public services can make a contribution, as well as providing financial support to families, continued efforts to help parents who can work into work, and looking to remove material deprivation.
National Standards, Local Action: Health and Social Care Standards and Planning Framework 2005/06–2007/08 (published July 2004)	This was a framework for all National Health Service (NHS) organisations and social service authorities to use in planning over the next three financial years. It included PCTs and local authorities and stated that they needed to lead community partnership by even closer joint working to take the NHS Improvement Plan forward.
The Chief Nursing Officer's review of the nursing, midwifery and health visiting (July 2004)	This looked at nursing, midwifery and health visiting's contribution to vulnerable children and young people – it examined the role of nursing, midwifery and health visiting when working with children at risk. This report sets out to identify the changes needed to improve the health and well-being of vulnerable children and young people.
The Healthy Living Blueprint (Oct 2004)	This outlined the health and well-being of children in schools as part of the National Healthy Living Standard.

The remaining 10 modules of the Children's NSF launched (Sept 2004)	Secretary of State for Health Dr John Reid launched the remaining 10 modules of the Children's NSF, setting future aspirations for the improvement of services across health, education and social care for women, children and their families over the next 10 years. The NSF is divided into three parts:
	▪ Standards 1–5 apply to services for all children and young people.
	▪ Standards 6–10 set standards in services for particular groups of children and young people, e.g. those with disabilities, complex needs, mental health, etc.
	▪ Standard 11 relates specifically to maternity services.
	An information strategy was also launched, addressing the key information technology challenges that need to be met in providing services for children and their families. The framework for children was to be implemented over the next 10 years.
Choosing Health: Making Healthy Choices Easier (2004)	This White Paper on public health set out the key principles for supporting the public to make healthier and more informed choices with regard to their health.
Supporting Local Delivery (Dec 2004)	This health element of the *Every Child Matters: Change for Children* documents was launched alongside documents for education, social care and the justice system. It outlined the activities that national government would undertake to support local service providers in delivering the NSF, and specifically the 'Be Healthy' outcome of the *Every Child Matters* agenda.

9.6 Policy affecting practice

What do we mean by policy? Why do we have policy? These are questions you may have asked yourselves at times in a decade when policy has had such a profound effect on the provision of childcare services in the UK.

What do we mean by policy?

Policy is summarised by Levin (1997), cited in Baldock, Fitzgerald and Kay (2004), in four ways:

1. a stated intention – for example transferring responsibility from one agency to another

2. an action – steps being taken to improve an area which has been identified as having a need

3. an organisation or administrative practice – for example the government sets up a funding regime and needs policies to ensure everyone knows where the money will be going

4. an indication of the formal status of a course of action – an example is a manifesto published for a general election.

Levin also tells us that policy helps an organisation to think in a coherent way about what it is trying to achieve and how it is going to achieve it. All policies have certain characteristics suggested by Baldock, Fitzgerald and Kay (2004):

- underlying assumptions about values and facts
- clear broad objectives
- costs need to be known for those responsible for implementation
- plans need to be made for communicating the policy
- structural arrangements need to be made to meet the objectives
- the policy has to be compatible with other policies
- there is a regular review of the policy.

Why do we have policy?

Most policies are in written format, which helps to clarify ideas and make sure there is no disagreement. When the policy is written down and communicated to all concerned everyone is then aware of the objectives of the policy, and new people (parents, families and staff) who join later can also read the same policy. In order for a policy to be effective it needs to be used regularly and implemented, not just put on a shelf gathering dust while everyone goes their own way or ignores the fundamental objectives of the policy.

Table 9.2. Advantages and disadvantages of policy

Advantages	Disadvantages
It makes us think about what we are doing and why we are doing it when we write a policy.	We do not use a policy on a regular basis – it gathers dust on a shelf or is covered up on a noticeboard so no one can see it.
Policy gives everyone clear guidance on a particular area of work – e.g. child protection or health and safety.	Policies are not regularly reviewed and they are outdated and ineffective.
When people come into the organisation or use services of the organisation they can be sure they are working to the same objectives.	Policies are given to new people but not explained properly.
Policy can protect – e.g. if a member of staff is nervous about asking a parent not to smoke on the premises.	If policies are ignored or not enforced by management, people who do adhere to them become frustrated.

Why do we need policy?

Recent and historic early years policy in the UK has helped change attitudes and practice in the sector. It has had an impact on the everyday lives of children and their families and has provided:

- better standards of health and welfare for all children
- a reduction in anti-social behaviour and crime

- improved educational standards

- an awareness of the needs of children and their families and the vulnerability of children and young people

- support for our values systems.

Points for reflective practice

Think about the ways in which policy affects your practice – are there ways in which you can improve your use of policy in your setting?

There is no doubt then that policy which is well thought through and has clear objectives is an effective working tool for all settings. Policy which is regularly updated and reviewed to inform and support good practice is essential in maintaining a structure which supports good-quality provision.

Conclusion

This chapter has briefly looked at a wide range of issues that managers and leaders will have to both understand and work with to provide good-quality experiences for children and young people. The last 20 years have seen far-reaching and wide-ranging changes in the sector and these will no doubt lead to substantial and immense changes in the next decade. Managers and leaders have to be abreast of these changes; they need to move with them and embrace them in order to provide children and young people with the protection and life chances they deserve. We have looked at some of the issues that can have an adverse effect on a child or young person's life and the ways in which we might, as professionals, improve the situation by using the latest legislation and policy to support us. As professionals working in the sector it is also important to be proactive and involved in working at a local level to drive forward initiatives which will improve life chances.

Check your understanding

What are the key pieces of government legislation affecting practice?

How are children addressed in the UNCRC?

How does the Common Assessment Framework (CAF) support safeguarding children and young people?

When working with children, young people and their families, what are the most effective ways of implementing a multi-agency approach?

In what ways can professionals support and promote good health?

References and further reading

Abbott, L. and Moylett, H. (2004) *Working with the Under 3s: responding to children's needs*. Buckingham: Open University Press.

Abbott, L. and Langston, A. (2005). *Birth to Three Matters: Supporting the Framework of Effective Practice*. Maidenhead: Open University Press.

Baldock, Fitzgerald and Kay (2004) TO COME

Bell, A. (1808) The Madras School. London: J. Murray.

Bruce, T. (2004) *Developing Learning in Early Childhood*. London: Paul Chapman.

Carpenter, B. (2006) *Families in Context*. London: David Fulton.

Commission for Racial Equality (1997) *From Cradle to School: A Practical Guide to Racial Equality in Early Childhood*. London: CRE.

Commission for Racial Equality (2002) *A Guide for Schools*. London: CRE.

Cullen, D. and Lane, M. (2003) *Child Care Law. A Summary of the Law in England and Wales*. London: British Association for Adoption and Fostering.

Daycare Trust (2007) *Listening to parents of disabled children – a report for the London Development Agency*. Available at www.daycaretrust.org.uk.

Department for Education and Skills (2003a) *Every Child Matters*. London: DfES. Available at www.dcsf.gov.uk.

Department for Education and Skills (2003b) *Aiming High: Raising the Achievement of Minority Ethnic Pupils*. Consultation Summary. London: DfES. Available at www.standards.dcsf.gov.uk.

Department for Education and Skills (2003c) *National Standards for Under 8s Day Care and Childminding*.

Department of Health (2006) *Sure Start Children's Centres Practice Guidance*. Nottingham: DfES.

Dowling, M. (2000) *Young Children's Personal, Social and Emotional Development*. London: Paul Chapman.

Dunn, J. (2006) *Children's Friendships – The Beginnings of Intimacy*. Oxford: Blackwell.

Elkin, F. (1960) *The Child and Society: The Process of Socialization*. New York: Random House.

Gaine, C. (1995) *Still No Problems Here*. Stoke-on-Trent: Trentham Books.

Greene, S and Hogan, D (2006). *Researching Children's Experiences*. London: Sage Publications.

Joseph Rowntree Foundation (2006) *Report – Inclusion of children in primary school playgrounds*. Available at www.jrf.org.uk.

Lane, J. (1998) *Action for Racial Equality in the Early Years*. London: National Early Years Network.

Lord Laming (2003) *The Victoria Climbié Inquiry*. Report of an Inquiry. Available at www.victoria-climbie-inquiry.org.uk/finreport/finreport.htm.

McNaughton, G. (2006) *Shaping Early Childhood*. London: Open University Press.

Ofsted (2003) *Early Years: The First National Picture*. London: Ofsted. Available at www.ofsted.gov.uk.

Pugh, G. and Duffy, B. (2007) *Contemporary Issues in the Early Years*. London: Sage Publications.

Riley, J. (2006) *Learning in the Early Years*. London: Paul Chapman.

Schaffer, H.R. (1996) *Social Development*. London: Blackwell.

Smith, P. and Bond, H. (1999) *Social Psychology Across Cultures*. London: Harvester Wheatsheaf.

Smith, P., Cowie, H. and Blades, M. (2003) *Understanding Children's Development* (4th edn). Oxford; Blackwell.

Tassoni, P. (2003) *Supporting Special Needs: Understanding Inclusion in the Early Years*. Oxford: Heinemann.

Willan, J., Parker-Rees, R. and Savage, J. (eds) (2005) *Early Childhood Studies*. Exeter: Learning Matters.

Useful websites

Children's Information Service (CIS): www.childrensinformationservice.org

Children's Trusts: www.dfes.gov.uk

Commission for Racial Equality: www.cre.gov.uk

Daycare Trust: www.daycaretrust.org.uk

Extended schools: www.teachernet.gov.uk

Foundation degrees: www. foundationdegree.org.uk

Innocenti Research Centre: www.unicef-irc.org

Mellow Parenting: www.mellowparenting.org

National Service Framework: www.dh.gov.uk

Ofsted: www.ofsted.gov.uk

Parents as First Teachers: www. parentsasfirstteachers.org.uk

PEEP: www.peep.org.uk

Race Equality Foundation: www.reu.org.uk

Save the Children: www.savethechildren.org.uk

Sure Start: www.surestart.gov.uk

Triple P (Positive Parenting Program: www.triplep.net

UN Committee/Convention on the Rights of the Child: www2.ohchr.org

Index

Professional Development Series

Inclusion, Equality and Diversity in Working with Children

How to turn good intentions into effective anti-discriminatory practice

- Takes a sensitive, holistic approach to promoting inclusion, equality and diversity when working with children of all ages.

- Practical examples from a wide selection of childcare settings show how to put the principles into practice.

- Written by Sue Griffin, a respected figure with many years of experience in the children's workforce.

978 0 435402 40 2   **Sue Griffin**

How to Observe Children, 2nd edition

The second edition of *How to Observe Children* is fully revised and updated to support the Early Years Foundation Stage

- Retains the popular, practical approach of the first edition, making it ideal for practitioners to dip in and out of for day-to-day guidance and in-depth enough for students learning the theory and skills for the first time.

- Includes updated information relating to the Primary National Strategy to support effective observations in schools.

- Examples of observations throughout enable students and practitioners to relate the theory and techniques to their setting.

978 0 435987 66 4   **Sheila Riddall-Leech**

For more information and details on other titles in the Professional Development Series, visit
www.heinemann.co.uk/childcare